Writing Travel
Series Editor, Jeanne Moskal

Writing Travel
Series Editor, Jeanne Moskal

The series publishes manuscripts related to the new field of travel studies, including works of original travel writing; editions of out-of-print travel books or previously unpublished travel memoirs; English translations of important travel books in other languages; theoretical and historical treatments of ways in which travel and travel writing engage such questions as religion, nationalism/cosmopolitanism, and empire; gender and sexuality; race, ethnicity, and immigration; and the history of the book, print culture, and translation; biographies of significant travelers or groups of travelers (including but not limited to pilgrims, missionaries, anthropologists, tourists, explorers, immigrants); critical studies of the works of significant travelers or groups of travelers; and pedagogy of travel and travel literature and its place in curricula.

Other Books in the Series

Vienna Voices: A Traveler Listens to the City of Dreams, Jill Knight Weinberger
Eating Europe: A Meta-Nonfiction Love Story, Jon Volkmer

Sarah Heckford

A Lady Trader in the Transvaal

Edited by
Carole G. Silver

Parlor Press
West Lafayette, Indiana
www.parlorpress.com

Parlor Press LLC, West Lafayette, Indiana 47906

© 2008 by Parlor Press
All rights reserved.
Printed in the United States of America

SAN: 254-8879

Library of Congress Cataloging-in-Publication Data

Heckford, Sarah, 1839-1903.
  Sarah Heckford : a lady trader in the Transvaal / edited by Carole G. Silver.
    p. cm. -- (Writing travel)
  Includes bibliographical references.
  ISBN 978-1-60235-082-3 (pbk. : alk. paper) -- ISBN 978-1-60235-083-0 (hardcover : alk. paper) -- ISBN 978-1-60235-084-7 (adobe ebook)
  1. Transvaal (South Africa)--Description and travel. 2. Heckford, Sarah, 1839-1903--Travel. I. Silver, Carole G. II. Title.
  DT2310.H43 2008
  916.8204'45092--dc22
  [B]
                              2008038417

Cover design by David Blakesley.
Printed on acid-free paper.

Parlor Press, LLC is an independent publisher of scholarly and trade titles in print and multimedia formats. This book is available in paper, cloth and Adobe eBook formats from Parlor Press on the World Wide Web at http://www.parlorpress.com or through online and brick-and-mortar bookstores. For submission information or to find out about Parlor Press publications, write to Parlor Press, 816 Robinson St., West Lafayette, Indiana, 47906, or e-mail editor@parlorpress.com.

Contents

Acknowledgments	*vii*
Introduction	*ix*
Carole G. Silver	
Chronology of Sarah Heckford	
(1839–1903)	*lxvii*
Chapter 1	*3*
Chapter 2	*8*
Chapter 3	*12*
Chapter 4	*21*
Chapter 5	*28*
Chapter 6	*37*
Chapter 7	*42*
Chapter 8	*45*
Chapter 9	*49*
Chapter 10	*59*
Chapter 11	*68*
Chapter 12	*75*
Chapter 13	*79*
Chapter 14	*83*
Chapter 15	*88*
Chapter 16	*96*
Chapter 17	*105*
Chapter 18	*109*
Chapter 19	*114*
Chapter 20	*118*
Chapter 21	*128*
Chapter 22	*134*
Chapter 23	*141*

Chapter 24	*152*
Chapter 25	*158*
Chapter 26	*169*
Chapter 27	*175*
Chapter 28	*180*
Chapter 29	*191*
Chapter 30	*200*
Chapter 31	*217*
Chapter 32	*234*
Notes	*241*
About the Editor	*247*

Illustrations

Figure 1. Photograph of Sarah Heckford in the early 1870s.	*viii*
Figure 2. Nathaniel Heckford, from a portrait presented to the East London Hospital.	*xi*
Figure 3. "Festival at the East London Hospital for Children on New Year's Eve."	*xiv*
Figure 4. "Crossing a Drift in Natal." Thomas Baines (c.1870).	*xl*
Figure 5. "Boer Commandoes." An unsigned, unidentified illustration of the techniques utilized by the Afrikaner forces during the first South African War.	*xliii*
Figure 6. Sarah Heckford shortly before her death, drawn by her friend, Lady Sarah Nicholson.	*lxi*

Acknowledgments

Creating a new edition of Sarah Heckford's provocative and unusual travel book would have been impossible without the help of a number of institutions and individuals. First, I am truly grateful to the excellent staff of the Cape Town Campus of the South African National Library and for the use of its facilities. Here, with the invaluable assistance of reference librarians Najwa Hendrickse, Zaidah Sirkhotte, and Petrie Le Roux and Special Collections librarian Melanie Geustyn, I was able to do most of my research on Heckford and her world. I am also indebted to the South African National Gallery in Cape Town, both for the help given to me by curator Hayden Proud and for permission to use material in its collection. The British Library was, as usual, an extraordinary resource and I am particularly indebted to the National Library of Scotland in Edinburgh—holders of what appears to be the sole surviving copy of Heckford's book on *Christ and Communism*—for welcoming me and permitting me to use it. The New York Public Library and the libraries of my own institution, Yeshiva University, have been extremely helpful and resourceful. In addition, I must thank Stern College for Women of Yeshiva University and its remarkable Dean, Karen Bacon, for the technical, financial and intellectual support they have provided throughout this project.

My appreciation and thanks must also go to a number of people. My summer research assistant and former student, Rebecca Rosenberg, was largely responsible for the chronology of Heckford's life and for many of the notes to *Lady Trader*. Working with her was a delightful experience. Vivien Allen, Heckford's biographer, whose volume, *Lady Trader: A Biography of Mrs. Sarah Heckford*, is soon to be republished, has been a major resource, graciously providing permissions and sharing information throughout this project. Friends and colleagues on two continents have been helpful readers, adding comments and making suggestions. I am especially grateful to Ellen Schrecker, Frinde Maher, Jill Landimore, and Norman Levy.

Lastly, I wish to thank the editors and staff of Parlor Press for their patient and helpful assistance in the production of this book. I am grateful to Jeanne Moskal for including it in the Writing Travel series and especially to David Blakesley, Publisher, for making this edition possible.

Figure 1. Photograph of Sarah Heckford in the early 1870s. Reprinted with the kind permission of Vivien Allen, author of *Sarah Heckford: Lady Trader*. Courtesy of the National Library of South Africa.

Introduction

Carole G. Silver

Three days after Sarah Heckford's death on 18 April 1903, a correspondent for the *Times* of London announced: "The news [...] comes as a terrible shock to all who knew her; and even those who know a tenth of her adventures and achievements will feel that her country is much the poorer for her loss. It is not an extravagance, indeed, to describe her as one of the most extraordinary women to whom the British nation has given birth" ("Obituary" 8). The lengthy and eulogistic obituary concludes by saying, "her life will remain an inspiration to noble, disinterested, and patriotic endeavour; and her country cannot afford to let it pass into oblivion" (9). Yet Heckford and her life have been almost entirely forgotten, and, in republishing her remarkable book, my intention is to re-inscribe her name in the annals of South African and British History.

Born in Dublin on 30 June 1839, Sarah Maud Goff, as she was then known, was the youngest of the three daughters of William Goff, formerly governor of the bank of Ireland and descendent of one of Oliver Cromwell's generals.[1] Her mother was Mary Clibborn, William's cousin as well as his wife. In 1842 Goff and his family left Ireland for the Continent, settling in Dresden. Mary Goff died in 1845, followed soon after by her oldest daughter, Jane. Mary's sister, Abigail Clibborn became surrogate mother to the surviving girls, Annie and Sarah. Rich enough to enjoy living on and touring the Continent, the Goffs spent two years in Switzerland and then in 1848 moved to Paris—where they were inadvertently caught in the 1848 French revolution. Returning to London, the family rented rooms in Eaton Square, perhaps to be close to William's bachelor brother Robert, whom William appointed as his daughters' guardian. Shortly after Sarah's ninth birthday, William killed himself. At roughly the same time, Sarah contracted tuberculosis of the spine (Pott's Disease), which left her hunchbacked (her left shoulder was deformed) and slightly lame. Raised by pious Aunt Abigail and worldly Uncle Robert, Sarah and Annie were deprived of part of the serious education their father had intended for them. Instead, they were "finished," trained in the "accomplishments" necessary to make them "ornaments of society" and thus marriageable. So, Sarah learned her foreign languages, studied piano, painted (even visiting the National Gallery to copy its pictures), and became an excellent horsewoman.

After Aunt Abigail died in 1859, the sisters, now without a chaperone, took a house together in Warwick Square, Pimlico, London. They were rich, each inheriting some fifteen thousand pounds sterling from their parents; they were serious and they were unusually independent. In the late 1850s, Sarah came in contact with some of the leaders of the burgeoning women's movement and was sufficiently influenced by their ideas to become a feminist, if a slightly unconventional one. Concerned, as were others in the movement, with women's rights to work outside the home and to enter the professions, her ambition was to become a medical doctor, emulating Elizabeth Blackwell, who had qualified as a doctor in America and was placed on the British Medical Register in 1859. It was at this point that Sarah, as she later put it, began to leap over "the barriers of young-lady-dom" despite the disapproval of her remaining family. Like George Eliot before her, she ceased to attend church; like Octavia Hill,[2] whom she much admired, she began to apply herself to social work, visiting and attempting to aid poor women and children. Slightly later, she began to visit the East End—something "a young lady" did not do—and to be distressed by the poverty and illness she found there.

As she later noted, "at two and twenty, I found myself possessed of a good fortune and absolutely my own mistress" (qtd. in Allen 6). An unhappy love affair with an older man, a friend of her uncle Robert, did not deter her from social action, but ironically, it was the cholera epidemic of 1866 which freed and empowered her. Both Goff sisters responded to the appeal for "lady nurses" made by Catherine Gladstone, the wife of the future Prime Minister. Sarah was sent to work at the Wapping Fever hospital, near the London Docks, where she met the man who was to become her husband, Nathaniel Heckford, one of the doctors in charge. He found her reading medical texts as she sat on night duty, encouraged her to study medicine, even offering to tutor her, and, after a short and unconventional courtship, married her on 28 January 1867. Significantly, they were wed in a Unitarian Chapel, with her sister Annie and Nathaniel's colleague at the Fever Hospital as witnesses.

Figure 2. Nathaniel Heckford, from a portrait presented to the East London Hospital. With the kind permission of Vivien Allen, author of *Sarah Heckford: Lady Trader*. Courtesy of the National Library of South Africa.

Heckford himself remains an interesting and slightly enigmatic figure. Born in Calcutta in 1842, he was three years younger than Sarah, darkly handsome, and apparently quite charming. He was part Indian, for though his father Nathaniel Heckford was a British Master Mariner of ancient lineage; his mother appears to have been Eurasian. The child of his father's second marriage, he had been raised and well educated in India, coming to England at the age of sixteen. Possessing both what friends described as "Eastern looks" and what Sarah calls an "Oriental" perspective on the world, he appears to have been influenced by both Hinduism and Buddhism. Sarah comments that "his ideas and even his modes of expression were tinged with Orientalism"*(Hospital* xii). Did she, plain herself, marry him for his charm and good looks, what she describes as his "unusual beauty of disposition and form" (xii)—overlooking the fact that in the eyes of society he was not entirely "white"? Did he marry her, in part, for her money? She tells us he was not affluent, even asking her to take on a consumptive young woman as a servant since he could not afford to. They were, as Sarah Heckford later wrote in describing their plan to create a hospital, in agreement "that we must do something to show how much happiness might ensue if persons of means and culture would devote themselves to elevating those less fortunate than they" *(Hospital* xiv). Whatever their initial impulses—and both marital partners were connected by their seriousness about medicine and devotion to social service as well as by their shared love of music and of poetry—the marriage though brief, appears to have been an extremely good one, a union that was both "romantic" and "companionate."

> In that part of London which lies East, North-East, and South-East of the Bank, there is to be found a network of streets whose peculiar dingy look it is impossible to describe and which must be seen in order to be appreciated. It is as though the accumulated dust which maids-of-all-work have for years been sweeping into corners [. . .] had, in despair of ever being put into a dustpan, forced itself through the bricks [. . .]. An unenlightened enquirer, as he walks through these streets, must always wonder who lives in them, and, even if he sees their inhabitants, must always wonder *how* they live. (qtd. in Allen 111)

Thus Sarah Heckford later described the area in which, with her money, the newlyweds bought two disused warehouses (in Ratcliff Highway near the docks) and began the work of establishing the East London Hospital for Children and Dispensary for Women. One year later, on 28 January 1868, their wedding anniversary, they opened the doors of the tiny institution. It began with only ten beds, but grew in size and importance; one of the only children's facilities in the East End, it was also the only hospital that accepted infants. Nurses willingly worked hard for meager wages or, as Sarah Heckford reports, turned down more lucrative positions to stay with the facility. An additional doctor, young and female, the first British woman to be accepted in the Medical Register, joined Nathaniel, while Sarah and others created outpatient facilities, attending women in their slum dwellings during their confinements. The Heckfords even adopted one of their orphans, ten-year-old Marian Matthews. But the hospital, run on a shoestring, was virtually bankrupt until it received help through the agency of the very famous Charles Dickens.

In an article subtitled "A Small Star in the East," signed by Dickens and published in the magazine he edited, *All the Year Round* (19 December 1868), Dickens described a grim ramble in London's East End: "a wilderness of dirt, rags, and hunger. A mud-desert chiefly inhabited by a tribe from whom employment has departed" (61)—and related how he came upon the Heckfords' hospital. In reality, he had been asked to visit by some mutual friends. After hearing of and witnessing the terrible plight of the poor and unemployed, he reports that the thought of their children, suffering and dying, leaves him feeling "unmanned." Just at that moment, he "accidentally" sees the sign that reads "East London Children's Hospital." Entering a building he sees as rough and simple, he finds within it, "the sufferings both of infancy and childhood tenderly assuaged" (65). " I heard the little patients answering to pet playful names," he continues, "the light touch of a delicate lady [Sarah, no doubt] laid bare the wasted sticks of arms for me to pity; and the claw-like little hands, as she did so, twined themselves lovingly around her wedding-ring" (65). Thus Dickens transforms Sarah into the epitome of the tenderly maternal angel in the house he himself so desired. One rare, pretty child (most have the "pinched" look of poverty) seems to implore him to tell the story of the little hospital—and so he does, never mentioning the names of the "gentleman and lady, a young husband and wife, [who] have bought and fitted up

Figure 3. "Festival at the East London Hospital for Children on New Year's Eve." *The Illustrated London News*, January 8, 1870. Sarah Heckford is the figure on the extreme left, offering a doll to a sick child. Nathaniel is directly behind her. Courtesy of the National Library of South Africa.

this building for its present noble use, and have quietly settled themselves in it as its medical officers and directors" (65). Transforming the Heckfords into paragons of perfect philanthropy, he notes that:

> With every qualification to lure them away, with youth and accomplishments and tastes and habits that can have no response in any breast near them, close begirt by every repulsive circumstance inseparable from such a neighbourhood, there they dwell [. . .]. The lady's piano, drawing materials, books, and other such evidences of refinement, are as much a part of this rough place as the iron bedsteads of the little patients." (65)

Dickens praises the couple for "their contented manner of making the best of the things around them"(65), for their innocent pride in the things they have built and the arrangements they have made, even for the mongrel dog they have adopted, euphemistically named Poodles. He is impressed by their medical approach, noting the qualifications of both and equally impressed by their common sense and generosity. He comments that "insufficient food and unwholesome living conditions being the main causes of disease among the children of the poor, the staff wisely provides nourishment, cleanliness and ventilation—and it is entirely free" (66). Finally, he compares Nathaniel to the hero of a Paris play, "The Children's Doctor." Dickens sees "in his pensive face, in the flow of his dark hair, in his eyelashes, in the very turn of his moustache, the exact realization of the Paris artist's ideal as it was presented on the stage" (66). But truth is better than fiction, even than romantic drama, says Dickens, the icon-maker. And "no romancer [. . .] has had the boldness to prefigure the life and home of this young husband and young wife, in the Children's Hospital in the East of London" (66). Dickens comes away, moved and heartened, sending others to visit as he has, and hopefully to contribute to the institution's upkeep.

But Dickens was neither the only visitor to the hospital nor its sole promoter. *The Illustrated London News* featured and pictured a fund-raising New Year's Eve party in its 8 January 1870 issue. It explained that its selection of this hospital, then enlarged to forty beds, was because the facility "was obliged to appeal to the public for funds to provide a more suitable building." Describing the party, the anonymous reporter noted that the guests were comprised of patients well enough to attend as well as two hundred children who had formerly been patients, that entertainment included a Punch and Judy show given in the wards—for those too ill too leave their beds—and that "a supper and all that could be desired in the eating way was not the least part of the evening's enjoyment." Commenting that the expenses of the evening were defrayed by the founders of the hospital [the Heckfords] and a few friends, the reporter adds: "It was indeed a sight to rejoice the hearts of those who were thus providing for these poor a few hours of unwonted pleasure." The end of the brief article announces the great achievements of the little hospital: "The out-patients relieved at this institution during the two years [of its existence] number 7155, and the in-patients, 597" (54). The illustration, worth more than the few hundred words of the text, shows in the left foreground, among the crowd, a glorified and beautified Sarah, bending over to offer a doll to a sick little girl.

Not only did the hospital receive an excellent report in the *British Medical Journal* but an "entertainment" at a London theatre raised additional funds and, much to Sarah's surprise, resulted in an anonymous donation of a thousand pounds, just when the Hospital needed it most. And in February 1870, *Macmillan's Magazine* published an article by Agnes T. Harrison closely imitative of Dickens' piece and clearly devoted to fundraising. Calling the hospital "An Ark by the Riverside" (rather than "A Star in the East"), Harrison recapitulates Dickens' ramble, again emphasizing the squalor of the East End and especially its "barefooted, blue-faced children" (355). She too has much to say of the noble sacrifices this upper-middle class couple has made. Describing Nathaniel as "a young physician, who was just entering on what his friends predicted would be a brilliant professional career at the West End" (355) while depicting Sarah as "the doctor's young wife, who had put her enthusiasm to the test of a strict medical examination as nurse," Harrison praises them fulsomely. Sarah is again perceived as a domestic angel—even as the image of Charity herself (often depicted with babies, symbolizing good deeds, around her). Readers are shown Sarah's tenderness to the young sufferers and are introduced to "the child of the hospital," a little boy named Georgie, who "clung to the hands of the doctor's wife, and nestled his head in the folds of her dress," or rested in her arms "with his small hand in her soft hair or fondling her cheek" (358).

Noting that the Heckfords have chosen to live in the East End—in the hospital itself—as well as work there, Harrison comments: "For some rare hearts there are stronger claims than those made by 'society', or the graces of life, and such were those who left so much behind them and cast in their lot with the inhabitants of Stepney and Wapping" (355). Like Dickens too, she remarks on the difference between the clean, cheerful but simple wards of the hospital and the Heckford's parlor, marked by "handsome pieces of carved furniture [. . .] and other touches of refinement as unmistakable in the aspect of places as the subtle definitions of accent and manner in people" (356). Harrison's descriptions of the child patients are even more sentimental than Dickens'. She points to "the babies, ten more little cribs full! What a sight!—too pathetic to be seen for tears, by eyes that see it for the first time" (356) and depicts the quiet, "pinched" and pale-faced infant, the "angelic baby face, surrounded by a halo of silky golden hair," the "little face, with the colour just returning to its baby cheek" (356–57) and, of course, "the little empty bed," with its identifying card turned to the wall. And, stressing the impact the Hospital has had on the neighborhood surrounding it, she asks her readers to contribute to its work. The hospital is very poor, she says; it deserves the fullest support of all who can contribute, for it is "an ark in the midst of a dreary sea of suffering and hunger and cold." (358). Like Dickens she ends with a plea that her readers visit—to do so will wring the hardest of hearts and open the tightest of pocketbooks.

Years later, by the time Heckford came to write about the institution (in "The Story of the East London Hospital for Children"[1887])—as part of a fundraising effort to help finance and expand its facilities at Shadwell—it was well established and well-known. It had moved and been rebuilt in 1876; it was officially opened in May 1877 by the Duchess of Teck. In addition to the Duchess, its patrons included Queen Victoria (as of 1886) and Princess Louise; among its vice presidents was Gladstone; contributors to the *Voluntaries* fundraising volume included such well-known authors as W.E. Henley, Robert Louis Stevenson, Andrew Lang, and May Kendall. Thus Sarah could turn her account of its history into a somewhat personal tale, particularly into an encomium for Nathaniel who, in her eyes, had given his life for the Hospital. He had died of tuberculosis in December 1871, after insisting that they return to the cold of a London winter so that the site at Glamis Road could be purchased.

Heckford's account provides an excellent insight into both her emotions and her ideas. She had already installed a memorial to Nathaniel which reads: "He Founded This Institution At His Own Cost" (though with her money) and continues: "He Lived For It And Died A Few Days After the Site Of This Building was Purchased by the Committee of Management of the Hospital" (*Hospital* ix). What she suggests by the later phrase is that "he lived for it and died for it." She recounts a dramatic scene—something out of a Victorian novel—in which her husband insists that they return to London from Amalfi, where they had gone for his shattered health, knowing that the return would kill him. Viewing him as a Christ-like sacrifice, she tells readers that he chose to "right the hospital by a supreme effort, and die" (xxxix). "We will go home," he tells her; "I shall not see next year, but the hospital will be saved! What is my life against the good of numbers"(xl). A true prophet, in her eyes at least, he was dead—age twenty-nine—before the year was out. She says too that he accepted his death, feeling that broken in health he would not be useful. "You will be able to do much more good without me than with me," he argued, strangely remarking, "You will not be long in following me, but you must see the hospital settled"(xliii). Nathaniel was only half-right, for by autumn 1876 the new building was finished and Sarah had abdicated her guardianship over what she considered their "child" (xliv). But she was not to follow him to the grave for many years and she had several new and exciting lives to lead.

Intellectually, the hospital experience had an important influence on Sarah Heckford's social ideas. At the beginning of her medical career she was quite conventional in her attitudes towards class differences and the class system. At first acquaintance, the inhabitants of the East End were as alien and "other" to her as the peoples of South Africa would be. Her attitude to philanthropic work begins as that of a "Lady Bountiful," as she implies when she describes herself as demonstrating "how much happiness might ensue if persons of means and culture would devote themselves to elevating those less fortunate than they" (xiv). Her thinking is vertical and hierarchical; she sees herself as raising and civilizing the working classes. Heckford's hospital experience radically modifies though it does not completely obliterate this attitude. Joining in hard work with nurses and servants alike, Heckford sees them all as "a band of friends, with but little distinction of social rank kept up between . . . [them]." She comments that they shared "friendship without familiarity" (xix) and that they worked generously and cooperatively as a unit. No longer does she believe the falsehood "that the distinction of rank lies below the surface, and that it is not merely a difference of polish" (xxi). That it *is* mere polish becomes evident when circumstances arise that unite those of all classes in the common interest. Then, she continues, people come to "understand that there is as much refinement and elevation of thought to be found in the homes of the poor as of the rich" (xxi). What the Hospital has come to signify, she explains, is "a system by which widely different classes of society might come to appreciate their unity, and learn to develop the good which is in all alike, disguised under varied aspects" (xxxvii). She has learned that the poor feel as strongly, as deeply as the rich, that they show in action what the more affluent verbalize or dramatize and that it is the rich who must strive to understand and to give.

Introduction   xix

    This idea lies at the core of her eccentric and revealing book of 1873, *The Life of Christ and Its Bearings on the Doctrines of Communism,* and was to alter and reshape her life. Working on plans for the new hospital, serving as a "lady visitor" in the Ratcliff facility, and writing her brief volume occupied her for the first few years after Nathaniel's tragic death. However, his demise left her temporarily devastated, perhaps even suicidal (it seems more than coincidental that she defends the right to end one's own life, arguing that Jesus did so, in her book on Christ and Communism). Heckford's volume is a revelation of her emotional condition but, more important, an insight into her philosophy and a direct indication of the ways in which she was to choose to lead her remaining years.

    Dedicating the volume to her adopted daughter, Marian, Heckford broadly reinterprets both the life of Jesus and the doctrines of communism. Eschewing "faith in the divinity of Jesus Christ" while simultaneously rejecting "that form of scepticism which attempts to lower and to discover faults in His sublime character" (*Christ* 6), she attempts to picture an ideal "human being." It is no surprise that the person who most resembles him is the recently deceased Nathaniel and that part of the subtext of the volume is an extended eulogy to her late husband. But the stated purpose of the volume is to show how Christ's precepts "may be followed in dealing with the social problems of this age" (10). Refusing to discuss Christ's miraculous birth, life after death or miracles, she offers her readers a brief, untheologized series of pictures of a "man," tempted to lead a revolution of the oppressed, refusing to buy freedom with bloodshed, loving the beauty of the world he chooses to leave, and dying as a noble sacrifice and suicide. His "gentleness, patience, unselfishness and [. . .] forgiveness of injuries" (24), his "serving of many"(46) connect him to her glorified image of Nathaniel. To her, the essence of Jesus' teaching lies in his valuing of motive rather than outcome, and of virtuous action, even of the smallest variety, over inaction (31).

    Her redefinition of communism is even more radical than her reinvention of Jesus. Clearly affected by the Paris Commune of 1870, valuing many of its ideals but deploring the violence that accompanied it, she voices her belief in an impending revolution. However, she wants "the most educated portion of the community to lead the revolution which is coming and to make it a purely moral one" (56–7). Arguing that communism as practiced when controlled by the poor has been unsuccessful and injurious, she protests that "it is a code of morality which might have been approved of by Christ himself" (57–8). At its heart is Christ's admonition "to sell all thou hast and give unto the poor" (58). To her, this commandment actually means: "Give all you have to those who are in want and come and earn your living in the most noble way [. . .] by curing the sick and teaching the ignorant" (64). Telling readers that she is writing to and for "the *rich* and *idle*" (58), she proceeds to redefine the class structure of England. There are only two classes, she states, the working class and the idle class. Her unorthodox working class includes "the wealthy banker, the prime minister, the elegant and fascinating wife" (of the latter) "who really keeps his 'party' together" (59) along with dockworkers and the good mothers who care for their own children. She finds members of the *idle* class in all strata of society, in workhouses and alleys as well as in mansions, among the "thoughtless and the frivolous" of all varieties. Stopping a moment to consider the daughters of the rich, "to whom good useful work would be a luxury, but to whom prejudice denies it" (60), she reveals her ardent feminism. After a diatribe in the spirit of Thomas Carlyle and John Ruskin, attacking hedonists and libertines, she returns to her main subject in addressing her appeal to those who have capital. It is their duty, she insists, "*to work for their livelihood and to give others the means of living* [my italics], that is, if they possess such means"(65). After redefining poverty to mean the "deserving poor" and to include the hard-working middle class, she argues that it is the obligation of the "rich and idle" to aid them. She was to act on these principles repeatedly, giving away much of her capital to the Children's Hospital, divesting herself of shares, and even—on her return from South Africa in the 1880s—founding and running a cooperative store in Woolwich.

Especially concerned with the role ladies can play, she insists that there are ways of their obtaining the happiness that comes from "rational and useful employment" (73). Her answer is voluntarism, not a popular idea in our day, but quite acceptable in hers. "Voluntarily doing work for those who cannot pay" gives one the right to a certain amount of the money that one has inherited, she argues. Speaking specifically to ladies, she tells them that "being grave and benevolent" (76), acting like professional do-gooders, is counter-productive. To look attractive and elegant, to be amusing and bright is not offensive to the poor; it helps not hinders giving and receiving. She insists, however, that voluntary, unpaid work should be only for the men and women who do not have and cannot acquire a profession, for real, professional work is best.

Heckford is most interesting and unorthodox when she raises the question of the proper distribution of wealth. She argues that "the more labour is employed, the more services are rendered, the more will wealth not only be diffused, but be actually increased" (84). The general wealth will be augmented, she notes, for each person gets what he or she most needs. It is "the duty, and should also be the pride, of every human being to work for his livelihood" (65). She ends her argument by quoting Octavia Hill and seconding Hill's admonition: "Let each of us not attempt too much, but take some little bit of work, and, doing it simply, thoroughly, and lovingly, wait patiently for the gradual spread of good" (90).

Christ and Communism is notable both for its feminism, much in the vein of Mary Wollstonecraft's *Vindication of the Rights of Woman*, and for its awareness of the realities of economic life under the capitalism of Heckford's era. Long before Olive Schreiner's *Woman and Labour* (1911), Heckford argues for women's right to "honoured and socially useful human toil" (Schreiner 27). She points to the social prohibitions that prevent "the daughters of the rich" from doing the "good useful work" which would be "a luxury" for them. She insists on good and equal education for women, so that "no more half-taught girls" will be forced to go out "as second-rate governesses" (63). She argues that both men and women must have the right to pursue and acquire professions. Believing that work can and should be pleasurable, and thus anticipating the argument made by William Morris ten years later, she insists "that the happiness coming from rational and useful employment must be the same to women as to men" (73). And, disliking dour and sober-sided female do-gooders, she remarks that women of means can still do "good works" and enjoy parties, theatres and elegant dress.

Her grasp of Marxist or socialist economics is unexpected. She recognizes that the disparity in the distribution of wealth is at the root of society's problems, and that wage labor is a social relation between the person who sells his or her labor, the employer and other workers in general. She notes that capital becomes "capital" only when it is employed for profit or acquired through the labor of others; that "real" wealth, honest wealth (and she makes the distinction clear) is increased by the production of goods, not by the amassing of stocks or money. However, it is her understanding of the condition of the working class that shows how far she has come from the elitism of her early years. She insists that the more "capital" that is amassed, the more stocks that are exchanged, the worse is the position of workers performing honest labor. She notes that the problems of the working poor are almost insurmountable. They are increasingly less educated. It is not just that they cannot afford to send their children even to free schools, but that when children enter wage labor themselves, their minds are dulled by the drudgery of their jobs. Thus, she says, they become a permanent underclass. Unable to entertain abstract ideas, too tired and downtrodden to think clearly, they become the tools of demagogues. "The labour market is [. . .] glutted with men who are too ignorant to do anything but the commonest work; too ignorant to understand even the simplest abstract idea of justice, or any other principle of action" (86). Unless society changes, their ignorance and poverty, their incitement "to plunder the rich" will lead to a bloody revolution quite different from the moral one she desires. The resonance with Marx's views is notable.

By 1876, Heckford was ready to get on with her life. Following the doctrines that she had enunciated in *Christ and Communism,* she had given away most of her capital and was determined to follow the "duty of every human being to work for his livelihood" (65). Nevertheless, she had kept sufficient funds for travel and for life abroad. First she went with Marian, aged seventeen, to Naples, perhaps as a way of recapturing the Italian idyll she had shared with Nathaniel. There, after a whirlwind courtship, Marian wed a young Italian lawyer. There, too, Sarah, unwell but incapable of being inactive, doctored the neighborhood poor, treated those suffering from malaria, and campaigned to prevent cruelty to the city's overworked carthorses. After Marian's wedding, Sarah went to India, traveling through and visiting Egypt on the way. Influenced by Nathaniel's heritage, perhaps interested in locating other members of his mother's family as well as his childhood friends, she visited Calcutta, his birthplace. Again, she did not merely tour, she worked. She became involved with a charity called the Zenana Mission, offering medical aid to women in purdah, something only other females could do. Next she traveled through Central India, ending up in the princely state of Bhopal, where she became the resident medical adviser to the female ruler, Shah Jahan Begam.

Introduction

By the middle of 1878, stricken with malaria, Heckford returned to England. Her timing was extraordinary, for by 1878, the Transvaal had been annexed, plans for developing England's newest colony had proliferated, and all had proclaimed its potential—in terms of both wealth and health. It was the perfect place, said news reports and advertisements, for speculation and recuperation. Uncharacteristically, she purchased a hundred shares in the Transvaal Farming, Mining and Trading Association, determined to learn Afrikaans, study farming methods, and purchase land. She embarked for South Africa, leaving her friends and family bewildered and amazed. It is at this point that the narrative of *Lady Trader,* a travel book unlike most others, begins.

The events of the book themselves are not outstandingly dramatic though Heckford has come at an exciting time in the history of South Africa, an era that will shape and change an emerging nation. Her account is less of adventure than of endurance, less of success than of disappointment, struggle and resolution. Intending to be a farmer, she arrives in Durban, travels to Pretoria, the sole woman in a party of new settlers, only to find that the scheme in which she has invested is fraudulent, and the farm she has bought is non-existent. Almost insolvent, she is forced to spend two years as a governess,[3] teaching on a farm called Nooitgedacht. Fortunately, however, her employers became her close friends, even helping her to learn to farm. To raise the funds needed to buy land of her own, she embarks on an occupation almost never undertaken by a woman; she becomes a *smous,* a peddler or trader—travelling with a wagon, a team of oxen, and trade goods to the northern bush-veldt. With only a native driver and a small boy to lead the team, she treks to the Zoutspanberg in the Northern Transvaal and successfully sells her goods to both Afrikaners and Africans. Successful in business, making money and enjoying the unconventional life she had chosen, she is caught in the First South African War. Trapped by the siege of Pretoria, she both participates in its events and begins the writing of her experiences as a "lady trader." Angered at the retrocession of the Transvaal in April 1881, ruined financially by a war she now viewed as pointless and ignoble, she returned to England. Her book ends with a sad—though unknowingly temporary—farewell to South Africa.

Published in 1882 in London by Sampson Low, *A Lady Trader in the Transvaal* was a considerable success. Although not as popular as Charles Du Val's account of his South African adventures, *With a Show through Southern Africa,* which, like Heckford's volume, partially focused on the siege of Pretoria, it nevertheless did well. A belated review of Heckford's book in the *Academy* 1889 (21:56) describes it as "an amusing and interesting book" and announces:

> One would wish to know something more about the antecedents of this vigorous lady who suddenly, without friends or relations, lands at Durban in December 1878, and [is] equal to anything, from nursing, teaching, and cooking, to grooming her horses and ordering and superintending the flogging of a Kaffir. We learn incidentally that she was born in Ireland and has been in India, and incidentally, also that she went out to learn farming in the Transvaal. (56)

Other reviews were equally laudatory. *A Lady Trader* was, however, to be Heckford's only literary success. No trace of *Excelsior,* her autobiographical novel of 1884, published in London, remains. Evidence of Heckford's other later writings is also lacking; these include a collection of stories about the gold fields called *True Transvaal Tales* (1891) and a belletristic essay about Nooitgedacht, published in a South African magazine.

Upon her return to England in 1881, Heckford continued to work for "good causes." At the same time, she became involved in spiritualism, not surprisingly since she had shared an interest in the mystical and occult with her deceased husband. Moreover, she believed that, in common with many of Scottish and Irish stock, she had the power of second sight. With her friend, Lady Sarah Nicolson, she participated in séances, an activity popular among both "ordinary folks" and such eminent Victorians as Elizabeth Barrett Browning, Alfred Lord Tennyson, Florence Nightingale and the Queen herself. Like Mrs. William Butler Yeats, a few years later, she produced examples of what she believed was "automatic writing." One wonders if her trances and writings made her feel closer to the dead Nathaniel.

Most important, she began campaigning on behalf of the English-speaking farmers and traders who had been ruined by the war and its outcome. Apparently, she had lost her heart to South Africa—along with her pocketbook—and had bought and left untended a farm, called Jackallsfontein, south of Pretoria. When in 1886, gold was discovered on the Witwatersrand, she hurried back, arriving in 1887, hoping to find gold on her land. She was not among the fortunate; but from 1887 on, most of her remaining days were spent in the land she had adopted.

Inventive, indefatigable, versatile, she worked at anything and everything. As ever, she had a goal: to provide education and medical care for those in the rural farming communities. It was to crystallize into a farm-school scheme, a self-sufficient educational and commodity producing co-op which would help the isolated, ignorant farmwives and children, Boer and English alike. But for this, she needed capital. So, unable to sell her farm, she went to Johannesburg and, calling herself a share broker, sold mining shares. But her timing was bad (the gold was mixed with pyrite and difficult to extract until the invention of a new process) and by March 1889, her business had collapsed and she was bankrupt. Once again she became a *smous*. Her skills served her well and the business flourished. With the profits, she bought a farm in the Zoutspansberg, which she named Ravenshill, and settled her English cousin, Sarah Eland and Sarah's son on the land. Her action was both altruistic and self-serving, for the terms of the land grant stipulated that the property must always be inhabited, and Heckford was often away on her trading ventures. Continuing her work as a *smous* and plying her trade in the mining camps, her desire for adventure and need for cash led her to try prospecting on the Klein Letaba goldfields in the winter of 1891. There, at Barbarton, and at the "Birthday" mine, she managed to pan a small amount of gold—worth about forty pounds sterling.

By 1893, she was ready to give up this rather demanding life. She rented a farm near Ravenshill on which to live and work while she had a house built on her own adjoining property. Here, she became the friend and supporter of the "Rain Queen," Madjadje, and one of the only Caucasians to be permitted in the Queen's sacred kraal. The life of the Rain Queen would have made an excellent subject for another book by Heckford; unfortunately she never wrote it.

The queen ruled the Lovedu—peaceful, gentle people especially skilled in metal crafts. She was primarily a priestess rather than a potentate. But her power to make rain for her people and to withhold it from their enemies made her a goddess on earth. (Several commentators suggest that the Rain Queen is the original of H. Rider Haggard's *She.*) Not only her role as "Transformer of the Clouds," but her powers as changer of the seasons and maintainer of their regularity, and her ability to control violent thunder storms and to deal with broken taboos, gave her enormous status (Krige 271). Her responsibilities were equally great; her rainmaking required constant ritual and continuous care, as well as the good will of her ancestors and the assistance of male rain-doctors. The artifacts, charms and medicines associated with her work were sacred; the ways in which she used them were her secrets, to be given to her successor in this matrilineal society only at the point of her death. She was to be supplicated through gifts or dances; she was to be kept content, lest her upset stop the rains (Krige 279), but she was also to remain in seclusion and not to leave her people. Though some of the rituals have changed, a Rain Queen and the Lovedu belief in her powers remain to this day.

Madjadje II was the daughter/sister of her father, Chief Mugudo and the woman who had been Madjadje I. Already old when Sarah met her, she was to commit ritual suicide in 1896, a practice thought necessary for the continued fertility of the land, and a requirement of her rule. A number of Madjadje's people had kraals on the land Heckford rented; many were Heckford's agricultural workers. When the Boers again began to expropriate African land in 1888, Madjadje was caught up in the conflict. Although other tribes had rebelled, the Lovedu had not. Nevertheless, the Queen and her people were told to move to a new "location," much too small to hold them. Angered at the injustice, Heckford intervened to the point where the Boers labeled her "Madjajde's lawyer." She pleaded with the Superintendent of Native Affairs; she paid the hut taxes for the kraals on her farms (reluctantly agreeing, both for the workers' sake and her own, to accept repayment in harvested crops); she accepted the custom of the workers' attending initiation schools (losing their services for two or three months). As tensions heightened and angry Africans retaliated by looting white farms, Modjajde sent a message telling Sarah not to be afraid: "that she counted me as her sister and her people as my children and that they would defend me as such" (Allen 186). Unfortunately, the Queen was unable to do so. When white-owned farms were burned, the innocent Lovedu were ordered to disarm, fined several thousand head of cattle, and humiliated. This last blow took the form of forcing the Rain Queen—always secluded and sacred—to publicly exhibit herself in the Boer camp. As the violence increased, Heckford too was forced to leave the area and make her way to the city.

By 1895 her health was beginning to fail and the hard work of farming was becoming too much for a woman in her fifties. Sad but resolute, she left Ravenshill in good hands, those of Sarah and her son, Frank Eland. Undecided about what to do next, she returned to Nooitgedacht, where she had been a governess some fifteen years earlier, this time to teach the children of her former pupils. At Nooitgedacht when the South African War broke out in October 1899, she once again offered her services to the empire. This time, unlike her offers to help during the siege of Pretoria, they were accepted. Twice she carried messages about Boer troop movements to Lord Roberts, Commander in Chief of the British forces. On the second occasion, aged sixty, ill and alone, she rode the forty miles to Pretoria on a winter's day, stopping to warn the troops at Commandonek of another rumored attack.

Unable to return to her farm, she again remained in Pretoria; needing "useful work" to do, she helped to reorganize and open the schools closed at the war's beginning. Still thinking about and promoting her "farm-school" idea, she authored a major report on the educational needs of the Transvaal Colony for the Transvaal Women's Educational Union (an organization she had founded), hopefully to be used by the Colony's education department. The report, completed in March 1901, was forwarded to London.

Heckford herself returned to England in 1901, now in pursuit of a project that had arisen out of her awareness of the educational needs of the Transvaal colony as well as out of her belief that rural ignorance and lack of education were among the main causes of the war. Her idea? An adult education program mainly for rural Afrikaner women in the form of a series of popular lectures on history, enriched and made accessible through the use of magic lanterns and slides. In her scheme, lecturers would travel the rural areas, presenting the magic lantern shows, recommending books and organizing literacy groups for the many Afrikaner illiterates.

One segment of the lecture series written by Heckford survives. Published posthumously in 1905, its subject is the "Huguenots," and it is clearly for a general audience with little historical background. Beginning with Christian martyrs "condemned to be torn to pieces by wild beasts, snatched from the wilderness where they had been happy and harmless" (2)—the beasts, that is—Heckford proceeds to give an emotional, loosely historical account of Protestants victimized by state and church intolerance. Her sympathy for the animals "brought to the Arena by men more savage than they, and perverted into instruments of man's cruelty" (6) is in accord with her strongly held views on cruelty to animals, though a bit incongruous in this context.

Incorporating fifty-five slides, the surface text of "The Huguenots" stresses the need for tolerance and for an education that teaches it (she even condemns Calvin's burning of Servetus), but its sub-text is staunchly anti-Roman Catholic. Attacking "image worship" as a device used by priests and rulers to maintain the status quo, noting that persecutions arose from the fear that denial of the divine right of the Pope would lead to a similar disbelief in the absolute power of monarchs, Heckford makes it plain that her heroes, those to be emulated, are the simple, faithful Huguenots. Educating their children to be loyal to whatever nation sheltered them, they took with them into exile the best of France and they gave it to countries such as South Africa. Wherever they went, she concludes (flattering an audience that would include many of their descendants): "They carried with them those qualities which make the backbone of a nation, strong individuality, uprightness, industry and unswerving fidelity to their religious convictions" (30). There is no evidence that her lectures were effective, but her intentions are clear.

For this project, not the sort of enterprise an education department would fund, Heckford needed to raise money. However, while fundraising, she also began to support the British Women's Emigration Society, speaking on behalf of their projects and urging teachers in particular to begin new lives in South Africa. She became a well-known lecturer as well as a notable writer of letters to newspapers and journals on the matters that concerned her.

Beginning in 1890, she had spent much time and effort writing on South African issues: detailing Boer cruelty to native Africans, stressing the plight of those loyal to England (the "English Africanders" who had lost much in two recent wars), and pleading for more and better educational facilities. She became widely known and respected in England as a speaker and commentator on southern Africa. In particular, she established herself as an expert on the South African War and its problems

Heckford had much to say, partially from genuine compassion and partly in support of empire, about Boer mistreatment of the Africans. An article in the 5 January 1901 *Spectator* deals with Afrikaner cruelty

Introduction

to "natives," their belief that the British treat Africans "who are savages and murderers, as equals." "In the Colony," complains a Boer prisoner of war, "you will allow them to walk on the sidewalks. One might even have to sit next to a black woman in church"(qtd. in Allen 210). Heckford intelligently links this rage at the thought of permitting "natives" on the sidewalk with the similar upset of American Southerners before and during the Civil War. On Monday, 10 August 1901, the *Times* published a long letter she had written on "Boer Treatment of Kaffirs." (The term was still commonly applied to Africans, but did not yet have an openly pejorative connotation.) Writing to rather sharply correct statements made during a British Parliamentary debate, Heckford protests both the refusal to acknowledge Boer cruelty to natives and the attitudes of some members of Parliament themselves. She is angry that an insulting statement that "there were only two things a black man wanted [. . .] a bottle of brandy to get drunk [on] and a gun to shoot his neighbour" (*Times* 8) was greeted by amused and approving laughter. But more important, she must attack the British belief that "the original pass laws were only mild measures of the police," that the Boers instituted them to "protect" natives. (It was not apparent at the time that such Pass Laws protected mine owners by helping them to sustain their migrant labor force.) No, she says, again with the authority of someone who has seen the practice firsthand: any white person may stop any native and demand his pass. If the native has none, if it is not in order, if the African questioned is unable to name his *baas* (or for any other reason his interrogator chooses), the white may flog the native or tear up his pass. That the same powers would be held and used by white officials some eighty years later becomes an irony of history. That Heckford finds such laws offensive is much to her credit.

As to the hut taxes administered by the Boers,[4] Heckford's account of the punishments visited on natives who could not pay them is memorable, and again implies her belief in the superiority of British rule. She depicts one Afrikaner magistrate as "a fiend in human form" for imprisoning and starving natives who refused to sell their cattle (at unfair prices) to pay their taxes. At the center of Heckford's article is her account of the treatment of the Lovedu (as she spells it) and their Rain Queen. Noting that the purpose of a Boer raid on the peaceful tribe was actually to steal their livestock, she adds that a commander was told to "kill every male above childhood" if a native fired a single shot, to burn the kraals[5] on Heckford's land and to confiscate all "Kaffir cattle" (*Times* 8). The end result was horrible. Five thousand head were stolen, the kraals were destroyed; men, women and children were exposed to cold and rain; their mielies [maize], the staple of their diet, were saved only by Heckford's insisting they were her property. The Lovedu were "mercifully" treated by the vicious Boers, she sarcastically remarks, tribes that had rebelled had "droves of women, children and old men (some 1,500 to 2000) driven to Pretoria "in a way that it would be wrong to drive cattle" (*Times* 8); there, they would be partitioned among the Boers in a system of "apprenticeship" and servitude that was tantamount to slavery.

Heckford is equally impassioned about the plight of the "Loyal Afrikanders in South Africa," as she calls the English settlers. Her long letter in the *Times* of 18 February 1901 reiterates the statements of many others, that throughout both South African Wars, England has ignored or forgotten those loyal to her. Mrs. M. J. Moon, for example, described by the *Times* (20 July 1901) as once resident in the Transvaal but now a refugee in Cape Town argues the same case. While Boer men "openly chuckle that they have no encumbrance; that they are able to enjoy the 'picnic,' as they term this guerilla war," because their wives are safely in refugee camps (as she calls them), "thousands of poor women are in exile at the coast and elsewhere, and many of them have no homes to return to." Their lives ruined by "the cunning, hypocritical Boers," they are the people who deserve "the greatest sympathy" (*Times* 6), concludes Mrs. Moon. Ever loyal and courageous, English Afrikanders do not complain.

Although Heckford's argument is much the same, she is far more eloquent, providing readers with the case study of a family destroyed by two wars, her close friends, the Jennings. Beginning with the siege of Pretoria in 1881, she recounts the heartbreak of William and "the despairing cry" of his wife at the news of the retrocession: "And we trusted so in England." Returning to their ruined farm, their flocks and herds stolen, their fields untilled, they have had to bear the insults of the neighboring Afrikaners. By the outbreak of the next war (though William had died) the family had rebuilt, and were once again prosperous. This time, though living in the midst of Boer territory, they refused to bear arms against their British brothers. Risking their lives by their refusal to fight, they were forced to plough Afrikaner fields and to permit the guerillas to commandeer their cattle, sheep, and horses as well as to confiscate their produce. Loyal to England, they refused to capitulate and were forced to flee, knowing that flight would mean the destruction of their property. "These families are in Pretoria now," says Heckford; they are "refugees. Their houses are ruins, their farms desolated." Forced to take menial jobs, they can barely survive, but they are "as loyal as ever." Neither complaining of their treatment, nor demanding full compensation (on the grounds that farmers too should pay part of the cost of the war), they will be the backbone of a new nation. Nevertheless, Heckford insists, loyalists must be treated better than their conquered foes. "If we are to pardon rebels and give money to our enemies," she asks, "what does our honour require us to do for the number of truly loyal Afrikanders who have stood devotedly by the English flag" (*Times* 14)?

Support for the empire and the belief in justice for the Afrikaner loyalists and English-speaking settlers separates Heckford from those perceived as "pro-Boer." However, unlike Emily Hobhouse,[6] she stops short of condemning the concentration camps. The feeling that England has not done right even by those who fought on her side is perhaps the reason for her relative lack of sympathy for the Boer "victims" of the camps. In one of her least commendable newspaper campaigns, she contests Emily Hobhouse's depiction of the British camps of the Second South African War. However, her argument has been partially misconstrued. Heckford is irritated at Hobhouse's attacks on the camps made, in Heckford's view, after only brief visits to them and with little knowledge of South Africa, its people and their lifestyles. She accuses Hobhouse of a "do-gooder," tourist mentality. (Ironically, similar attacks on "do-gooders" and their "lack of understanding" would be made by the Afrikaner Nationalist Party government during the apartheid years.) The *Times*, supporting the British government's refusal to let Hobhouse revisit the camps with an official group of lady volunteers, predictably cites Heckford as a more reliable and impartial authority. In an introduction to her article of 5 August 1901, the editor notes "Mrs. Heckford settled in the South African Republic more than 20 years ago, and has passed through both Transvaal wars. Having lived as a farmer among farmers, she has naturally acquired a peculiarly intimate knowledge of the Boer character and way of life" (*Times* 6). In short, *she* is the expert, qualified to speak while, as Heckford says in her opening salvo, Emily Hobhouse is not!

Heckford argues that the camps are better in hygiene, sanitary conditions, population density, and comfort than many of the ordinary dwellings of Boers. (She has seen their tent life as a trader in the bushveldt.) She notes, realistically, if callously, that war always brings suffering and death and that it is usually the very young, the female, and the very old that die most quickly. Citing a nephew of Paul Kruger's, she comments that many of the Boer commandos considered confinement in a camp a favor, a way of protecting women and children from the ravages of war. Changing tack, she notes that the Afrikaner women should not be considered non-combatants, for they served as spies and couriers for their men folk and thus deserved to be confined. And, she adds that she wonders at Hobhouse's lack of sympathy with the English Afrikanders, "the loyal subjects of the Empire [. . .] driven from their homes, still enduring as much or more than the worst cases addressed by her amongst the Boer refugees" (*Times* 6).

In the article itself, Heckford again argues for loyalty to empire and support for the plight of the victims of the Transvaal retrocession. Once again, her solution to the problems of the Transvaal lies in education; only through it, she believes, will conditions change. Arguing that "education for adults, as well as for children, offered under conditions that would facilitate its acceptance, would do more to render the Boers loyal to the Empire [. . .] than all else" (6), she promotes her rural school scheme. Ignorance is the enemy, she insists; use the camps, while they still exist, to educate and indoctrinate. She closes with a letter from an English Afrikander who has started a night school for adults in the camp to which he has been assigned. Let us learn, she concludes, that there are better ways to be both loyal to empire and sympathetic to one's fellow humans (regardless of their political views) than by bewailing the inevitable suffering of war. Schooling the Afrikaners is not just an educational whim; it is a political necessity.

Like her contemporaries, the Fabian Socialists, Heckford found in education an answer to social and political problems and a source of societal change. She knew, first hand, the difference it could make. Well educated herself, though untrained as a teacher, she had found work as a governess when she was nearly destitute. Initially appalled by the isolation and ignorance of her pupils, she found them considerably improved by education and became increasingly convinced of its efficacy. Years later, in a lengthy letter to the *Spectator* of 20 April 1900 titled "How to Conquer South Africa in its Schools,"[7] (she commented that poor education was not only the problem of the Boers or the Transvaal, but was equally prevalent in the British Cape Colony, where few children went beyond Standard IV and most learned no relevant history or geography. Using as her motto the statement of a Boer farmer that "This war would never have been had we been better educated" (564), she argues for the political and social power of learning. "Why is it that so many Colony Dutch are disloyal?" she asks. "Why is it that anti-British agitators obtain so easy a success among them?" "Why is it that those Colonials who are thoroughly loyal to England in feeling cannot, as a rule, refute the abuse of her?" (564). Because, she answers, they know nothing of history. The teaching of all its varieties, even in junior classes is essential, for it will break down religious bigotry, inculcate morality and, above all, support the empire. Heckford's belief that the teaching of history will promote England's claims to power, assuage the anger of the Afrikaners, and create peace is almost touchingly naïve. But her recognition of the political power of education is remarkably sophisticated.

By the end of 1902, she was partially blind and failing in health, but insisted on returning to South Africa. She reached Pretoria in February 1903, only to die of "an affection of the bronchial tubes" on the 18th of April, two months before her sixty-third birthday. Her long battle with illness, "the long disease" that was her life was over. She is buried in the Old Cemetery on Church Street West in the plot reserved for Wesleyan Methodists and her simple monument—spare, unadorned, and understated—reads in part: "She adopted the Transvaal as her home and devoted herself to its best interests." Far from being consigned to oblivion, she was remembered in England as well. A few weeks after her death and her obituary in the *Times,* portraits of Heckford and of her beloved Nathaniel were unveiled by the Lord Mayor of London, who rode in state to the East End to place them in the Heckford Street Schools, institutions she had funded. Her epitaph in the *Pretoria News* described her as "a worker among women" whose death was "a serious loss" (qtd. in Allen 228) and whose life was something to remember. For twenty-first century readers, it is not her identification with empire (the blind spot of almost all the eminent Victorians), but her views on feminism, education, philanthropy, health, and the distribution of wealth that make her memorable.

Heckford as Traveler

Sarah Heckford was only one of the many "travellers in skirts"[8] or so *Punch* called them, who journeyed to Southern Africa in the late

1870s. More a "temporary resident" than a tourist, she differed from the usual visitors in a number of ways. Motivated by high principles and a passion for the "improvement" of its peoples, she did not come to see South Africa's natural wonders; she did not find the country especially beautiful; she did not visit Cape Town; she did not, for the most part, participate in the spotting or hunting of African wildlife.

Although, by the 1870s, many women toured and wrote of Southern Africa, it was still structured and perceived as essentially a man's country. Several of the travel narratives written at the same time as Heckford's are by men, and what Mary Hall (another woman traveler) describes as "big game romances" ("Preface"). E. F. Sandeman's *Eight Months in an Ox-Waggon,* published in the same era as *Lady Trader,* is typical of these. Sandeman covers the same time period and some of the same geographical terrain. But it is hard to imagine that the two travelers are visiting the same locations. Like Heckford, Sandeman comes for his health, not unusual since South Africa was considered an appropriate place to recover from "weakened constitutions." But, while he encounters and comments on Boers and Africans, his interest is primarily in hunting. Strikingly apolitical—at a time when English-Boer tensions were at the boil—he remarks, as many did, on Boer ignorance, squalor and, hospitality. His comments about Africans are equally stereotypical. They drink too much, are prone to sloth and cowardice and, through exposure to the white world, have lost their ancient hunting craft. A skillful writer, Sandeman entertains his audience with accounts of violent storms, raging grassfires, wagon accidents, and the ravages of flooded rivers, deadly snakes and tsetse flies. A good if sporadic naturalist, he provides interesting accounts of such creatures as the honey bird (a bird that leads humans to bees' nests in the trees). However, with the exception of his awareness of matters of trade (he tells readers what supplies he carried and what he paid for them and notes the lack of local manufactured goods), he is almost entirely involved with the sighting, chase and killing of the various animals he encounters. Not an especially good shot, he wounds endless numbers of bok, wildebeests, quaggas, and birds. His interests are considerably narrower than Heckford's; his insights concern hunting, and readers are told much about the retrieval, preparation, and eating of his prey. The sections on hunting in Lord Randolph Churchill's *Men, Mines and Animals in South Africa* (1892), published twelve years later are remarkably similar to, almost interchangeable with Sandeman's.

Introduction

Churchill too provides accounts of the honey bird and the horse sickness caused by tsetse flies, of the herds of bok and their slaughter, of grassfires and thunderstorms. Here too are stereotypes of Boers—idle, slothful, and cruel to natives—and of lazy, childlike Africans.

But what of other women travelers?[9] Many who visited and wrote of South Africa were of the same class as Heckford or even more aristocratic; they too were women of "independent means." Some, like her, were widows, coming in part for their health; others were "accidental tourists," accompanying their husbands on official business. Most came to travel; only a few came to work, and of this small number, almost all but Heckford were journalists. Writing about the Cape, its beauties and its exotic peoples had become something of a female tradition, starting with Lady Ann Barnard in 1798 and continuing, in Heckford's own time, with Lady Lucie Duff Gordon, whose *Last Letters from Egypt to Which are Added Letters from the Cape* had been published in 1875. Writing about the Transvaal was less common. Louisa Hutchinson, author of a book Olive Schreiner admired, found herself *In Tents in the Transvaal* (1879) at the same time as Heckford's visit. She shares Heckford's intrepid nature, choosing, despite obstacles, to join her military husband on his postings, purchasing a horse, living in a tent, and, when permitted, accompanying his regiment on its march. But traveling with a lady's maid and other officers' wives, she is neither independent nor alone.

Lady Florence Dixie came as a journalist; her mission: the defense of Cetawayo[10], the Zulu King conquered and imprisoned in the war of 1879, or so she writes in *The Land of Misfortune: A Defence of Zululand and its King* (1882). Sister of the infamous 9th Marquis of Queensbury and aunt of the "decadent" Lord Alfred Douglas, Dixie was not entirely an "ornament of empire." Sent to the Transvaal in 1880 by the *Morning Post* as a female war correspondent, she began her career as a great if unconventional beauty, a superb rider and sportswoman, a staunch imperialist, and a progressive Tory. Transformed by her visit to Zululand, she became unbendingly political and steadfast in her cause—the reinstatement of Cetawayo. Unsurprisingly, a Cape Town newspaper argued that the "misfortune" in "the land of misfortune" was her visit. Her travels changed her to a Liberal, a questioner of empire, a feminist, and, most surprisingly, an opponent of the blood sports she had once so reveled in. More sympathetic to Africans than to the Boers, she declaims that a largely naked Hottentot[11] "slave," called "Dog," is far superior to the Boer master who persecutes him (247). She never, however, loses her faith in the superiority of British rule or British morality. Even the Hottentot slave knows this, she says, quoting his wish that all were as kind as the English. Although they would differ on several political issues, Heckford might well have admired her.

Like Dixie's work, Lady Barker's book, *A Year's Housekeeping in South Africa* (1875) also has serious political underpinnings, although it never questions the values of empire. In a work marked by its graciousness in mood and expression, Lady Barker shows her admiration and sympathy for the Zulu people. Barker's respect for Zulu royalty (like Heckford's for the Rain Queen), her slightly condescending praise of Zulu dignity and elegance and of African customs in general—she much prefers a real Zulu wedding procession to an imitation "white" wedding—mark her as less overtly racist than most imperial female writers. Like Heckford, she is acutely class-conscious; inviting a Zulu princess to tea, she views the visit as one of near equals, even showing the princess "her Royals," pictures of the Queen and royal family. Yet, by her own admission, Lady Barker is both pampered and protected.

Ladies of the more conventional type, more passive and traditional, also visited South Africa at the same time as Heckford, publishing their accounts in the same years. For example, Mrs. Wilkinson's book, *A Lady's Life and Travels in Zululand and the Transvaal During Cetewayo's Reign* (1882) is an account of "the kind of life a lady is called on to lead when she leaves her English home for the purpose of aiding in the extension of Christ's kingdom in such a wild and savage country as Zululand" (vii). Although Wilkinson had died in 1877, her "simple," unaffected letters were published by her devoted husband, the Bishop of Zululand, along, of course, with his insights into politics and native culture. Her account of her life as a missionary wife—even Bishops' ladies taught, played the organ and piano in church, and doctored native sufferers—is not unusual, but one wonders if her travels freed or empowered her. Describing the way floors are prepared and smeared in Zululand, she is unable to write the word "dung," instead euphemizing it to "a substance" (73–4). Told by those at home in England that she is "too dainty for Africa," she attests to her toughness by informing them that she has learned, when necessary, to take coffee without either milk or sugar (147). However, as she complains about the servant problem and the weather, readers do not get the sense that she ever

Introduction   xxxvii

transcends her role as loyal helpmate to the Bishop. Although she is not analytical or colorful in writing, the Bishop's wife is not "silly"—not the sort of female traveler satirized by *Punch* or in an anonymous volume titled *Lispings from Low Lattitudes or, extracts from the Journal Of the Hon. Impulsia Gushington*.[12]

Unlike Sarah Heckford or Lady Florence Dixie or even Mrs. Wilkinson, many women traveled simply to see—and to be seen—for adventures and experiences rather than to work. Alice Blanche Balfour, sister of the Prime Minister, trekked *Twelve Hundred Miles in a Waggon* (1895)—from Kimberley to Umtali—with three companions, essentially for the fun of it. Rich, independent, feminist, she comments on both the physical beauty and the wide spread ill treatment of African women. Unlike other travel writers of both sexes, Balfour carefully puts the word "boy" in quotes when describing Africans. Her lively book is less frivolous than it first appears though her London publisher disempowered her by omitting almost all her references to politics. By the turn of the century, female visitors had become so numerous and their visits so frequent, that they no longer found it necessary to describe South Africa.

Heckford's attitudes and experiences are different from other women travelers, even those with missions and occupations. Other women travel with much equipment and with retinues. Mary Hall, author of *A Woman's Trek From the Cape to Cairo* (1907) may be proud of being a "woman travelling alone," but she neglects to mention the numerous colonial officials who aid her, the Africans who serve as her interpreters, and the many bearers who support both her and her equipment. (At one point, she employs forty porters). Heckford, on the other hand, often travels with only a drover and a single servant or, at times, with a young man named Jimmy whom she must protect. Not for her is the vast amount of paraphernalia ladies usually required on expeditions. There are no accounts of camp-beds, folding baths, mosquito nets or elaborate tents; we do not see her change to formal dress for dinner. She sometimes sleeps under the wagon and sometimes in the open air. There are few complaints about bad food, bad weather, or bad accommodation, though she clearly suffers from all three.

Nevertheless, Heckford is a product of her era and her culture, and like many other women travelers she mingles what Susan L. Blake calls "endorsements of empire and accounts of personal experience that undercut it" (20). Like other women too, she differs from male travelers in the way she narrates incidents, that is, in the way she sees others—more as subject to subject, more as people in reciprocal relations than as subject to object or master to servant. She would be viewed by most of those who encountered her as superior in race but inferior in gender, and to some extent she uses these perceptions to her own advantage. Except for moments when it suits her purpose, she does not play the vulnerable or deferential or submissive female. She seldom uses racial superiority as a source of power. Instead she uses class superiority. Her relations with those she encounters are based on status; with chiefs and leaders they are reciprocal, with servants and porters, authoritarian but not impersonal. Blake believes that women's divided and self-contradictory position in English society leads to their having an implicitly anti-imperial relationship to Africa (21); in Heckford's case this does not occur. Although Heckford avoids jingoism and at times, questions imperial policy and action, she is firmly persuaded of the overall rightness and justice of British rule.

What does make Heckford somewhat unusual, however, is her identification with and emulation of male manners, values, and behavior (as Adler suggests [36]). Her behavior is marked by true gender ambiguity, as she constantly manifests the "masculine" virtues of strength, decisiveness, initiative, endurance, and assertiveness on the road and on the farm, while becoming "feminized" in towns and villages. When she is trekking and trading, she uses masculinity as protective coloring, as a way of maintaining independence and asserting herself, a way of having power and authority in a man's world. She sleeps under her wagon, wrapped in a blanket, sharing food and brandy with men she has encountered. She orders and witnesses the flogging of a servant; she rides alone, a pistol at her waist and another on her saddle, through wild territory.

Yet, when she enters towns and cities, she dons a mask of feminine decorum. Going in search of a hotel one night, only to find it full, she informs the manager that she cannot return to her wagon since the men will "be asleep in it"(*Lady Trader* 31). He promptly ejects a "rough-looking man" and gives "the lady" his room. She dismisses Pretoria's two hotels as unsuitable for lodging, since they both have bars, and "loud-talking men [. . .] lounging in front of them" (33). She describes herself as needing to "take heart" (33), to walk through the bar to the restaurant and is rewarded by being sent to a private room in which to dine. Yet this same woman rides alone in the veldt, bargains

Introduction

and deals with men of every class, and controls and manages drunks of varied races,

For nineteenth-century women, poised between the private or domestic sphere and the public sphere, travel writing could be especially problematic (Foster 174). Heckford does what many women traveler-writers do, that is, she establishes herself both as a conscious narrator, analyzing what she has seen, and as a woman in the midst of things, engaged in the experiences she undergoes. There is always a dichotomy between the two aspects of self; in this case it is between the decorous, feminine creature she thinks her audience expects and the assertive, active person who travels and who trades.

Intrepid and unsinkable, Heckford is a splendid traveler, uncomplaining, accepting of difficult conditions, interested in the people she meets and the sights she sees. Perhaps, as one contemporary explains (of British women travelers in general), her skill is due to the domestic nature of Englishwomen's lives which inculcates in them the "four cardinal virtues of travelling—activity, punctuality, courage and independence" (qtd. in Foster 5). More likely, it is the result of Heckford's personal history of overcoming obstacles, both physical and mental, to lead the richest fullest life she can.

HECKFORD AS TRADER

In becoming a *smous* or itinerant trader, Heckford overleaps both the barriers of class and of gender. Although excluded like most other women from the institutions of empire—she cannot serve in the military nor is she eligible for the Civil Service or government office—she has come to South Africa to do "useful" work. Moreover, hers is not among the conventional women's occupations (private and domestic or service-oriented); she has come to farm and thus make money. Yet why did an Anglo-Irish lady, acknowledged by all as a gentlewoman, choose to become a *smous?* Why does she join the class of people described in a South African newspaper of 1865 as engaged in "the very lowest occupation an unfortunate wretch can apply himself to," and "only marginally superior to the *meester* (or itinerant teacher)?" (qtd. in Shain 13). To be "in trade" was in itself a questionable occupation among the Victorian upper or aspiring middle classes; to be a female peddler and to write about it should have been beyond the pale. Heckford's implicit answer is both "necessity" and her belief, firmly held, that supplying goods to struggling farmers and to natives was the kind of useful and socially productive labor in which she could participate. It accorded with what she had argued in *Christ and Communism*. She would sell real products; she would be honest in her dealings; she would use her profits first to improve her trade and later to buy and work a farm.

Figure 4. "Crossing a Drift in Natal." Thomas Baines (c.1870). With the permission of The South African National Gallery, Cape Town. The wagon and team are typical of those used by traders like Heckford.

A few years later, she again worked as a *smous* even when many of her fellow traders were recent Russian and Polish Jewish emigrants, despised by the local South African population. But in 1880, this group had not yet arrived and peddlers were sometimes English or German Jews (assimilated to South Africa) and sometimes emigrants from the nations of Western Europe. The *smous* was certainly useful and the role could be perceived as noble. One historian sees *smouses* as bringing "to the isolated farmer living in semi-primitive conditions the material goods and also some of the cultural wares of civilization" (Saron 183). Another comments, "these commercial pioneers supplied almost all the requirements of the farming population, from agricultural implements and patent medicines to low-priced furniture and oleographs"[13] (Abrahams 27). The *smous,* in effect, enabled the farmer to survive and even prosper in remote areas.

Like other traders, Heckford must have carried paraffin and lamps, candles and soap, shovels and hoes, axes and tools, needles and thread and pins and fabrics; combs and mirrors, and hats and caps and boots, gloves, shoes, shirts, collars, and trousers as well as pots and pans, crockery, tea, sugar, patent medicines, and brandy. She mentions most of these when she speaks of her "Boer goods." She notes that the Afrikaners, often short on or unwilling to pay cash would barter, offering hides and skins, ostrich feathers and ivory, and, on one occasion, addled eggs. She also carried "Kaffir Goods" and found them even more profitable. She had fabrics and shirts and blankets, brightly colored cloth, beads and mirrors, and coils of shiny wire, which she traded for grain and for mielies, the maize that formed the mainstay of the Africans' diet and could be resold for a good profit in the towns. Her account of trading in a kraal is amusing, as she compares the buying practices she finds among Africans—the preening, modeling, and seeking and obtaining of advice—to the scenes and figures at a London department store.

Heckford's trading experiences constitute some of the most interesting incidents in her book. Determined to go to the bush-veldt of the northern Transvaal where the Boers go in winter to graze their herds and flocks, she learns about their lives and customs. "The Boers greatly enjoy this annual picnic; the men hunting, the women and children sitting and playing about under the trees" (63), she says. They travel long distances in their wagons and live in tents as comfortable or more so than their unpleasant everyday houses (123). (Because of this fact she will later see the housing in concentration camps as no worse than ordinary Afrikaner habitations). She quickly recognizes that people in a holiday mood, living close together in tents and wagons (instead of on isolated farms) will be conducive to trade. Her initial plan to go with Egerton, the fallen "gentleman" she likes, a German employee and two Africans to serve respectively as driver and *foreloper,* goes awry.[14] With insufficient and untrained help, inexperienced herself, she feels both the risk of her venture and the excitement of the challenge.

The risks and challenges are real. Heckford must learn an entirely new "profession," for which nothing in her previous life has prepared her. She begins by selling forage, seed oats, pumpkins and fowls, collecting the goods she has imported from England, selecting and buying other goods, and pricing them all. After much delay and several mishaps, she obtains the services of Hendrick, a half-caste driver and Hans, a Hottentot *foreloper* who comes with a little Khoisan boy who has been left in his charge. She tells readers of her first sales on the road, pipes for smoking and sugar for coffee, bought by two men in a wagon loaded with hides. Handicapped by her initial inability to speak the language of the Boers, she soon learns Afrikaans, both because she needs the language for trade and because she wishes to know about the people with whom she trades. Painfully honest herself, she is distressed by what she sees as cheating and stealing among the Boers, telling readers of a girl who lies about a price, of another who tries to remove a valuable ring from her finger, and of a third, whose gloves are stolen almost as soon as she buys them.

To the annoyance of the Afrikaner men, she does not, at first, sell liquor. On a second expedition and on the advice of other traders, she carries a barrel of Cape brandy. She will not sell drinks by the glass, only bottles, and has trouble persuading the magistrate who gives her the necessary license that she will stick to the letter of the law. Refusing to kowtow to authority, annoyed that her integrity is questioned, Heckford tells the magistrate that he may fine her as heavily as he chooses if he catches her breaking the law. She sticks to the agreement despite pressures, and rejects the pernicious advice of the shopkeeper who sells her the brandy: "When you get well out from amongst the Boers," he tells her, "just fill up the cask with water; the Kaffirs won't remark it. I wouldn't advise you to put tobacco into it; that I don't think right. But just fill up with water; it won't pay well enough if you don't" (161). She will no sooner cheat Africans than Afrikaners!

Although selling liquor is legal, Heckford finds it more nuisance than profit; she must deal with Boer men begging her to sell or give them "tots" or glassfuls (which her license does not allow) or else clubbing together to buy bottles and getting rapidly drunk and rowdy. She finds it nearly impossible to sell her brandy to Africans, since these potential customers seldom have the containers to put it in. Brandy is in such demand, however, that when she loses the key to the tap on the keg, and thus cannot pour it, her otherwise uninventive customers find other ways of extracting it.

Successful enough to buy a second and larger wagon, Heckford ends her first trading venture when she is laid up with fever, threatened

Introduction

by the outbreak of the Basuto War, and rich enough to buy a farm. It is not the end of her experiences as a *smous,* however, for she returns to trading when she reenters South Africa in the late 1880s. But she does not write of her later adventures. She has already made her point: one can be both a "lady" and a "trader."

HECKFORD AND WAR

Sarah Heckford's comments on three South African wars add interesting footnotes, at the least, to the historiography of the period. She arrived in South Africa at the beginning of one conflict (the Anglo-Zulu), was deeply involved in a second (the First South African War of 1880–81) and survived a third (the Second South African War of 1899–1902). Her involvement in the Zulu War was peripheral; she merely comments that "volunteers" (many of whom would die at the battles of Isandlwana and Rorke's Drift) had boarded her ship at East London and bought up most of the available horses when they disembarked at Durban. The impact of the war was far greater than she recognized, for the ineptness of the British forces in that set of battles served to embolden the Boers who would fight against them the next year.[15]

Boer Method of Fighting.

Figure 5. "Boer Commandoes." An unsigned, unidentified illustration of the techniques utilized by the Afrikaner forces during the first South African War. From Charles Du Val, *With a Show Through Southern Africa,* Volume 2 (London: 1881). Courtesy of the National Library of South Africa.

"The Transvaal problem" began in 1877, the same year that saw Victoria made Empress of India, when Disraeli and the British Parliament annexed the South African Republic for the first time as part of a plan to federate the territories that then comprised South Africa. Although the Afrikaners of the Transvaal had no intention of having their land made part of a British federation, they were initially too weak and divided to contest the issue. By 1880 matters were different. Gladstone and his Liberals were once again in power and were seemingly less interested in building the empire than was the Tory, Disraeli. The Boers took advantage of a weak administration and an inept system of taxation and declared their independence in December 1880. They declared war and, in the next two months, shattered the myth of British military supremacy by soundly beating the English forces at Laing's Nek, Ingogo and Majuba. As they besieged the small British garrisons in Pretoria, Potschefstroom and Lydenburg, British General George Colley marched with troops from Natal, falsely believing that women and children were starving in beleaguered Pretoria, and was badly defeated at Laing's Nek.

H. Rider Haggard was in South Africa at the same time as Heckford although there is no evidence that they ever met. He was running an ostrich farm near Newcastle, close to the Transvaal border, when he heard gunfire announcing the battles. All on the farm except Haggard mistook it for thunder. He knew, long before Heckford, who was besieged in Pretoria, that Colley and his troops had been virtually destroyed at the battle of Majuba.

But even before the British defeat at Majuba, Gladstone had begun negotiating with the Boer ruling triumvirate, Paul Kruger, Piet Joubert and Hermanus Pretorius, and when the Pretoria Convention was finally signed in late 1881, it once again granted independence to the Transvaal. The Boers had won the right to self-determination, albeit briefly. To the British and the settlers of English stock (or English Afrikanders), the retrocession was a humiliating loss; they could not forget either the slaughter at Majuba or the betrayal the empire had visited upon English settlers and "loyal" Boers alike. Haggard, who had been present at the beginning of the process—he had hoisted the British flag at the annexation—ironically, was present at its ending. His farm was used by the Retrocession Commission, which metaphorically, at least, was forced to lower the British flag.

Introduction	xlv

Heckford's role in the First South African War was considerably more central. She was trapped in Pretoria during all hundred days of the siege and her account of it is significant both historically and as narrative. She provides a detailed record of life in the camp and a realistic, uninflated account of the sorties and battles in the area. Hers is only one report, however; Charles Du Val, an Irish entertainer, well known for his one-man shows, was another among the besieged. Co-editor of a thrice-weekly paper called the *News of the Camp* and volunteer cavalryman with a group of locals known as "The Pretoria Mounted Carabineers," he encountered and described Heckford at the beginning of the siege:

> With all the relief of an editor who has just got his paper safely out, I walked down to the Garrison Office, where I arrived just in time to hear a little, delicate lame lady offer her services to Colonel Gildea to try to run the blockade with dispatches to Sir George Colley, in Natal, on whom our hopes of relief were now fixed. (*With a Show* 2:31–32)

His initial tone of condescension toward the "little, delicate lame lady" gives way quickly; after noting that the offer was declined, he goes on to comment that "subsequent knowledge of the lady (a Mrs. H——) led me to believe [she] would have been successful" (2:32).

Du Val "was much interested in this little woman—in all respects a lady, and who was undoubtedly a figure in our camp—she being allowed to retain two of her horses, for her own use and that of a Kaffir servant, who invariably followed after her wherever she rode. I often thought what a sensation she might have created in the 'Lady's Mile,' with those two rough African ponies and her wooly-headed Jeames" (2:32). One wonders what he knew of Heckford's past. Was he aware that she had once been one of the fashionable equestrians of London's "Rotten Row"? He did know that she too was engaged in writing about the war and made haste, when the conflict ended, to get his book, *With a Show Through Southern Africa,* out before hers.[16]

Heckford's chronicle of the siege differs greatly from Du Val's (which occupies most of his second volume). Gender, of course, plays a role in differentiating the two accounts; Du Val could and did go out and fight; Heckford, though an excellent shot and equestrian, could not. His story is of sorties and action, of adventure and excitement and comedy. He is at the center of it all and readers learn much of his newspaper and his role in battles. The subtitle of the paper (published from a tent on the camp premises): *a journal of Fancies, Notifications, Gossip And General Chit Chat,* is an accurate description of both Du Val's book and his contributions to the newspaper. He wrote much of the material for *News of the Camp;* he includes his own light verse (often parodic), early chapters of *With a Show,* and much "General Chit Chat." But the paper's specific, detailed accounts of the military actions around Pretoria make it historically useful. And, though it often struggles for wit, it is sometimes amusing.

Instead of the concern with individuals and camp conditions that Heckford exhibits, Du Val's "Personal Reminiscences of the Transvaal War" (in Volume 2 of *With a Show*) are filled with battle scenes and comedies. There is a humorous anecdote about the confusion between the doctor's bell and a local cow-bell; there are jokes about gold mining told by men digging earthworks; there are comments on the colorful if vulgar language and amusing squabbles of the ordinary soldiers' wives. Du Val is a showman, and his account was far more popular than Heckford's. *With a Show Through Southern Africa* sold 25,000 copies in its first two months of publication.

What immediately strikes a reader is the difference in attitude and approach between Du Val and Heckford. His book is surprisingly devoid of political and military analysis; his people are stereotypes. All Africans are "niggers" (1:47); Cetchwayo, the former Zulu King whom he earlier sees in Cape Town, is "his royal duskiness" depicted as semi-naked (in token of his "savage" nature) and as suffering from loneliness since only five of his wives are with him (1:52). Though Du Val recognizes that the "colonial anti-Kaffir does as much harm by his ill-treatment of the native races as the Exeter Hall sympathizer" (1:94) does by his extravagant claims of black equality, it is clear that he views Africans as an inferior, even a separate race. After seeing an African albino, he remarks, "the negro's blackness is a blessing, as it helps to conceal his unprepossessing lineaments" (1:40).

His attitude toward the Boers is equally stereotypical. They are slow, slovenly, lazy and ignorant; though he grants them excellence as marksmen. Unlike Heckford, he never questions the "rightness" of the way the Transvaal was annexed. For him, much of the blame for lost battles in particular and the British failure in general, lies with the "Intelligence Department"—colored scouts and spies whose "informa-

Introduction   xlvii

tion was always unreliable, often totally false, and whose 'intelligence' appeared to be only exhibited in successful forays upon farm-yards" (2:28).

While Heckford's war activities were limited by her circumstances, she actively observed and commented upon much of what she saw, including the fighting. Her account of the Transvaal affair is factual and yet personal, intelligent and compassionate, fair and noteworthy for its judgments of people and events. Remarking that she wrote most of her book during the siege, she gives us a sense of her daily routine. Rising at dawn, she takes care of her animals, fetches her rations, and spends much of her day in the village (that is, Pretoria) working, relaxing or writing. Her care and concern for her horses and oxen, her attempt to preserve them while others died, seems foremost in her mind.[17] She also fetches her own food supply, for she quickly learns that "by going myself instead of sending a boy, I got better rations" (222). Coming "home to dinner at about five;" she again checks on the well being of her animals and "then paid visits" (222). Life was not quite as boring as it appears, for she knew many people in the camp, was invited to dinners, was assiduous in gathering the local news, and remarks elsewhere that evenings at least were cheery. Du Val reports that there were band concerts almost every night and Sarah comments:

> Against this picture [that is, of the camp on a depressing, rainy morning], I may set that of a fine evening, after the band had ceased playing. Then all the various habitations were alight, and one caught glimpses of illuminated interiors, with dashes of bright colour in them, arranged in long vistas. The camp-fires burnt cheerily, and one heard nothing but merry voices and laughter from the groups of coloured people assembled round them and from the promenaders, whilst here and there a gay party would be assembled, and one would hear snatches of song–and even, in one bungalow, the sound of a piano. (219)

Making the best of things was part of Heckford's own nature and of the spirit of the camp. She never complains; her real concern is with the plight of others, especially the women. She does speak of the "plagues" of camp life: ranging from comic and petty disputes over smoke from one person's fire annoying the people whose tent or wagon was next to it, arguments over lights and "lights out," through gossip and scandal, to the miserable weather and the infestations of fleas. Again, refusing to complain, she says that the camp was better in sanitary matters, disease control, and comfort than might have been expected. But the weather was dreadful; it rained incessantly and Heckford speaks of walking on dismal mornings, covered by her "waterproof," the water running over her boots. However, her focus is on the discomfort of others, especially that of the women. She describes:

> Women of various ranks emerging from their tents, or from their wagons, slipping in the mud, or plashing into the water so soon as they stepped on the ground; making their coffee, or preparing the breakfast over the little fire some shivering Kaffir was trying to blow into a blaze, while a little child, perhaps, held on to them and cried, or bewailed itself from within the tent. (219)

Her admiration for such women manifests itself in vignettes of their stoic courage. She is especially impressed by the wives of the volunteers who almost daily watched their husbands go off to scout or fight and then spent the day waiting to see if their men returned. "I used to admire these women!" she says. "There was no ostentatious anxiety or grief, but you would see their poor trembling lips, and nervously clasped hands, and eyes strained bravely to keep back their tears, as they hastened to where they could get tidings of those who might perhaps be destined never to return, or to return only to die" (225).

Aware of the hazards of war, Heckford paints sad but not melodramatic pictures of the deaths she witnesses. "Children and delicate people suffered severely. Many a coffin was taken in a cart to the little graveyard with s few mourners walking after it; a few flowers plucked from some deserted garden strewn on it" (222–23). In an abrupt change of tone, she notes realistically, if matter-of-factly, that as the number of deaths increased "there was difficulty in obtaining planks for the coffins, and those earthworks in which wood had been used as a support, had to be demolished" (223). Her description of the fate of Desiderius Erasmus is especially poignant. The handsome young son of a Boer family loyal to England, "Deesy" had insisted on fighting—as "a matter of honour"—(228) only to be wounded, captured by the Boers, exchanged as a prisoner, and sent home to die of his wounds.[18]

Heckford's scorn is reserved for the inefficiency of some in authority. In this case, she is scathing about the retrocession of the land so many had died for. Her annoyance at the foolishness of military control is often masked by the humor with which she describes it. When she first follows the instructions to enter the camp, she slogs through a storm only to discover that, without telling the populace, the authorities have postponed their entry till the next day. On first arriving in the camp, she asks where she should stable her thirty-eight oxen and is told to let them loose in the camp square. After thanking the officer for his advice, she entirely disregards it, commenting "how singularly beneficial to all parties it would be to have thirty-eight oxen, maddened with fear, rushing about in a small space that was being desperately defended; unless" (she adds sarcastically) "one looked upon the arrangement from a Boer point of view" (213). Nevertheless, she is fair-minded enough to be concerned about the rounding up and incarceration of people thought to be Afrikaner sympathizers on mere suspicion and the flimsiest of evidence.

As to the conduct of the war itself, she is concerned about the way both volunteers and regular troops are deployed. She observes that the volunteer brigades, "Nourse's Horse" and the "Pretoria Carabineers" are sent out first, without sufficient backup, while the regular troops, better trained and eager for action, are kept back. Brutally honest about the conduct of the war, she notes that the first sortie was the sole British success and factually comments on the Boer victories in two other battles, especially the Red House kraal.

"Poor, inglorious martyrs, sacrificed for nothing" (223) is her verdict on the deaths of the British and colonial soldiers when she learns that the Transvaal is to be returned to the Boers. Yet, not an unthinking daughter of empire, she has questioned the annexation in the first place. "It has always been my opinion that although the English Government were perfectly justified in annexing the Transvaal, *the manner in which it was annexed was not only an unjustifiable blunder but an unjust act*" (205, emphasis added). And she feels free to say this to her Boer neighbors, while explaining that she would nevertheless side with the English, not because of nationality, but because of her belief that the action was correct in principle. Although she too is ruined by the retrocession, she considers herself "luckier than most." Her oxen are alive, her horses are well and she is unhurt. "I was the luckiest person in camp," she says, "and I felt almost as if I were selfish as I walked through the lines of tents and wagons [. . .] thinking of the ruin that had fallen on almost all in them" (231). Her concern is with others, the many she knows who have lost everything. Above all, it is with the disgrace to England. "It was not for myself that I felt the bitter ache at my heart, it was for the honour of England, a thousand times worse than any pain caused by personal loss" (230). About the defeat of the imperial dream, she could do nothing, she says, while she can retrieve her personal ruin "by courage and steadiness" (230). In her eyes, the real sufferers are the loyal Afrikander and the loyal Boer. As she was to write in her newspaper articles, these people had been robbed, not just of personal possessions but of home and country.

In all, Heckford's account of the war, though perhaps flawed by her concern for "the honour of England" is a splendid but overlooked contribution to history and narrative art.

Heckford on the Boers

Not unexpectedly, Heckford's attitude to the Afrikaners she encounters during the war and in peace is a combination of the stereotypical and atypical. On the one hand, she accepts the conventional view that Boers are dirty, ignorant, and lazy, by their very nature inferior to the British (and herself). On the other hand, she can, at times, transcend the cultural differences between herself and Afrikaners, especially once she has learned their language and come to understand the rigors of farm life. At best, she is ambivalent about them. She is more astute about and sympathetic to the wives and daughters of the farmers than to the men. Nevertheless, she can never quite forgive or forget the cruelty of both sexes to Africans. After telling of the brutal flogging of an African woman about to give birth, Heckford stops to relate tales of other Boer brutalities. She specifically indicts Paul Kruger, having heard numerous stories of his cold-blooded murders of African women and children. She adds her own tales to the stock; one of an Afrikaner man she knows who dragged an African to death behind his horse and boasted of it; another, of a native, sick with fever, who was ordered by a Boer magistrate to be flogged more severely than the usual sentence demanded because Heckford "had the bad taste to interfere on behalf of a Kaffir" ("Boer Treatment of Kaffirs" 8). She is equally horrified by the attitude of two Boer women witnessing the whipping—and nonchalantly sipping coffee.

Her responses to Afrikaners are often negative but become less stereotypical as she has more contact with them, especially in her capacity as a *smous*. There is a progression in her views; she ceases to generalize so frequently and begins to recognize how much the Boers are conditioned by their environment. Her first view, however, is typical of British middle and upper-class visitors. The remote farmhouse in which she must spend the night is, she reports "squalor in the midst of plenty." After shaking hands with everyone, Heckford remarks that "all the hands were very dirty" (22). There are fourteen children, and the family is "rich in flocks and herds, and yet all but the father, mother, and two eldest sons were barefooted; none had stockings; none appeared to be possessed of a brush and comb, or of soap" (22). Such accounts of the slovenly, backward Boers at home are almost set pieces in the works of English commentators. What follows is equally stereotypic. A small basin and dirty cloth are passed first to guests and then down the ladder of family (the girls, Heckford notices, do not get to wash). Then, after a long grace, comes a meager, ill-cooked meal. The guest sleeps "in a dark little closet, in which there was a big very dirty-looking bed" (23). She sleeps alone, for she is an honored visitor, but her bed is "the domicile of innumerable insects." Fortunately, she has slept with her clothing on, since the Boers do not undress for sleep and "think it the height of impropriety to do so" (24). Her modesty has reduced the number of insect bites she must endure.

Culturally, she is a world away from them. She speaks of the mixed blessing of Afrikaner hospitality, of how the Boers can be both kind and annoying at the same time. They have no respect for privacy and when she is staying with or renting space from them, invade her incessantly. Famous for their lack of courtesy, they do treat her with more respect than they afford most people or so she remarks. Is it her infirmity or their awareness of her class superiority that makes them courteous and formal rather than excessively familiar? They are seldom either "coarse and impertinent" to her (202).

But it is as a *smous* that Heckford really gets to know the Afrikaners and she tells us, candidly, of what she believed, before she could speak their language. She had heard them described as "a treacherous, lying, hypocritical people, with all the faults but with none of the virtues supposed to belong to rough peasants" (144). But she meets honest, kind and candid people too.[19] Her experiences as a trader alter, but do not entirely contradict her preconceptions. She does learn that Afrikaners are not as ignorant or stupid as the British like to think, although some do believe the earth is flat and the stars were made as lamps for human benefit. She finds that some are sharp, dishonest traders; that girls and women are sometimes "light fingered," that promises made are not always kept. But, on the other hand, she learns that Afrikaners want to know and help her, that they are capable of generosity as well as of acts of kindness and concern. A Boer couple rescue, feed and care for her lost dog, refusing to sell him "because they wanted to find his true owner" (156). Moreover, these "good Samaritans" break the mold, for they are "clean and tidy in all their arrangements" and their child is "as neat and fresh as any English child could be" (156). For Heckford, cleanliness (to her a British attribute) is a moral as well as physical virtue.

When Heckford interacts with Afrikaners on a personal level her perceptions of them change radically. She becomes friendly with the interwoven families of the De Clercs, with whose men she candidly discusses politics, and the De Plessis. "They are the best Boers I have come across," says she of the latter family. Young De Plessis, merry, bold and free, is "a sure-shot, a daring hunter, and a first rate horseman; yet always ready to help his wife with the baby [. . .] and, withal a most diligent and energetic farmer" (164). His wife is equally attractive, "doing all sorts of little domestic work with the air of a Juno" (164), but more serenely than the goddess, Heckford adds. She is neat and tidy, Heckford's cardinal virtue, and even the couple's infant is spotless. All this, despite the fact that they are very poor. From knowledge of such people and of their lives grows respect for them. Surprisingly, Heckford can remain friendly with Afrikaners even when they attempt to cheat her—though she scolds them and offers moral lessons. She is truly grieved at the losses suffered by the "loyal Boers," moved by such figures as the mourning mother of Deesy Erasmus. And she never fails to admire the courage and the skill in battle of the Afrikaner men. Despite her bitterness at the retrocession of the Transvaal, Heckford can approach a Boer commando whom she knows and say, "I am sorry for the peace [. . .] it is a disgrace to my country; but [. . .] I heartily congratulate you; you have fought well and have got your reward" (232).

Her insights are sharpest when directed towards Afrikaner women. Even relatively early in her experiences, she comes to respect their strength and integrity. Her admiration for a Boer female farmer, the widow of three husbands, is considerable. Though "like all Boer women and men, she regarded husbands and wives as articles so necessary to household comfort that no time must be lost in replacing them" (80), the widow manifests the virtues that Sarah Heckford (and after her, Olive Schreiner) sees as ideal. On the trim farm she has created, the widow is "hospitable and free-handed to all, of whatever nation they might be." Yet, she is a hard worker and "a frugal manager." "If her oxen stuck in a difficult drift, she would tuck up her petticoats, pull off her boots [. . .] and drive the team through herself. If labour was scarce at harvest time, or when water had to be led on the lands, she thought nothing of doing the necessary work. But she attended to her household duties withal" (80). Heckford, true to the dicta expressed in *Christ and Communism,* praises Boer women for their useful and productive work, foreshadowing what Olive Schreiner will say in *Woman and Labour.*

However, like other imperial travel writers and fiction writers of the period, she deplores the way many Boer women are forced to live, their low status in their families, their marriages of convenience, their lives of endless childbearing and backbreaking toil. Discussing another family named De Plessis (but no relation to the "best Boers"), she again describes the dirty children, and "slatternly women with loud voices," but stops to explain the reasons for the condition of which these are symptoms, the "depression" common to Boer women:

> With a life of dull toil stretching from childhood to the grave, it is no wonder that it should be so; and yet, those who have known the peasantry of other lands, must feel the question arise in their minds, 'Why should the Boer peasant-woman look depressed, when the South Italian peasant-woman (for instance) does not?' I think the answer to the question is, 'Look at the men.' (201)

Heckford continues: "It is not the want of education, or rather of book-learning, that makes a life of toil dull, and the men and women who live such lives, generation after generation, incarnations of dullness." The problem, for Heckford, is Boer men. "The women of a race will not look depressed if the men be not 'dull;' and *vice versa,* if the women look depressed the men must be 'dull'" (201). Depression is the stamp on the faces of the vast majority of Afrikaner women, Heckford believes, though among the elder ones, "the tendency to fat" can give "an appearance of jollity." She concludes, however, that "cheerful women amongst the Boers [. . .] are rare exceptions" (202). Her remedy (not yet formulated) for this gender-induced depression was to be education and communication *within* a community of women through organizations such as the Transvaal Women's Educational Union. In the end, conditioned by her class, status, identification with empire, and moral convictions, Heckford's attitudes toward the Boers remain conflicted and inconsistent but not unsympathetic.

Heckford on Africans

As with the Afrikaners, Heckford's views of Africans combine the stereotypical and the iconoclastic. Natives are "Kaffirs," the term ordinarily used for them by Europeans; the adult males who work for her, to some of whom she is deeply attached, are "boys." In an era when virtually all whites, no matter how advanced, did not perceive Africans as equals, she too, accepts the racial myths propagated by empire. But she is not a Social Darwinist; to her, Africans are inferior, but they are not a separate species nor do they have inherent or immutable characteristics; they may be uncivilized at present but they are civilizable. Unlike most other commentators, she is fond of those she labels Hottentots—again, the usual name for the Khoikhoi or Khoisan people—and does not have the usual contempt for half-castes. (She believes that they make excellent, intelligent servants.)

But she begins her South African adventures with the usual preconceptions. She thinks of Africans as drunks, as childlike, as beastlike in many traits, as especially cruel to animals, but soon reveals an interesting combination of compassion, condescension and empathy towards them. Just as she has initially seen the East End poor as nearly different in nature and must learn firsthand of "the good which is in all alike, disguised under varied aspects" (*Hospital* xxxvii), so too with Africans. Once again, experience teaches her. Early in her travels, she watches a white man beating the drunken driver of the vehicle in which she is supposed to ride. The whipping ("he struck the Kaffir across the head, arms, and breast, with his heavy stinging ox-hide whip" [18]) amazes Heckford, new to the mistreatment of Africans. She is equally astonished by the lack of response: "The fellow barely stirred a muscle. I could hardly at the time think that he felt much, but Kaffirs will sometimes bear a beating that *does* hurt in that way" (18).

By the end of her stay she recognizes that Africans suffer pain just as Caucasians do and admires their stoic endurance of it.

Unlike many of the other travelers to South Africa, Heckford sees her African servants and associates as people—who have names, and traits, and personalities. She does not often write about "boys" and servants but instead about Fiervaree, the young and mischievous groom, about Maikee and Vittaree of Nooitgedacht, about Sannee, the housemaid, and the old woman, Krid. Readers get to know Hendrick, the drover, and little Hans, and Clas, and the unfortunate Pete; all are described without mockery and condescension. And, as with the Boers, when Heckford knows Africans as individuals they become something other than "Other."

Heckford is idiosyncratic in her acceptance or dislike of various groups and tribes. Always concerned with "class" herself, she is amused by intra-African class snobbery, by the tensions between "raw Kaffirs" and "Urlams" or "civilized" Africans who dress and eat like Europeans and attend the mission schools. Annoyed at the attitude of a black woman who announces that "when she came back from school and had been made a Christian," she, being superior, "would not let the raw Kaffirs eat with her" (52), Heckford does not recognize her own snobbery. In her relations with African chiefs, and tribal rulers, she minimizes racial and cultural difference—in part by reaffirming their mutual status. She meets African rulers as one aristocrat to another. Thus, she shakes hands with and gives brandy to one chief, and is deeply interested in the sad life and reduced circumstances of another.

For example, her account of a "Kaffir idyll," (Chapter 17) reveals an interesting combination of feeling, personal insight and empathy. Here, as she discusses Mangwan, son and heir of chief Mosilikatz (that is, Mzilikazi)[20] of the Mantatees, she retells a tale of a world lost for love and its less romantic consequences. Mangwan, who has married his dead father's favorite wife and is thus subject to the forfeiture of his life and inheritance, is forced to flee with his beloved to the property of Heckford's friends. There, because it is beneath his dignity to work, he loses his wealth, his slaves, and all his stores. By the time he becomes Heckford's tenant, he is an old man "very skinny and ugly, and the woman he had given up his kingdom for was a hideous specimen of humanity." Heckford dislikes the shrewish wife, admires their son, "a very pretty, active, and graceful boy" (106) and respects the innate aristocracy, the dignity and "stateliness" of Mangwan himself. She comments on the steadfastness of his love for the woman who cost him so much, noticing that the only time he gives way to anger is when his beloved is annoyed or insulted. Comparing him in exile to the great Italian poet, Dante, Heckford remarks: "whether to a European or a Kaffir the sense of having to ask for favours when you once dispensed them, to obey where you once commanded—the feeling of dependence upon a stranger—must always be bitter" (107). Here, transcending her prejudices, she sees Mangwan as very like herself in his love for a spouse, his exile, and his reduced circumstances. Ironically, her class snobbery—he was, after all, a chief—makes her empathetic and compassionate.

She dislikes most of the Makatees, as she calls them (they are actually the Mantatees, a Zulu people) who migrated to the northern Transvaal.[21] Told by the missionary who works with them that even the Christians among them are deceitful, disobedient and grasping, she remarks that they are "nasty." But she is impressed with the kindness and dignity of a random group of Africans, on their way to the diamond-fields at Kimberley, who she finds resting under a tree. Inquiring about where to find water for her thirsty horses, she is led to a distant spring by a volunteer among the tired men. Yet, to her amazement, he refuses payment. "I have brought you to the spring," he tells her. "I did not want any money" (166). Surprised that the man is satisfied with thanks, Sarah offers him and his companions some brandy. They accept and thank her graciously; though "very raw Kaffirs," they are "wonderful in the matter of courtesy" (166).

Heckford cannot pardon either the mistreatment of children or of animals; she is extraordinarily sentimental about the latter. In one case, her medical skills lead to her being called on to help a seriously ill child. It is the little girl of a Westernized father, Andreas, and his wife. The father is greatly distressed at the child's illness, while the mother seems unconcerned. A tragic tale of vengeance unfolds, and Heckford, convinced that the mother has poisoned her own daughter, learns that the act is revenge for Andreas' poisoning of his brother. She is filled with sorrow, less for the child than for its suffering father. "The poor fellow had no thought for himself, but with anguish in his face and voice he besought me to save his child" (72), she reports. But she cannot. Like Medea, Andreas' unhappy wife has murdered her own offspring and Heckford is horrified to learn that some in the tribe believe

Introduction

her action is fit retribution. This incident and one other mark the low ebb of Sarah's feelings about Africans; she finds it appalling "that Kaffir women were quite capable of poisoning their own children in revenge upon their husbands" (74).

She is even more upset by the climax of her visit to chief Makapan's kraal in response to his invitation to a tribal ritual. A thoroughly modern chief, Makapan wears European costume, lives in Western style, and does not observe the ceremoniousness of the more traditional tribal leaders. He lacks belief in his "special powers," and Heckford comments that like her, he does not believe that he can conjure up the rain. Far less class-conscious than Heckford, he shakes hands with her drover, leading her to wonder if the chief's lack of formality loses him .the respect of his people. Attending the ceremony, Heckford enjoys the dancing, finds the young men attractive and "picturesque" (175) and admires their acting and miming. However, she leaves before the feast itself, for she is enraged when she learns that it involves the torture of the animal to be slaughtered (304). Truly disgusted with the behavior of people to whom she has felt friendly, she tells her servants to refuse the meat of the animal, even though all are hungry. "We would rather starve than encourage such an atrocity" (179), she announces. Although Makapan denies the story and the practice, she finds it difficult to shake his hand when they next meet, not because he is an African, but because he has permitted the tormenting of an ox.

Heckford's rather puritanical sense of justice leads to one of the moments in her book most difficult for modern readers to accept. On the one hand, she hates what she sees as injustice, even condemning the common practice of using Africans as unpaid tenant labor. She does not like the fact that Africans are seldom paid, that they are often virtual serfs, whose landlords have the right to their labor in return for their presence on the farm. On the other hand, she believes in following the letter of the law, in strictly maintaining her word regardless of consequences. The incident of her punishing her servant Pete—in her eyes a just act—is the most regrettable in the book, though her Victorian audience would have praised her for it. She has warned Pete twice of his misbehavior, reminding him that she does not like to punish either her servants or her animals, but that when she does, she gives them something to remember. She informs readers: "I have always found the giving of a certain grace a good plan with European servants, I have found it a bad plan with African servants" (171). She comments that at the time she warned Pete, she did not yet believe this and so gave him "the benefit of the doubt" (171). Pete's third offence is severely punished. He has abandoned the oxen left in his charge in a place that grows poisonous plants and has disappeared. Heckford, having threatened to give him twenty-five lashes, goes to the local Boer magistrate for assistance. "Looking like a hunted baboon" (185), Pete is caught and earns Heckford's contempt by groveling to her. A crowd of Boers gathers and she notices how pleased and gratified they are at witnessing the punishment. One looks like "a weasel that has caught sight of a rat" (186), another has a "bloodthirsty look" and gloats "hungrily" at Pete. The spectators are just as bestial as Pete, and Heckford finds the way the Boers begin to torment him, "like hounds round a fox," "a disgusting spectacle" (187). She warns the crowd that he is to be punished not tortured. Feeling obliged to witness the flogging, she does so, gives Pete his pay and fires him. Only then does she learn that he has been stealing and reselling her trade goods. Brought in for questioning, Pete is this time committed for trial. When he refuses to confess, he is sentenced to twenty-five more lashes and six months of labor, but (mercifully) escapes before the sentence can be carried out.

This incident reveals more about Heckford as a rigid moralist than as a racist (though that element is undeniably present), for she condemns almost equally the offense of Pete and the base enjoyment of his punishment by the Boers. She believes she has been just in her accusations, is justified in her behavior, and that justice has been done. It is justice without mercy, however, and predicated upon an innate belief in the inferiority and bestiality of African servants and on a sense of her own superiority.

Heckford has less to do with African women than with African men both as a *smous* and as a farmer. However, unlike other women travelers of the time, she does not use them as examples against which to gauge her own social power or political progress. She is also somewhat unusual in not depicting them as victims of tribal oppression. Perhaps because she too works hard (and esteems such labor), she does not see their strenuous work as punitive. Her responses to African women are mainly esthetic; she describes some as "pretty and graceful," (250) often comparing them to European works of art or sculpture; she views others as unattractive. Not a "maternal" imperialist or an embodiment of a benevolent mothering force, she does not see their lives as wretched or question their tribal status as females.

The Private Heckford

In all, Sarah Heckford is an odd mixture of traits and responses. Although she is already staunchly individualistic before she begins her travels, she finds in South Africa an even fuller sense of personal identity. In addition to being a social worker, medical worker, teacher and farmer, she becomes an astute and successful trader—a businesswoman to be reckoned with. While in this sense she is the paradigm of a thoroughly modern woman, assertive, strong, confident and commanding, she retains the moral structures and strictures we associate with the Victorians. She insists on respectability and adopts, when necessary, all the subterfuges of the "lady." For instance, while it is clear that she is attracted to Egerton (Heckford's biographer speculates on an affair between them), she never mentions or even suggests her sexuality or that of others. While she can and does transcend racial and cultural biases, she is thoroughly class-conscious. Her responses are always conditioned by social position; she never forgets that she is white, upper class and Anglo-Irish. For her the divide is less between black and white than between gentry and plebian. Hence, she will do almost anything for Egerton, a "fallen" gentleman, whom others believe has lost his status; she will feed and maintain Mangwan, the son of the great chief, Mzilikatzi, and she will offer her friendship and aid to the Rain Queen. However, she redefines gentility. She is quick to see the innate aristocracy in people of all groups and races, Boers and Africans included. Gentility is a matter of natural courtesy and refinement, whether exhibited by the farm wife, Mrs. Higgins, who drops her "haitches" or by the unknown "Kaffir" who leads her and her horses to a distant spring. She is generally both kind and fair to those who serve her, though she treats them with patriarchal rather than maternal authority. She may demand obedience and honesty but if food is scarce she will go without dinner or share her own with a servant.

Heckford is fulsome and sentimental about animals, and her love and concern for her horses and dogs and even her oxen is prominent in her narrative. She sees such concern as a mark both of class and of "civilization." How one cares for one's animals is to her an indication of one's morality. De Plessis, the Boer she admires, is the only one of his "race" who carefully grooms his horse at night, as she does. Natives show their inferiority by refusing to tend to her horses and by what she discerns as a lack of concern for their own animals. Cruelty to beasts is an unforgivable sin. Significantly, feelings like Heckford's created the

Royal Society for the Prevention of Cruelty to Animals (RSPCA) at just about the time she writes.

Her viewpoints are indeed colored by the inherent colonialism of Victorian social and political thought. Although the colonial state is a male state in its social base, personnel and laws, Heckford accepts and supports it. But she does not passively submit to men's authority nor is she silent in the face of what she deems stupid or unjust. She believes in the empire at large, but she does not fully internalize the circumscribed role allotted to women within it. A woman of initiative and capability, she enjoys organizing and running her own life, and has little tolerance for hampering social contacts. Becoming a trader allows her to circumvent a number of them. While she can play traditional female roles, her goals are not the "caring professions," mothering, teaching, nursing or domestic service. Although capable of exhibiting the sentiment and "feminine" kindness that define women in the imperialist construct, she simultaneously displays the competitive nature, adventurous spirit, and rational mind that the paradigm ascribes to men. She manifests true gender ambiguity, demonstrating the "masculine" virtues of initiative, decisiveness, endurance, and assertion on the road and on the farm, while becoming decorous and "feminized" in towns and villages.

Heckford has a clear, if unromantic, sense of self, even telling readers that she is plain and lame. Visibly disabled, she is neither self-pitying nor self-aggrandizing because of it. Although she can be haughty and arrogant and humble and compassionate in quick succession, she seldom mocks or effaces herself, at least in print. Unlike most other women travelers, Heckford does not apologize for writing.

Her book, *A Lady Trader in the Transvaal* is both highly intelligent and unflinchingly honest. Perhaps these two traits are among its most striking virtues. As readers, we may disagree with Heckford's biases; we may dislike the strictness of her moral code, we may repudiate the narrowness that sometimes clouds her vision, but we can never question her integrity. Her honesty, her courage, her endurance can still speak to us today.

Figure 6. Sarah Heckford shortly before her death, drawn by her friend, Lady Sarah Nicholson. Reprinted with the kind permission of Vivien Allen. Courtesy of the National Library of South Africa.

NOTES

[1] For most of the biographical information in this introduction I am indebted to Heckford's only biographer, Vivien Allen, whose book *Lady Trader: A Biography of Sarah Heckford* and whose entry in the *Oxford Dictionary of National Biography* have been most helpful.

[2] Hill (1838–1912) becomes famous as an early "housing reformer," buying up, renovating, and providing low cost housing for the poor of the London slums; she is considered a founder of social work as a profession.

[3] Heckford is initially unhappy about having to accept this position. "I had always pitied governesses," she remarks, "and had always objected to

be[ing] an object of pity myself, even to myself" (*Lady Trader*, 45). She is a success at it, however, and notes that she is always treated "not like a governess, but like a welcome guest" (53). She is to give her pupils what is called "a good English education, and to teach them to play the piano, to draw, and to sing" (50). However, she finds her students distressingly ignorant. Even the sixteen-year old must be taught to spell monosyllabic words; all are deficient in grammar, vocabulary, and, to her surprise, the use of a compass. Their lives, like her own there (which she describes as "monotonous, but not unpleasant" [51]) are so limited that it is difficult to explain ordinary things to them. Her experiences as a teacher were to shape her later views on the political power of education.

[4] Heckford is either unaware of or chooses to ignore that fact that hut taxes were products of the British mine owners' desire to maintain the flow to the mines of African migrant labor.

[5] Traditional African villages or settlements; the term is also used for enclosures for livestock.

[6] Emily Hobhouse (1860–1926) became a female hero to Afrikaners and anti-imperialists for her exposure of life-threatening conditions in the concentration camps to which Boer women and children were confined during the Second South African War. She briefly visited the camps early in 1901 but was refused permission to revisit them on her second trip to South Africa in 1902.

[7] Later reprinted in the *Natal Witness* as "Shaping the Future."

[8] The poem reads, in part: "A traveller in skirts? / The notion's just a trifle too seraphic" and suggests that women "stay and mind the babies, or hem our ragged shirts/ But they mustn't, can't and shan't be geographic" (qtd. in Adler 26).

[9] There are a larger number of books by women about travel and/ or residence in South Africa written in this period than has been noticed. Among the most interesting are: Charlotte Barter's *Home in South Africa*. (London, 1867). This is a barely fictionalized advertisement for working-class emigration; something of a tract, it suggests that "a man with a good pair of hands, a tolerable head, and a fair start—can become independent if he keeps steady and has a good wife" (87). Far more sensational is *Bush Life: A Woman's Adventures Among the Caffres* (London, 1892). This is Mrs. Fenton Aylmer's edition (and perhaps transformation) of the earlier experiences of Helen, Mrs. Colonel Somerset, shipwrecked in the 1860s and rescued by "bush-men." To her, the Caffres prove that there are "as noble hearts beating beneath the dark bosom of the African as that which throbs under the laced vest of the European" (175). By the turn of the century there is a great spate of travel books by women. Important, if not entirely accurate is Mary Hall, *A Woman's Trek from the Cape to Cairo* (London, 1907). Also of interest is Rosamond Southey's *Storm and Sunshine in South Africa*. Published in 1910

Introduction   lxiii

in London, it describes her visits to South Africa from 1893–1904 and her sister, Mrs. Bruce Steers' trip alone through Zululand by ox-cart.

[10] Cetawayo also spelled Cetewayo and Cetshwayo etc, ruled the Zulu kingdom from 1826 until 1879, restoring much of its power and rebuilding its military might. When the British moved to "contain" his kingdom, in effect, to move further into the interior and expand the borders of their colony in Natal, he was given an ultimatum to disband his army at the command of the British High Commissioner. He refused to do so and British and colonial forces entered Zululand (the Anglo-Zulu War of 1879) and ultimately defeated his troops. He was imprisoned in Cape Town and the kingdom was divided into thirteen separate chieftainships. He was reinstated in a greatly diminished role and with considerably less territory in 1883, a year before his death. Zululand was annexed to Natal in 1897.

[11] The name applied to the Khoikhoi people by the early Dutch settlers on account of the "clicks" which give their speech its distinctive character; it is supposedly derived from the term "huttentut" meaning "stammerer" or "stutterer." Not pejorative in the 19th century, it is now an insulting form of reference to a person of mixed-race.

[12] Perhaps only Mrs. M. A. Pringle deserves the title; she is in the minority and is only occasionally "foolish." As she travels *Toward the Mountains of the Moon* (London, 1884), she laments the fact that she cannot use the eggs she has obtained for lack of an eggcup to eat them from. However, despite moments such as these she has a worthy purpose—to accompany her husband on an investigation of a Scottish mission station—and a fresh and lively literary style.

[13] An oleograph is an inexpensive print colored to imitate an oil painting.

[14] *Foreloperl,forelooper* is an Afrikaans term for the man or boy who walks alongside the foremost pair of a team of oxen, in order to guide them. It is worth noting that the same elitism that makes Heckford fire other workers because they do not respect Egerton's status as a gentleman, leads her to assertions about the unfortunate lack of class structure in South Africa and the need to keep proper distance between master and servant. Class tensions play a role in others' perceptions too. Egerton is seen by those who work with him as a man who has forfeited his right to social superiority, while Heckford believes that he should be allowed to redeem himself—through humility and hard work He proves himself a gentleman when, realizing that travelling alone with Heckford is compromising her and harming her business, he insists on leaving.

[15] In 1879 the long threatened Zulu War broke out, a war that included the great Zulu victory at Isandhlwana; the famous battle of Rorke's Drift where the Zulu invasion of Natal was averted, and the death of the Prince Imperial of France who was serving on Lord Chelmsford's staff. Benjamin

Disraeli was reported to have complained that the Zulu "convert our Bishops [referring to Bishop Colenso], defeat our Generals, and put an end to our dynasties." The war came to an end with the defeat of the *impis* (Zulu regiments) at Ulundi by Chelmsford. See also note 10 above.

[16] Heckford's attitude to Du Val is more problematic; she never mentions him. It is likely that she read *News of the Camp;* but she would have had little tolerance for Du Val's professional "Irish" charm and somewhat vulgar, egocentric manners.

[17] Heckford's passion for animals, her valuing them at times above people may seem excessive, yet it makes sense both psychologically and culturally, for this is the era of the founding of the RSPCA and of the first recoil against blood-sports in England. Limited though it is, her approval of missionaries rests on the fact that they oppose cruelty to animals and teach humane slaughter to Africans.

[18] Du Val writes of the same incident, but he focuses on the fact that Deesy's father had once refused to halt the execution of Boer rebels and thus, that the death of his son was an example of the avenging stroke of Nemesis come home (2:141).

[19] She is amused, however, at some of the Afrikaners' social pretensions. Although "adverse to the English, [they] are very proud if they can induce Englishmen to marry into their families" (*Lady Trader* 32), she tells readers. She relates the comic anecdote of the young, insolvent Englishman who flirted recklessly with a young, rich Boer heiress, decamped, and cleverly induced her irate father to give her an enormous dowry.

[20] Properly Mzilikazi, founder of the Ndebele people. See note 21.

[21] George W. Stowe, in *The Native Races of South Africa* (London, 1905) provides the material from which I derive my explanation. His Mantatees fled Tshaka Zulu under Moselekatze (as he and Heckford transliterate Mzilikazi) and traveled north. They perpetuated their customs and language, says Stowe, among the alien Bantu tribes whom they subjugated and they ultimately became the Ndebele. On the way, however, they trekked over and remained in the high veldt of the Transvaal, settling for a while near Pretoria. Chased by the Boer colonists, they crossed the Limpopo river and created a kingdom on the other side (now Zimbabwe). Another group, led by Manukuz, ended up in the eastern Transvaal near the Zoutspanberg mountains and Pilgrim's Rest.

Works Cited

Abrahams, Israel. "Western Province Jewry 1870–1902." *The Jews in South Africa: A History.* Ed. Gustav Saron and Louis Hotz. London: Oxford UP, 1955. 12–28.

Adler, Michelle. "'In a Man's Country': British Women Travellers in Nineteenth- Century South Africa." *The Societies of Southern Africa in the 19th and 20th Centuries*. Vol. 19. London: U of London P, 1992. 26–40.

Allen, Vivien. *Lady Trader, A Biography of Mrs. Sarah Heckford.* London: Collins, 1979.

Balfour, Alice Blanche. *Twelve Hundred Miles in a Waggon.* 1895. Rpt. Salisbury: The Pioneer Head, 1970.

Barker, Lady. *A Year's Housekeeping in South Africa.* London: MacMillan, 1879.

Barnard, Lady Anne. *The Letters of Lady Anne Barnard to Henry Dundas: From the Cape and Elsewhere 1793–1803*. Ed. A. M. Lewin Robinson. Cape Town: Balkema, 1973.

Blake, Susan L. "A Woman's Trek: What Difference Does Gender Make?" *Western Women and Imperialism: Complicity and Resistance.* Ed. Nupur Chaudhurit and Margaret Strobel. Bloomington: Indiana UP, 1992. 9–34.

Churchill, Lord Randolph S. *Men, Mines and Animals in South Africa.* London: Sampson Low, 1892.

Dickens, Charles. "New Uncommercial Samples: A Small Star in the East," *All the Year Round.* December 19, 1868: 61–66.

Dixie, Lady Florence. *In the Land of Misfortune: A Defence of Zululand and its King.* London: Richard Bentley, 1882.

Duff Gordon, Lady [Lucie]. *Last Letters from Egypt to Which Are Added Letters from the Cape: With a Memoir by her Daughter Mrs. Ross.* London: Macmillan, 1875.

Du Val, Charles. *With a Show Through Southern Africa.* 2 vols. London: 1881.

—, ed. *News of the Camp, a Journal of Fancies, Notifications, Gossip and General Chit Chat Published in the Military Camp of Her Majesty's Forces Defending the Beleaguered Inhabitants of Pretoria.* Pretoria: n.p., 1881.

"Festival at the East London Hospital for Children." *Illustrated London News*, January 8, 1870: 53–54.

Foster, Shirley. *Across New Worlds: Nineteenth-Century Women Travellers and their Writings.* London: Harvester, Wheatsheaf, 1990.

Haggard, H. Rider. "Introduction." *Diary of an African Journey: The Return of Rider Haggard.* Ed. Stephen Coan. New York: New York UP, 2001. 11–13.

Hall, Mary. *A Woman's Trek from the Cape to Cairo.* London: Methuen, 1907

Harrison, Agnes T. "An Ark By the Riverside." *Macmillan's Magazine.* (February 1870): 355–58.

Heckford, Mrs. (Sarah). *A Lady Trader in the Transvaal.* London: Sampson Low, 1882.

—. "Boer Cruelty to Natives." *Spectator*, January 5, 1901: 48.

—. "Boer Treatment of Kaffirs." *Times*, August 19, 1901: 8 col. 5.

—. "The Concentration Camps." *Times,* August 5, 1901: 6 col. 2.
—. "How to Conquer South Africa in its Schools." *Spectator,* April 20, 1900: 564.
—. *The Huguenots: Historical Sketch.* London: George Philip, 1905
—. *The Life of Christ, and Its Bearings on the Doctrines of Communism.* London: Field and Tuer, 1873
—. "Loyal Afrikanders in South Africa." *Times,* February 18, 1902: 14. col. 6.
—. "The Story of the East London Hospital for Children." *Voluntaries for an East London Hospital.* Ed. Earl of Lytton, et. al. London: David Stott, 1887. ix-lxix.
Hutchinson, Mrs. (Louisa). *In Tents in the Transvaal.* London: Bentley, 1879.
Krige, Jensen E. *The Realm of a Rain-Queen: A Study of the Pattern of Lovedu Society.* Wynberg, Cape: Rustica Press, 1980.
Moon, Mrs. M. J. "Letter." *Times,* July 20, 1901: 6. col. 3.
"Obituary: Mrs. Heckford." *Times.* April 21, 1903: 8–9. col.1, 5.
Pringle, M. A. *Towards the Mountains of the Moon: A Journey in East Africa.* Edinburgh: Blackwoods, 1884.
Sandeman, E. F. *Eight Months in an Ox-Waggon: Reminiscences of Boer Life.* London: Griffith & Farrar, 1880.
Saron, Gustav. "Boers, Uitlanders, Jews." *The Jews in South Africa: A History.* Ed. Gustav Saron and Louis Hotz. London: Oxford UP, 1955. 179–212.
Schreiner, Olive. *Woman and Labour.* (1911*).* Rpt. Commemorative Edition. Johannesburg: Cosmos, 1975.
Shain, Milton. *The Roots of Anti-Semitism in South Africa.* Virginia: UP of Virginia, 1994.
Wilkinson, Mrs. *A Lady's Life and Travels in Zululand and the Transvaal During Cetewayo's Reign.* London: n.p., 1882.

Chronology of Sarah Heckford (1839–1903)

1833   Marriage of William Goff and Mary Clibborn

1839   Birth of Sarah, the third daughter of William and Mary Goff, in Dublin, Ireland.

1842   Goff family moves to Dresden, Germany

1845   Death of Mary Clibborn Goff; death of oldest daughter, Jane

1846   William and surviving daughters, Annie and Sarah, move to Switzerland. Joined by Abigail Clibborn (Mary's sister).

1847   Goff family moves to Paris. Caught in the 1848 Revolution, the family moves to London in 1848.

1849   Death of William by suicide. Annie and Sarah reside with uncle, Robert Goff and aunt Abigail Clibborn

1850   Death of Abigail Clibborn, leading to independent residence in London of Sarah and Annie.

1866   Cholera epidemic in London leads to Sarah's volunteer work at the Wapping Fever Hospital where she meets Dr. Nathaniel Heckford, her future husband. Death of Robert Goff (uncle).

1867   Marriage to Dr. Nathaniel Heckford (1842–1870), born in Calcutta of an English father and Eurasian mother.

1868   Heckfords found East London Hospital for Children and Dispensary for Women in two warehouses at the Ratcliffe Highway and live on the premises. Charles Dickens praises the hospital as "A Small Star in the East" in *All The Year Round*.

1871   Death of Nathaniel Heckford of tuberculosis at age 29

1873   Heckford's book, *The Life of Christ and Its Bearings on the Doctrines of Communism* published in London.

1876   Completion of new hospital facilities in Shadwell. Heckford and adopted daughter Marian Matthews Heckford travel to Naples.

1877   Marian wed in Naples. Heckford travels to India, stopping off in Egypt. In Calcutta, she works for Zenana Mission providing medical care for women in purdah. Becomes resident medical adviser to the begum of Bhopal.

British annex the Transvaal in South Africa.

1878   Heckford returns to England after a bout of malaria. In December 1878 travels to South Africa, ostensibly for reasons of health, and sets out for the Transvaal to become a farmer.

1879   Outbreak of the Anglo-Zulu War.

Heckford discovers farm scheme is fraudulent; financial needs lead to her residence at Nooitgedacht as a governess. Tries and fails at farming at Groenfontein nearby.

1880   Becomes a trader or *smous* traveling to the bushveldt with peddler's goods and an ox-cart. Outbreak of the First South African War, December 1880.

1881   Heckford trapped for one hundred days in the siege of Pretoria. Much of *Lady Trader* written there.

Boers win battle of Majuba, February.

Armistice and return of the Transvaal to Afrikaner rule, April.

Heckford returns to England.

1882   *A Lady Trader in the Transvaal* published in London. Heckford in England till 1887.

1884   *Excelsior,* Heckford's autobiographical novel published in England, receives little attention.

1886   Discovery of gold on Witwatersrand in South Africa.

1887   "The Story of the East London Hospital," published as part of a fundraising campaign for Shadwell facility. Heckford leaves for South Africa.

Chronology of Sarah Heckford

1889	Heckford becomes share broker for gold mining shares in Johannesburg; business crashes. She returns to trading; with profits, buys farm, Ravenshill, in the Zoutspanberg.
1891	Trading and panning for gold in Klein Letaba goldfields.
1893	Friendship with Modjadje, the "Rain Queen." Rents farm near Ravenshill till house there is built.
1894	Leaves area because of Boer-African conflicts.
1895	Jameson Raid.
1896	Heckford returns to England to raise money for farm-school scheme.
1897	Back in South Africa, works on farm-school scheme.
1898	Founds Transvaal Women's Educational Union. Returns as governess at Nooitgedacht.
1899	Outbreak of the Second South African War. Heckford at Nooitgedacht as governess. Carries messages on Boer troop movements to British forces in Pretoria.
1900	Letters to *Spectator* and *Times* on education in South Africa and treatment of "English Africander Loyalists." Returns to Pretoria in June when British take the city.
1901	Writes report on "The Educational Needs of the Transvaal Colony." Falls seriously ill and returns to England. In England, becomes well-known speaker on South African affairs. Writes to *Times* on Boer mistreatment of Africans. Opposes Emily Hobhouse's view of concentration camps. Begins raising funds for adult education program and becomes active in the British Women's Emigration Society.
1902	War ends with Treaty of Vereeniging, May. Heckford, ill and partially blind, completes lectures and slides for adult education scheme.
1903	Returns to South Africa. Dies, 18th April in Pretoria. Burial in Church Street West Cemetery.
1905	Publication in London of slide lecture text, *The Huguenots*, for adult education.

A Lady Trader in the Transvaal

Chapter 1

On a fine breezy morning, early in December, 1878, a number of passengers, and volunteers for the Zulu war, crowded the deck of one of the Union Company's steamships, then lying off the Port of D'Urban [Durban],* or Port Natal.¹ She had been for some days unable to land her passengers owing to the roughness of the "bar," that terrible difficulty presented by all southeast African seaports; but early on this particular morning the joyful intelligence that the tug was coming was made known, and the excitement was great in consequence.

The volunteers had all come on board at East London, a very sparely populated and commonplace-looking seaside village on the African coast. They were more or less prepared for what lay before them, for they knew what life in South Africa is; but to the majority of the passengers the low-lying, jungly-looking shore on which the breakers were beating was like the drop-scene of an unknown opera. What lay behind it was a mystery to all those who were then for the first time landing in South Africa—at least one half of the number assembled on deck. Most of them, no doubt, felt this; but there was one, at least, who did not. This was a young gentleman who went by the name of "Dick." He was a strapping youngster of about eighteen, who, I am inclined to think, had been shipped to Africa because nothing could be done with him at home. The new life before him presented no difficulties to his mind; he knew exactly how he was going to manage. He would buy a horse at D'Urban, put a few things in his saddlebags, strap his tent on his horse's crupper, and ride to Rustemberg [Rustenburg] (his destination) with a Kaffir for his guide. There he would rapidly make his fortune, principally by trading amongst the Kaffirs, to which end he had, before leaving England, provided himself with a stock of little machines, which (if my memory serves me rightly) are labelled in shop windows "A cup of tea in five minutes." This invention consists of a piece of sponge covered with wire gauze and encased in a metal cover, so that the apparatus can be carried in the pocket until it is required to perform the part of a spirit-lamp². The contrivance is more complicated than I describe, and decidedly ingenious. Dick had a store of these things in perfect order, and was confident of doing a roaring trade in them amongst the Kaffirs.

Dick was now, however, troubled with a difficulty; it was this: he had two dogs, one an English bull terrier—it had cost him 5*l.* to bring the animal from England—the other a Kaffir mongrel, for which he had paid a sovereign to the owner, who had come on board at Cape Town. The owner was a Kaffir, and had brought his dog on board without asking any questions, and probably would have taken him off without any being asked of him; but when Dick bought the dog, the captain and chief officer declared that he must pay the full fare for the animal, and on his indignant refusal, threatened to seize his saddle. Poor Dick was in an agony, honestly believing they meant what they said, and being much troubled in his mind as to how his new acquisition, a very large and lively dog, was to be got into the tug. The method of conveying the passengers from the steamship to the tug was certainly enough to alarm the poor mongrel, and Dick was justified in thinking it likely that he would object to it. A strongly-made basket, large enough to hold three or four persons crouching down, was being periodically hauled up to the side and swung over to the deck of the ship, filled with passengers, and then lowered away, until, amidst much laughter and shouting, its unlucky occupants were let bump down on the deck of the little tug that was bobbing about by the side of her big sister, when they were immediately and very unceremoniously tumbled out if they were men. Women and children were somewhat more gently treated. It certainly struck me that it would be very easy to break one's legs in the operation, and when my turn came I was very glad to find myself safely on board the little vessel. She was a funny-looking little craft, made expressly for crossing the disagreeable bar, and we were all cautioned to sit fast and wedge ourselves in well, or we might be swept overboard as we passed it. I expected a frightful drenching at least, but nothing at all happened; it was the old story of the mountain and the mouse,³ and as such, it formed a fitting prelude to life in South Africa, where, so far as my experience goes, everything is exaggerated—dangers, difficulties, beauties, and advantages.

I believe that D'Urban is a pretty town, but it did not look pretty to me, for I was in a bad temper. I had arranged to travel with a party who were going up country to speculate, thinking that it might be difficult for a lady alone, unless blessed with large means, to travel in a country of which the languages and customs were unknown to her. It is, I think, rather trying for any one accustomed to manage for himself to submit to be managed for, unless the management be very good, which in this case it was not. I found it decidedly tried me, and when it came on to rain, and (there being a strike of the Kaffir porters on that day) my companions piled all the luggage in the middle of a tramway, seemingly unconscious of there being any unadvisability in its being so disposed of, I felt very uncharitable towards them. The result of this disposition of our joint property was, that after a while a number of Kaffirs, with that beautiful disregard of consequences which is one of the pleasing characteristics of the race, sent a line of empty railway trucks right into it. The acrobatic and athletic efforts then made to rescue individual boxes dear to the owners' hearts, were amusing to behold; but it would have been a great relief to one's feelings to have been able to vent one's wrath, if only in words, on those unpleasant Kaffirs, who looked on grinning; but it was no use abusing them, for they didn't understand English, and none of us spoke Zulu or any other Kaffir language. At last I got into an omnibus which runs between the Port and the village of D'Urban, taking "Jimmy"[4] with me. And here, as I shall have occasion to mention Jimmy again, let me introduce him.

Jimmy was a boy of nearly sixteen, whom I had known from the time he was very small. He belonged to the party with whom I had arranged to travel, and was the only member of it with whom I had any previous acquaintance when I went on board the Union Company's ship at Southampton. He was fresh from home and school, and not at all accustomed to roughing it, hence he was permitted to be a good deal with me, and was allowed certain little privileges not accorded to the men of the party, or even to another youngster not much older than Jimmy, but about twice his size and strength.

The omnibus set us down at the best hotel in D'Urban; but that does not say very much. The village consisted of a line of straggling cottages or small houses, some of them with things in the window for sale, a railway station, and a rather nice-looking building where the post office was. I say consisted, for it may be much changed since then. The hotel was a cottage standing in a garden. There was a sitting room with a piano in it, and a *table d'hote*[5] in an adjoining but separate room; but there were none of the other arrangements which one connects in one's mind with an hotel. The idea it gave me was that a small farmhouse had been suddenly called upon to accommodate several people, and that the owner was doing his best. On the whole, D'Urban did not strike me as a singularly delectable spot, and I was not sorry to leave it.

We departed by the train, which took us to Pine Town, a pretty little place, in the middle of scenery that reminded me of an Indian jungle.

Here we got into an omnibus. We were packed very tight, and had little parcels of various sorts crammed into every available spot. The road was rough, and the horses went at a rattling rate. I suppose it was what some of the people said, "miserable"; but I rather enjoyed it, for the scenery was fine. We stopped for dinner at a farmhouse, and got into Pieter-Maritzburg [Pietermaritzburg] at sunset. The town looked very pretty with the evening light on it, lying in the middle of a circle of hills; but it is not really a very pretty place, although I believe its inhabitants think it so. Pieter-Maritzburg in reality is, or was when I saw it, only a large village.

Before I proceed, I must warn my readers, that although I shall have to tell them of rocks and valleys and wooded ravines, &c, they must not picture to themselves anything analogous to what they may have seen in Switzerland or Italy. There are such things in this part of the world, but they are commonplace. It is necessary to come here to understand what a "commonplace" wooded ravine means, but once here one understands it perfectly. I have often tried to make out in what this want of beauty, where there ought to be beauty, consisted, and I think that to a considerable extent it is caused by a "want of atmosphere," to use a phrase common to artists. In this part of the world the sun rises, when the sky is cloudless, in a bright yellow halo. It is yellow—not the glorious gold of the Egyptian or Indian sunrise—and the light it throws on all around is simply a bright yellow light. There are no delicately shaded tints, as it fades into shadow, or plays over an uneven surface. The artist who would portray it need have but few colours in his paint box. If the sky be cloudy, he need only as a rule have plenty of grey, and enough red and yellow for a streak or two. It is very seldom one sees the beautiful rose-flecked sky which made the fanciful Greeks gift Aurora with rosy-tipped fingers. And then, where will a dweller here find the magnificent colouring of an Indian, or the ethereal blush of an Italian, sunset? The finest he will ever see here will not be equal to many that he will have seen in England.

The colouring of the scenery is monotonous. The grass when it is not yellow is a very vivid green; the trees have not much variety of hue or form; and the sky is very blue—a cobalt blue, deepening into indigo as it nears the horizon, but without a trace of the rose-pink which, when we first learn to put a brush on paper, we are so strenuously enjoined never to omit in an horizon. Even the moonlight is not so ethereal as in other countries, although it is often very bright.

So much for the scenery. Now, as to the life here, I can only compare it to a picture in which there is no central point for the eye to rest on, in which everything is equally prominent. It is moral atmosphere which is wanting, I am inclined to think. Life here is a jumble, to use an inelegant but expressive word. To me, and to many I fancy, there is much in the life which is attractive. It is, I believe, a fact, that people who have been here for some time and have longed to return to Europe, having done so, have come back to finish their days in Africa. But I doubt whether more than two or three of those persons even, could have told the characteristic charm which thus recalled them from their old homes.

Chapter 2

Jimmy and I left Pieter-Maritzburg on a fine afternoon, having been there about a week—the rest of the party, together with the two waggons which had been hired by the manager, having gone on in front—the men on foot, we on horseback, or rather on ponyback, for neither of our steeds was fifteen hands high. I had found it very hard to get serviceable animals at Pieter-Maritzburg, for at that time all the available, and many unavailable horses, were bought up by the volunteers. Dick had invested in a weedy-looking young mare, and he rode her to death, I heard, in about a fortnight, although he was not in the volunteers. Two of our party had left us to join the native contingent (then being raised) as volunteer officers. They spoke nothing but English, and their men nothing but a Kaffir dialect; so how they, and many others who joined like them, managed, I do not know. They had also bought miserable hacks. I cannot say much for my own two. One, which Jimmy bestrode, was a rough and ugly Basuto pony, very thin, but with good qualities. My pony was larger, fat, and handsome; he would have been very good, except for his laziness. I certainly never have seen so lazy a little horse. He would stand stock-still, unless forcibly reminded that he was wanted to walk; and when induced to canter, he would in five minutes fall into a walk. These two animals were the means of introducing me to the common domestic insect of this part of the world, namely, the "tick," or "bush-louse," as it is called by the Boers. There were hundreds on both the ponies, and the groom of the hotel being, as Kaffir grooms generally are, a useless addition to the stable, Jimmy and I had employed hours in ridding our ponies of the parasites. I had an idea that I knew what a "tick" was, on sheep in England; but the South African tick is a wonderful creature. There are grey, brown, whitish, and striped varieties, besides one exceedingly poisonous kind, yellow-green on the back, with a white line with symmetrical streaks of red on it running round the edge of the podgy little body, and the belly grey. These insects vary in size, from almost invisibility to the bulk of a hazelnut. They are very agile; and if you happen to be sitting on the grass, you have a good chance of seeing one walk nimbly towards you, with a hungry look pervading his small person. What the creatures live on when they don't happen to fall in with some living prey I do not know, but numbers of them certainly have their habitat in the grass.

Jimmy and I started on ponyback. With a vague idea that I was going into a wild country, and with a distinct one that Jimmy was not likely to afford me much protection, I had a revolver in a case strapped round my waist, and another in a holster on my saddle. The waggons had started in a hurry; and there having been some misunderstanding on my part as to when I was to have all my things loaded up, a good many things belonging to Jimmy and myself had been left behind, and these were crammed into our saddlebags, and tied on our saddles. However, we started, and having arrived at an even stretch of road halfway up the hill immediately beyond the village, Jimmy proposed a canter. It was not a particularly fast one, but the effect was disastrous. I was a little in front when I heard "Hilloa! I say, look what's happening!" and looking back, I beheld the road strewed with articles which had gradually fallen from Jimmy's various parcels. Jimmy looked disconsolate as he returned, and began to pick them up and tie them on again, while I sat on my pony and laughed. This was unfair, I must confess, for the loading up arrangement had been of my invention, not Jimmy's. Presently we came up to one of our party, sitting, hot and weary, on a big stone near to a hand-cart laden with miscellaneous articles, which had not arrived in time to be packed in the waggons. I must here observe, that the manager of our party had contracted for our being taken to Pretoria with our goods by a carrier, or what is here called a transport-rider, and the transport-rider was imperious about when he would "in and outspann,"[6] to use a South African phrase for putting the oxen into and letting them out of the yoke. I confess that, being at the time ignorant of the conditions of transport-riding, I thought our carrier unreasonable on this and many other occasions. But experience has taught me that in respect of his treatment of oxen in this one particular, he was altogether reasonable, for in travelling with an ox-waggon, even an inhuman man, and our driver was one, must consider his oxen, or else he will stick fast on the road.

The young gentleman who was sitting hot and weary on the stone, guarding the hand-cart while his companions in misfortune had gone to drink somewhere, must have been a very amiable person if he did not feel something akin to hatred of Jimmy and myself as we rode up, and after a few words rode on. He did his best to look cheerful; and this was creditable to him, although it was a failure, for who could be expected to look cheerful at being harnessed two abreast to a heavy hand-cart, and having to drag it uphill for miles in a broiling sun? Everything, however, has an end. Some time after Jimmy and I reached the place where the waggons were outspanned, the cart was brought in, the articles in it placed in the waggons, and the cart itself sent back—I forget how—to Pieter-Maritzburg. When the oxen were inspanned and we started once more, we felt that we were fairly *en route;* and being so, let me describe the waggons, which were to serve us as houses until we reached Pretoria. The one was an open buck-waggon, something of the same make as our large English hay-waggons, with a tarpaulin, or what is here called "a buck-sail," thrown over it to protect the goods. There were, I think, eighteen oxen in this waggon, which was driven principally by the Africander[7] transport-rider, a small man, with red whiskers and moustache. The other waggon was also a buck-waggon, or waggon with railings projecting from the sides for the support of goods; but on the back half of it there was a tent, formed of canvas stretched on bent laths, so as to form a complete covering at the sides and top. The ends were furnished with canvas flaps, to be shut, or opened at pleasure. With very few articles packed in a half-tent, its occupant, if there be but one, may be comfortable enough; but when, in addition to cases, the entire paraphernalia which a company of twelve men, most of them unaccustomed to travelling, think necessary to keep handy, is tumbled into it, the conditions are altered. Of course each man had a rifle, and these weapons had to be kept exceptionally handy, although they did not get us more than two or three brace of birds during our whole trek, and not even one buck. The result of twelve men and one woman (myself) having these things "handy" in a half-tent was this. The various articles underwent a rotatory movement every time one of them was wanted, and became well mixed up. Later on I was able to make canvas bags and tie them up to the sides of the tent, and so save my property from the general confusion, but at the outstart my goods contributed to it.

Our evening outspann was on a bleak hilltop, along which a thick, damp mist was beginning to sweep. It soon enveloped us, and rendered the cooking of the evening meal difficult. In agreeing with the transport-driver, no definite understanding had been come to as to what assistance the natives under his control were to render, hence they gave us very little, and the men had to bring water, fuel, &c, and make the fire themselves. This a native will do in pouring rain, but an Englishman, as a rule, is puzzled to do it even in a drizzling mist. Presently, through the mist, up rode the two of our party who had joined the volunteers; they came to bid their companions God-speed, and then rode off, as it was already late. I don't know what became of one of them; the other was massacred as he lay ill of fever in the hospital at Rorke's Drift.[8] In the meantime the tent for the men was pitched by them. I had a tent, but I think I only persuaded them to pitch it for my benefit four times, and 1 forgot whether this was one of those occasions. Presently supper made its appearance. The meal consisted of fried ham, bread, and coffee—without milk, be it understood. It does not sound badly, but I will describe it in the words of the man who cooked it: "Rancid tallow candle, with lots of salt in it." He would not eat of it; but I was very hungry, and did, although I confess the description was accurate.

Chapter 3

I shall not give a lengthened description of a journey in or with an ox-waggon, through a country whose leading feature is an utter absence of any objects of interest, except to the eye of a speculative farmer, and even he could not but be disagreeably impressed by the want of water. I will sum it up by saying, that we travelled over many miles of undulating country, starting early in the morning, outspanning in the middle of the day, and travelling again in the evening, during which time we were not particularly comfortable. The men generally walked; Jimmy and I rode. It was very rough, although after our first evening the food improved; but the want of milk was trying. Then, too, it is unpleasant when the weather is very hot not to be able to get a good wash, or to change one's linen often; and these were impossibilities for me, owing to my not being able to induce the men to pitch my tent. The waggon-tent was too much cumbered for even an active person, not to say one who is lame, as I am, to perform satisfactory ablutions in; and the absence of trees made an impromptu dressing room a thing not to be thought of. Sometimes we came to a little shanty called an hotel, and then I eagerly seized the opportunity for a wash; but these accommodations were very few, and far between.

One duty which devolved on me, many would, I daresay, consider a hardship, but I did not mind it; this was cleaning my horse. I was a new hand at grooming a horse then, having previously only had the brush and comb in my hands *en amateur,* and it is one thing to rub down a well-groomed horse for amusement, and another to clean a very dirty and hot one under a broiling sun; but I cannot say that I disliked this hardship, although I used to wish that our outspanning times were such as to allow of my grooming operations being carried on at some hour when the sun was low. At best, however, a midday outspann in a treeless country is objectionable; it is pleasanter to be moving than stationary during the process of being broiled. It is true that under the waggon there is a little shade, but in this case it was not available for me, being fully occupied by the tired men. It is, however, absolutely necessary for oxen to rest in the heat of the day if they are to work well; and, as I said before, our conductor in this respect was a good manager.

The first place that made an impression on my mind was Kar-Kloof. It is approached by a road that winds round a hillside, and then one is almost startled by the abruptness and length of the ascent in front. It seems almost impossible for oxen to drag a loaded waggon up so long and steep a hill. It is a picturesque place (for Africa), with deep gullies at the side of the rugged road, and with even a sprinkling of trees. On the top of this tremendous hill is a tiny iron house—an inn, and very glad I was that such a thing existed; for hardly were we at the top when a most terrific storm broke over us. There was even a stable, or what served the purpose of one, and in it, to my great relief, I was able to get shelter for the horses. The landlady, a most garrulous and inquisitive old person, was very kind to me; although she apparently regarded my companions as undesirable characters, and came down on them very sharp whenever she could. The storm ended in a thick mist, through which one of the men thought he saw a buck, and incontinently set forth, rifle in hand. The buck disappeared, and so did its would-be persecutor; the disappearance of the former being for good, and of the latter for the whole night, which he spent in forlornly wandering in continual dread of losing his footing amongst the rocks and gullies as completely as he had lost his way.

Then there was Estcourt, a place that looked pretty by moonlight, but not so well by daylight; and then there was the Drachensberg [Drakensberg], or Dragon Mountain. I had heard much of this terrible mountain, and dreadful accounts of what happened to waggons whilst attempting to cross it; I therefore approached it with a certain amount of respect.

The Drachensberg is not a single mountain, but a very long chain, as any one can see by looking at it on the map. At its foot the road coming from Natal divides into two, one branch leading across the mountain into the Free State, the other going to Newcastle. We were to go by the former, and I now learned that we were to go to Pretoria via Heilbronn [Heilbron] and Heidelberg. My knowledge of the geography of the country was not up to the mark, but it was sufficient to render this announcement startling to me, the taking Heilbronn *en route* to Heidelberg bringing me some sixty or seventy miles out of my way; however, the conductor said he had to go, and that was considered to be conclusive. I believe the reason he gave was, that having lost many of his oxen on the road, and thinking it likely he should lose more, he had to go to Heilbronn, where his home was, for fresh oxen; in reality, he went to pick up his wife, who wanted to pay a visit to Heidelberg. But whatever was the reason, he said he must go by Heilbronn; and we, having no previous contract as to the road by which he was to travel, had to obey. We left the hospitable little inn at the foot of the mountain in the afternoon. The preamble of our starting was as follows:—

My horse's withers having been touched by the saddle, and Jimmy's pony being also touched on the back, I said I would go in the waggon.

"If that be so," said the conductor, "your young friend had best go with you."

"Why?" I inquired.

"Because very likely the waggon may be upset," quoth the conductor.

What benefit I was to derive from Jimmy's presence in such a case I did not pause to inquire, but, as speedily as I could, descended from my destined conveyance—just in time to see a wretched sheep in its dying agonies, having been killed for our supper by one of the men, alongside of the waggon, to which it was speedily hung.

The innkeeper now provided a light carriage called a "spider," drawn by four oxen, for my benefit, in which I started some time after the waggons had done so.

The ascent of the Dragon Mountain is certainly picturesque, although the lack of trees is very much felt, but the effect of it was greatly marred by a thick mist which came on as evening drew in. Presently we came to our waggons, stuck in the mud amongst a lot of others all in the same predicament. It was a nice pleasant lookout! The spider deposited me in the mud; the men pitched their tent in the mud; and presently up came Jimmy leading the two ponies, all very muddy. The supper was what might be expected under the circumstances. I got Jimmy into the waggon with me, tied the horses to the back of it, and fed them from my hand—for the mud made it impossible to feed them on the ground, and I had no nose-bag for them—and then prepared to go to sleep. My remembrance of that night is, that it was a perpetual struggle to avoid slipping out at the back; for as there was no mattress, but only a blanket or two thrown on a mixed assortment of articles, prominent amongst which were the rifles of the party, and the waggon stood on a steep incline, not only oneself, but all one was lying on had a downward tendency.

Towards morning I heard dismal sounds from a member of our party who had attempted to sleep on the waggon, outside the tent but under the buck-sail, and then a clank which told me that his head must have come in collision with a certain tin box of mine.

"I can't stand this any longer," he groaned; and I heard him descend to where, under the waggon, some of his companions had been sleeping in the mud. This woke them, and they began making comparisons between the relative coldness of their backs, which so amused me that I completely woke up, to find the dawn breaking very sullenly. I found the poor ponies warm under their blankets, but slipping in the mud, which was by this time over their pasterns, and got them something to eat. Then with difficulty I woke Jimmy—who solemnly assured me he had not slept a wink all night—and suggested to him the advisability of saddling, and trying to push on to an inn on the Willow River, which I heard was about twelve miles distant. This we did, passing a waggon, all broken to pieces in its fall, a little way ahead of our waggons, which, with the rest of the party, did not get to our harbour of refuge by the Willow River for two days, having fearful weather on the mountains.

We were now in the Orange Free State, and during my stay at the little hostelry I heard much political talk, adverse to the English, from an old Free-Stater somewhat addicted to the bottle. I also had a conversation with a gentleman of a very inventive turn of mind, who told me some wonderful stories, to which I listened gravely. Whenever something suggested to him that my wonderment was getting too strong, he would appeal in a most artless manner to the memory of a friend of his who was there, and the friend always remembered. These two were dwellers in the Transvaal, but both, with delightful *naiveté*, cautioned me not to trust any Transvaalists, as they were all fearfully acute and untrustworthy.

On the morning after the arrival of our party at the Willow River, Jimmy and I started for Harrismith, the others, with the waggons having gone on before. We found them having breakfast, and stopped for a few minutes with them.

Harrismith looked like a dismal little attempt at a town. I was fresh from European and Indian cities and towns then. Now, after a little more than two years in the Transvaal, I have become sufficiently savage to think Harrismith, whenever I may next see it, quite a respectable attempt at one. There are two inns in the place; the one to which we went was fairly comfortable—at least the sitting room, dining room, and my bedroom adjoining the sitting room, were very good. I could see that the bedroom was the show bedroom, and I don't know what the others were. The stable was large, and crammed with horses—just tied to the manger, without any division between them, and so closely packed that it was difficult to get between them so as to clean one's own horse. And the dirt! The Augean stable[9] must have been a trifle to it!

From Harrismith we were to trek to Heilbronn, and when our party came up it was proposed that I should go there in the post-cart, leaving Jimmy in charge of my horse and his own. I was rather loath to trust my horse to the tender mercies of either Jimmy or any of the men; but I had two reasons for acceding to the proposal—first, that the horses' withers were touched by the saddle; secondly, that my companions were evidently looking forward with delight to the idea of getting rid of me, and I felt it would be ungenerous to disappoint them. So it was arranged that they were to start on the morning of, I think, Thursday, and I was to start on Friday in the post-cart.

Just as they were starting, I bethought me that it might be as well not to carry money with me during my solitary drive with the Kaffir post-boy, and keeping only enough for roadside expenses, I sent the rest of my possessions on in the waggon; and, bidding Jimmy and my pony farewell, I prepared to employ the remainder of the day as best I could. There were a few books on the round table in the sitting room, none of them worth reading but one, Dickens's "Great Expectations." With this to enjoy, I lay down on the sofa, and had a thorough rest.

The next morning I remained in bed until my coffee was brought to the door by a Kaffir; and I was dressing leisurely, when I was startled by hearing a voice I was sure was Jimmy's. I hurried out, and there, in good truth, was Jimmy, looking very tired. In answer to my astonished inquiry how he came to be there, he recounted the following story, which he believes in implicitly to the present day, but to which no one else has ever attached any credit.

He had ridden in front of the waggons, leaving my pony in charge of the men, and although believing himself to be on the right road, virtually lost his way. Being, I fancy, rather glad to ride his pony just as he liked, instead of under my inspection, he rode and dismounted, rode and dismounted, until evening began, to creep up, when it occurred to him as odd that the waggons were not coming up into sight. Just about this time he was close to a small stony hill or coppie [koppie], down which he saw three Kaffirs, armed with assegais,[10] coming. He looked at them with some suspicion, and rode on, looking behind every now and then, when he observed that they were following him. He then cantered, upon which they ran; then, according to his account, he caused his pony to gallop—a feat I don't think the pony was capable of; anyhow, he attained to a pace which appeared a very fast one to the rider, when one of the Kaffirs threw an assegai after him, which overshot him, and stuck quivering in the ground. Thereupon Jimmy struck across the veldt, and cantered or galloped along till night stopped him. He then dismounted and led the pony, feeding himself and his little steed with some gingerbread and other biscuits he had in his pocket; but as he had no idea where he was, it was not much use walking about leading a pony. However, he presently saw a light in the distance, and making for it, found it to proceed from the fire of a friendly waggoner, who told him he was some twenty miles from Harrismith, but far off the waggon-road to Heilbronn, and who advised him to go with him to Harrismith, whither he was bound, and to find me out. He then gave him some supper and a blanket, and tied the pony behind the waggon, so that Jimmy need not stir when the waggon started.

All I can say about the assegai story is, that the Free State was far from the seat of war, in a condition of profound peace, and that I was informed that it is unlawful in the Free State for Kaffirs to carry assegais. One thing was evident, Jimmy was there, and so was the pony. Jimmy was tired; the pony completely knocked up. The question was, what could I do? I had my ticket for the post-cart, which was to start at ten o'clock, and a few shillings over what my hotel bill would amount to—and the price of a place in the post-cart was four sovereigns! It was evident that money must be raised, and so I raised it by selling the pony; and then Jimmy and I awaited the arrival of the post-cart, which was supposed to take us to Heilbronn in two days. Its advent was heralded by very loud talking. A gentleman on horseback was alongside of it, who in excited tones drew the attention of another individual to the state of the hulking Kaffir driver of the vehicle.

"I can't think of allowing a lady to go with the drunken brute," he exclaimed. "We *must* get another driver."

Whereupon he jumped off his horse.

"I'll give you a jolly hiding, and send you to prison, you rascal. You stand there, and take that—and that—and that—and that," and he struck the Kaffir across the head, arms, and breast, with his heavy stinging ox-hide whip.

The fellow barely stirred a muscle. I could hardly at the time think that he felt much, but Kaffirs will sometimes bear a beating that *does* hurt in that way. There was a twitch of the month each time the whip fell—that was all.

"Now you take him away," quoth the excited man; "and you here, you must drive."

You here was a diminutive Hottentot.[11]

"I can't drive," said the Hottentot.

"Oh, never mind that," said the excited gentleman, who probably know this was not the case; "jump up!"

"And I don't know the road."

"Then you'll have to find it out. You drove the cart some time ago—you must know it; jump up!" and up the Hottentot jumped.

The vehicle into which he jumped, and into which I proceeded to scramble, had once been a dog-cart, but was now a ruin; the system of pieces of leather and cord, ingeniously twisted together, which attached it to the horses, had, I suppose, once been a set of harness; the horses once had certainly been very good, but now they were a pair of vicious, jibbing rips. How they did jib![12] and when the united efforts of the little Hottentot (who soon proved that he could drive) and some four or five other men had got them to move, how they did rush away with the little cart!

They were just sobering down to a reasonable pace at the outskirts of the village when my driver said, "Will you hold the reins? That's my house; I must say goodbye to my wife, and get my blanket." The small man could talk English. Upon his return from taking a fond adieu of Mrs. Hottentot, the horses steadily refused to move. Jimmy had to push the wheels, and there was a great to-do before, with a plunge, they got away again; but alas! there was a spruit, or small ravine with a brook running through it, before us!

The Hottentot in the meanwhile opened his heart to me. "It is very hard pressing me like this," he said. "I don't remember the road; and my ribs were broken the other day, and they are hardly well." I don't know whether the effect was that of the broken ribs or not, but as he spoke the little man foamed at the mouth like a champing horse, which was unpleasant when one was to leeward of him, as I was: I therefore discouraged conversation. A few minutes after brought us to the spruit, where the operations of coaxing, whipping, and pushing the jibbing horses, had to be resorted to. The road was very uneven, and this had to be repeated at every little hitch, we therefore got along rapidly. I was looking forward with anxiety to the change, but it only brought us even worse horses. Then the harness took to breaking, and was mended with little strips of leather and pieces of twine, produced out of his pocket by the little driver. Each change seemed to bring us worse horses. At last a pair of almost unbroken colts were put in. It was a terrible battle to get them to start at all, and then they went at a furious rate, but stopped at the first hitch, and plunged the harness nearly off, breaking it hopelessly in one place. The Hottentot's resources were exhausted; but fortunately I had a little hunting crop with me, and its lash did excellent service.

"We must be near the house where I ought to leave some letter[s]," said the Hottentot at one place; "but I don't know the road."

"Dear me," said I, with my European conscientiousness about letters still unimpaired. "What can you do?"

"Oh, I shall just go on," said the little man. "It isn't; my fault. 1 told him I didn't know the road."

Presently it began to get dusk and chilly. "I can't get to the right place for outspanning for the night," said the driver. "We must stop at the next house."

A Dutch farmhouse is very different from an English one. It is merely, as a rule, a wretched hovel, stuck down in the middle of a waste of grass.

The Free State farmhouses are particularly desolate-looking, owing to the Free State being unfit for agriculture, and given over to pasturing cattle, sheep, and horses. The cottage where we stopped, however, was rather a good specimen, and the people—a young man and a pretty woman, his wife—were very hospitable, and gave us a good supper, cleanly served, and, to me at least, a clean bed. There was a nice basin and jug, with a clean towel neatly folded over it, in my room; but they never thought of the water!

I cannot describe the country we travelled through, for there is nothing in it to describe; it is simply a wide expanse of grass, with spruits running through it at intervals—spruits with quantities of stones, but sometimes only a trickle of water in them. The flocks of sheep, and herds of cattle and horses, are striking features of the scene.

Through this scenery, if scenery it could be called, we took our way once more on Saturday morning. Our hosts would accept of no payment, only thanks. They gave us a cup of black coffee before we started, without either sugar or milk—I suppose the cows were not yet milked—and we were off once more.

Chapter 4

After a long drive we got to a small house, into whose one room a large and very dirty family were crowded. Here the woman gave us a bottle of milk, and a little farther on we got some bread—the man who gave it to us asking for payment, but not getting any, because I had only gold and he had no silver. The horses in the meantime were becoming from bad to worse, Jimmy and our charioteer having frequently to get out to push the wheels, the reins being delivered over to me; and many a laugh I had, although frightened, at the frantic rush these two would make after the cart when the horses at last bolted off, I doing my best to hold them in, so as to allow the little Hottentot (who in spite of his broken ribs was an active fellow) to jump in, and then extending a hand backwards to Jimmy, who had to take flying leaps up to the back seat.

The broken ribs of our driver occasioned him, much to his sorrow, to transgress the regulation laid down that, when approaching any dwelling, the driver of a post-cart is to blow a horn. A Hottentot delights in any row on a thing supposed to be a musical instrument, and our Jehu[13] so greatly deplored his inability to perform his duty, that I, not at that time appreciating the true cause of his grief, offered to endeavour to extract sounds from the old brass horn. My endeavours were, however, not crowned with success, nor were Jimmy's. We achieved a great puffing out of our cheeks and a peculiar snorting noise, but nothing more. By nightfall we arrived at a house, which impressed me as the most squalid I had ever seen—I do not mean the combination of poverty and dirt to be seen in London, but squalor in the midst of plenty. This is a common sight amongst the Boers,[14] but it was a new one then to me; and it remains stamped on my memory. We approached this dwelling by a road which was invisible to me; indeed I had long ceased to wonder at our driver having, as he said at starting, forgotten the "road," for often when he seemed undecided as to which he should take, I could discern none whatever over the bare, dried grass. It was a raw evening with a mist coming on, and the long low-roofed cabin stuck down in the middle of the veldt, with three stunted trees near it, looked cheerless in the extreme. Our advent was heralded by a barking chorus from a number of gaunt dogs; this brought out seven men and boys. The little Hottentot whispered, "You must shake hands with every one"; and I descended and instantly commenced operations. The oldest of the men led us into the house, where we shook hands with a woman and a number of girls, big and little, terminating with a small baby. All the hands were very dirty.

I leaned against the half-door and looked out at the three trees, wishing very much that I could speak to these people, and turning, saw Jimmy sitting disconsolately near me, whilst ranged round the room on benches, sat the family, regarding us gravely. It was absolutely necessary to say or do something, so I made a desperate effort to form some sounds resembling Dutch out of a combination of German and English. One of the little girls was a pretty curly-headed little creature with large serious eyes. I thought I would make her the subject of my remarks. I daresay that the expression of my face was more intelligible than my words, for the woman looked pleased, and the eldest of the men said something to the effect that she was his daughter.

The Hottentot appeared, and squatted on the step of the half-door, and he was able to act as interpreter. The family consisted of a man and his wife and their children. It seemed wonderful, for there really appeared to be less than ten years difference between the two eldest men: presently more gawky boys came in and shook hands, until the whole family being assembled, I discovered that there were, I think, fourteen children. They were rich in flocks and herds, and yet all but the father, mother, and two eldest sons were barefooted; none had stockings; none appeared to be possessed of a brush and comb, or of soap!

"I wonder if they are going to give us anything to eat," whispered Jimmy. "Ask them."

I did not like to do so, not knowing whether it might be considered a liberty, as I did not know whether payment for food would be accepted; but I wondered too, for I was very hungry, having eaten nothing but a little bread since morning.

Presently the eldest girl brought me a basin, with a small quantity of water in it, and a not over-clean-looking cloth. I had my own soap and towel, and washed; the same basin and water was presented to

Jimmy, who washed; it then passed to the father, who threw the water on his face and hands and wiped them with the cloth, and from him it passed in regular order down to the youngest boy, a lad of about eleven! The girls did not wash. A cloth was now laid on the table, and plates with bowls on them placed on it, a big basin full of milk, and a dish full of a sort of hard, crisp bread, peculiar to this country and very nice, was placed near it. Jimmy, the father, and I had knives, forks, and spoons, the rest had spoons only. It was dark now, and a tallow candle illumined the scene. The father said a long grace in Dutch, and then the mother helped all to milk and biscuits—the hard bread is called Boer biscuit here—whilst the eldest girl brought in a very small piece of boiled mutton. This the father cut into three pieces, giving one to Jimmy, one to me, and reserving one for himself. I enjoyed my supper, and ended my meat before my host had finished his. Seeing this, I saw him eye me thoughtfully for a minute or so with uplifted knife and fork, then he pushed his own plate over to me. I smiled, thanked him in German, and shook my head, whereupon he drew it back again with a look of relief, and ate the meat that remained on it. And this man had hundreds of fat wethers, and full-flanked oxen grazing on his farm!

I think grace was said when all was done, and shortly after various sheep and goat skins were spread on the floor, and on a bench by the side of the room; and then the mother signed to me to follow her, and led me into a dark little closet, in which was a big very dirty-looking bed, a number of little delft bowls on a shelf, and absolutely nothing else. On the bare rafters various articles, including rags of apparel, were hung. Here she left me, without a candle, the only light I received being from the candle in the sitting room, which showed over the top of the door. There was a window, or rather a small opening in the wall, with a shutter to it; this was open when I went in, and to it I trusted for light and air; but hardly had the woman left me, ere I heard it being barricaded, in some very secure manner judging from the noise, on the outside; then the candle went out in the sitting room, and I heard sounds of people lying down. I lay down dressed, and for a long time listened to such a chorus of snoring that I felt convinced the whole family were sleeping in the sitting room; and, such was indeed the case, as I learnt next morning from Jimmy. He slept with one of the sons on the bench. None of the party undressed. Boers never do when they go to bed, not even in case of illness; indeed, they think it the height of impropriety to do so—so much so that a Boer who travelled in the waggon of an English Africander, an acquaintance of mine, afterwards said to the wife of the latter,—

"I shall never travel in William's waggon again with him; it is so dreadful of him to take his trousers off when he goes to bed."

My bed was the domicile of innumerable insects.

We had coffee and a wash in the basin, and started early. The horses were of the usual description, the scenery of the usual description, and the delivery of letters of the usual description; and this reminds me that I have not described the operation. On arriving at a place where horses had to be changed, the little Hottentot would request me to stand up, and, opening the top of the seat he and I occupied, would take out a lot of rags and pieces of leather, which seemed to be considered as valuables to be kept, and then pull out the letters, parcels, and papers, and make them over to me to decipher their addresses. The addresses were generally badly written, the names Dutch, and the places unknown to me; hence I think it probable that a great many letters went astray. I know my audience, namely, the driver and a Boer or two, more than once said they did not know the name of the individual I read out. However, the little Hottentot settled the matter somehow, and I suppose there were no more letters left wrongly on this occasion than on any other. It has sometimes occurred to me to wonder how letters get to their destination at all in the Orange Free State, judging from my experience of the post-cart, and from the fact that I heard from several persons at Heilbronn that the usual driver of the post-cart, namely, the Kaffir with whom my excitable friend in Harrismith had dealt so summarily, lived in a constant state of intoxication, frequently lying for hours on the ground by the side of the post-cart, whilst the wretched horses grazed, glad enough to be rid of their tormentor, who, when he was in his seat, always drove at a gallop, flogging them without intermission.

I forget whether it was on this day, or on the previous one that we came to a small river with very steep banks, and that the small Hottentot informed us that we had better get out of the vehicle, as he felt sure it would be upset. I concurred in this opinion, although getting out meant fording the river on foot; and indeed, if there had been any weight behind them the horses would certainly have upset the concern; as it was, they jibbed and plunged on the sharp descent, and then bolted through the river and up the other side. How the cart held together during the frantic leaps it had to take over the big stones that strewed the bottom of the river, and the road beyond it, I don't know—the more so as one wheel had been shaky from the time we started. Jimmy and I waded through the river, which came up nearly to my knees, and had to climb into the cart as quickly as we could, and off we went again. It was Sunday now, and we ought to have been in Heilbronn on Saturday evening. We were to have two more changes of horses, and were to pass through the small town of Frankfurt [Frankfort] before reaching our destination.

Our last change but one brought us a pair of very fine horses, if they had been in good condition; but they were very thin, their chests raw from the pressure of the chest-strap (collars are not used here), and. they looked very vicious. It was hard work harnessing them, and then there was a pitched battle before they would start. It was no wonder, for it must have been dreadful pain to throw their raw chests against the band; the blood was running from them before the poor brutes chose *that* pain instead of the pain of the flogging they were getting from three men besides the driver. It really was dangerous work driving these horses, for they were very strong, hard-mouthed, and added kicking to the accomplishments of the animals we had before had; in fact, not far from our starting point one of them sent his hoof through the splash-board in unpleasant proximity to my knee. It was early in the afternoon when we reached Frankfurt. I was told there was a village there; but all I saw was a small white house, the post office; another small white house of a shape that suggested to me that it was a church, and which I learnt was one; and I think three little cottages with gardens, in a row at a little distance. There were some children and girls in their best dresses lounging near the post office, one of whom I particularly remember, owing to the strange incongruity of her attire with both her appearance and her surroundings. She was a podgy young lady of about sixteen, and was arrayed in a white skirt, over which a pink polonaise[15] of some miserable sort of stuff was put on, and a hat with bad imitation flowers in it.

The postmaster, or some one who I supposed was he, came out and received letters; told me also in answer to my inquiries that Heilbronn was not very far, but that we had a very ugly spruit to cross. I asked if we could not have other horses; but he said that was impossible—and we started again. We got the horses off well, and were bowling down a grassy decline towards the three cottages before named, when the little Hottentot discovered a letter by his side which he had not left. He pulled up the horses, and the postmaster and another man—a little short man, with black hair and whiskers, a black coat, and a white collar—came running up. Now the question was to start the horses again. They evidently thought that having started once they had done their duty; they had no idea of doing it for a second time, and proceeded to display all their accomplishments. In the meantime the little black man, who had a very goodnatured broad face, favoured us with descriptions of the spruit in front of us.

"The cart is generally upset there," he said cheerfully. "Very often, at least," said the postmaster; "it was upset last time."

"I really think you are bound to find me other horses," I said then. "The persons who have the management of this post-cart are certainly responsible for any damage a passenger may receive, when such horses as you see these to be are kept in it. There must be some other horses here, and you are in duty bound to take these out."

The two men looked somewhat convinced.

"I would ask Mr. —— to lend his horses," said the postmaster, "but they are in the veldt, and would have to be sent for, and there would be great delay; you are a day behind time already."

I very nearly laughed.

"Well," I said, "not so much delay as if we are upset and the cart broken in the spruit; and you must see that is what will probably take place with these horses."

My listeners seemed suddenly convinced; the effect of my words was magical! It was instantly agreed that the horses should be sent for to the veldt, and my cheerful-looking little friend in black requested me to descend and accept of his hospitality. He offered his arm, and asked abruptly whether I was a member of the Established Church?[16] My reply in the negative completely stunned him, or completely satisfied him; he made no further remark, but led me to one of the three white cottages. This reminded me of an English farmhouse, and was a very pleasant relief. Some neighbours, who all talked English, dropped in, and we had tea and bread and butter.

Poor Jimmy had not been asked in, and I felt very sorry for him whilst eating my bread and butter, for I knew he must be very hungry. It was getting somewhat late in the afternoon when we started once more, the owner of the horses which had replaced the vicious pair using his own harness and driving himself, whilst the Hottentot drove his steeds walking behind them. The spruit was a very ugly one, but we got over it all right, thanks to this kind Frankfurtian, whose name I forget. He left us at the house where we got our last change. The horses were good, and we got into Heilbronn by dark without farther adventure.

Chapter 5

Whatever it may be now I do not know, but then Heilbronn consisted of a square of fifteen small houses, and a few outstanding ones, stuck on a slope in the middle of a perfectly bare country. If you walked to the upper side of the village, you could look along a grassy expanse to where it touched the horizon, whichever way you turned your head. The hotel was a long low cottage. The entrance door led you straight into the sitting room, from whence a step led you into the dining room at the back. Two doors at each side of the sitting room, each led you into a small bedroom. That is the plan of pretty nearly all Boer houses that have any pretensions—the architects of the nation can conceive nothing grander. The size may vary, but the plan remains. There were other tiny bedrooms built at the back, to get to which one had to go from the dining room into the yard. Two of these were appropriated to Jimmy's and my use.

The people of the inn—a man and wife with a large family—were good sort of people, I think, and wished to make us as comfortable as they could. They had two other boarders, unmarried men who had some employment in the village, and a good many men came there to dine. It was a strange gathering at meals, and the conversation was amusing. Very odd, too, it appeared to me, to hear shopkeepers in this funny little town looked upon as magnates in the land. Of course everybody knew everybody, and was free and easy with everybody, and of course Heilbronn delighted in gossip; what small place does not?

We arrived two days before Christmas Day, and on Christmas Eve mine hosts gave a dance in the public sitting room. Amongst the guests were the judge of the place, and the magistrate, or landroost, a shopkeeper or two, some of their assistants, and a dressmaker. During the pauses of dancing a musical box played—the dance music itself was performed on a fiddle—and there were some songs. But oh, the dancing! Whilst it was going on, I sat a spectator in the dining room.

They all danced with great gravity and ponderosity, if I may use such a word; but some clung to each other as they hopped heavily round and round to a waltz tune; others charged round savagely with outstretched arms, to the imminent danger of their neighbours; others held their arms stretched down so tightly that they looked as if they were mutually desirous of dislocating each other's shoulders; whilst one couple, a chubby little man and woman, regardless of the time of either the music or the dancing of the others, with a stolid smile on each fat little face, turned slowly round and round as on a pivot. I cannot say how they managed it; their progression was very slow, and they seemed quite regardless of the collisions they came in for. I saw them get a thump from one of the chargers which would have knocked a less steady couple down, but only caused them to totter; but the comicality of their appearance at last tickled me so much that I felt I must laugh if I stayed, and so I took myself off to bed.

The entire town of Heilbronn was going out on a picnic (a combined picnic) on Christmas Day. Great had been the preparations, and hence great was the woe when Christmas Day broke with a drizzling rain. The great question, to go or not to go? was discussed until ten o'clock, when there being a slight diminution of the drizzle, it was unanimously decided that it was going to clear up, and the whole white population of Heilbronn went off in waggons and carts. Of course there had been great discussion as to who was to go in whose waggon, and whose cart was to take up whom; and the arrangements had been slightly complicated at the last moment by two young gentlemen having brought their cart and horses up to the door of the hotel, and there upset it and broken it—leading one to the conclusion that the festivities of the previous night had been too much for them. However, everything was at last arranged, and Heilbronn was deserted for the nonce by its inhabitants. The landlady informed me that she had killed two fowls, picked a dish of peas, and made a plum pudding, for the benefit of Jimmy and myself, and had given her Hottentot girl strict injunctions to make us comfortable. This was her parting blessing, and we were left alone.

There was nothing very amusing to be done. There was the musical box, and it seemed to afford some entertainment to Jimmy, for he kept it playing nearly all day, driving me almost to insanity thereby; and there were some children's stories of good and bad children, and a mutilated copy of "Ivanhoe."[17] The rain came down heavily after the picnic party had started, and appeared likely to continue coming down. Presently we had dinner, minus the peas, which I suppose the Hottentot girl kept for herself.

In the afternoon, rather late, the weather cleared, and Jimmy and I walked a little outside the village, and I gave him his first lesson in pistol shooting. As we were returning I was accosted by a man, who asked me if I were not the lady that was going up country with a party of gentlemen who were expected in Heilbronn daily. I answered in the affirmative; and he then told me that he was the proprietor of one of the spans of oxen our conductor had. (I think he was in some sort a partner of his.) He said he heard that many of them were dead of red-water,[18] and that our conductor flogged them cruelly, and had beaten a Kaffir who was with him severely. I said it was all true. It was this man who told me the real reason of our conductor bringing us to Heilbronn. He asked us to go to his cottage, which stood a little apart from the village; and we went, and found his wife (a pretty young woman) and his baby there. The man was an Englishman with a pleasant English face. He was, as he looked and spoke, of the small farmer class. His wife was colonial born. They were very kind and hospitable, and gave us a very nice tea.

On our return to the hotel we found the party had returned in very bad humour. I should not think picnicking under a tarpaulin stretched between two waggons in a thick drizzling rain on a dead flat likely to conduce to good temper; and then there were all the little jealousies and envyings sure to arise on such occasions—Mr. So-and-so had done this and said that, and so on. The picnic had set the whole little town by the ears!

A day or two after, our party arrived bringing my pony with them. I had heard that the horse-sickness was likely to be bad as soon as we crossed the Vaal, so I sold him at Heilbronn to my pleasant-looking English acquaintance, and resolved to travel thenceforth in the waggon. A good many things belonging to the conductor were taken out of it at Heilbronn, and it was made much more comfortable in consequence.

The evening that we were to start, I went to take tea with the purchaser of my pony, and I have a vivid recollection of the excellent pancakes I was eating, when one of our party tapped at the door and said the waggon was waiting for me. Certainly a kind welcome given to a stranger travelling alone in a wild country, is one of the things the angel who records good actions ought always to make a note of.

I missed my pony very much. To jolt hour after hour in an ox-waggon along a dead flat under a broiling sun is objectionable: and being now always with the waggon, the spectacle of the brutality of our conductor to his oxen, and the fearful language used by him, were very hard to bear.

We crossed the Vaal on Now Year's eve, and I shall never forget his wanton cruelty on the occasion. The river separated us, or, powerless as I was, I should have felt called upon to, interfere, as no one else seemed disposed to do so.

We were now in the Transvaal, and a day more took us to Heidelberg. We arrived there rather late at night, and I proceeded with Jimmy to the hotel. The waggon was outspanned a little outside the small town, but I was told that I could easily find the hotel by the moonlight, and that it would be open [. . .] .

Little Heidelberg, sleeping in the moonlight, with the hills around showing brown against the clear sky, looked refreshing after the dreary Free State. We got to the hotel presently. It was shut up, but I was emboldened to knock by two considerations; the first, that I could not go back to the waggon, because the men I knew would already be asleep in it; the second, that I had met the proprietor of the hotel at the Willow River, and he had told me to be sure to come to his house. I knocked, and knocked, until Jimmy said, "How can you go on knocking like that? Well, I never thought you could do such a thing." At last a man's voice from within asked, "What do you want? Who are you?"

"A traveller," I cried in return. "Can't I have a bed?"

The door was unbolted, and I saw my roadside acquaintance, who had evidently just got out of bed. "I can't give you a bed," he said; "we're full."

"Oh, Mr. Dubois," said I, "don't you remember telling me that I must come here? Do, please, let me in. I can't go back to the waggon, the men will all be asleep in it." Mr. Dubois was mollified. He let me into the room, where I saw a rough-looking man sitting up between the blankets on a sofa-bedstead.

"Here," said Mr. Dubois, "you must put your boots on and you can sleep in there," pointing to a backroom, "and let the lady have your place." So the rough-looking man tumbled out; and Jimmy said goodnight, and had to go back to the waggon; Mr. Dubois brought me a piece of candle, and I tumbled into bed, and went very fast asleep in a minute.

Nothing particular occurred during our trek from Heidelberg to Pretoria, until we were quite close to the latter place. I think it was at our last outspann that a man, who, in spite of a rakish look, was more like a gentleman than any one I had seen during my travels, rode up to the waggon, and dismounting, entered into conversation. His manners and address confirmed what his appearance had suggested to me. Long after, I heard something of this individual's story, which still farther confirmed my first impression; the end of it is worth telling, as illustrative of habits and customs out here. It is an odd thing that Boers, although adverse to the English, are very proud if they can induce Englishmen to marry into their families. Our roadside acquaintance, who had earned for himself the sobriquet of "mad" amongst his intimates, was sane enough to make use of this little peculiarity. Being very completely on his beam ends for about the hundredth time, he wooed and won a young Boeress, whose father was prepared to give a handsome portion. Having used all his fascinations so as completely to infatuate his wife and make her think herself the happiest of women, he suddenly decamped, and had got to the Vaal river, on his way into the Free State, when his father-in-law overtook him. The old gentleman was in an agony of rage and anxiety for his daughter, who of course was doing what old women call "taking on" pretty considerably; the husband was quite cool. He told the story of himself.

"What's your figure?" he asked of his infuriated relative. "Make it high enough, and I'll go back, otherwise I'm off!"

"Will five hundred sheep do?" gasped the old gentleman. The younger shook his head.

"No," he said, "not enough; just consider how dreadfully I shall be bored. Make it a thousand, and I'll say done." And the old fellow made it a thousand.

This individual told us that he was out in command of volunteers, as it was thought that the Boers might break out next day, when they said they meant to come armed into Pretoria. Of course they did not come into Pretoria. Personally I, writing this in the besieged camp of Pretoria, don't believe they ever will do so; but it made one feel a pleasant sort of excitement to think that they might, and that we should be just in time to see them do it.

We came into Pretoria through a Poort, or opening between the hills, called, I think, Bobian Poort, literally Baboon Entrance. There are no baboons on the hills now, but I suppose there were, not long ago. Little Pretoria, with its blue gums and willow trees, and its surrounding hills, looked very pretty in the light of the fast-setting sun. It was nearly dark by the time we had outspanned on a common at the upper end of the town. I asked the manager if he had inquired which hotel was the best for a lady to lodge at. He said he had; that the "European" was the one recommended; and I started off with Jimmy. I had to ask my way from a gentleman I saw sitting under his verandah on the outskirts of the town, and then to walk down a longish road, with rose hedges at each side, and with a sound of running water to be heard, which, although it was too dark to see them, told me that there must be rivulets at both sides too. The cottages, standing back in their gardens, with lights in the windows, looked pleasant and home-like, and I was almost sorry when the pretty road ended in the market square, with an ugly white church in the middle of it. There were lights in two buildings forming one of the corners of this square—low long cottages, and I rightly guessed them both to be hotels. Neither of these appeared to be suited for a lady's lodging—the bar being the leading feature in both, and a number of loud-talking men, in broad hats, short coats, and riding boots, lounging in front of them. I asked a passerby which was the "European," and he showed me the one which had a verandah, and appeared the fuller of the two. I could see that it had a public dining room, which seemed crammed, but the only entrance was through the bar; so, taking heart of grace, into the bar I walked. It was as full as it could be of men of the kind who frequent bars; but, luckily for me, behind the bar itself stood a man who was a gentleman—the then proprietor of the "European," since dead (he was killed by lightning, together with the horses he was driving). I asked this gentleman whether I could obtain a lodging at his hotel, telling him at the same time how I had just arrived, a stranger, in Pretoria, and had been told that the "European" was the best hotel for a lady to go to. "Well," he said courteously, "you have been misinformed; it is completely a man's hotel. In fact it is not an hotel, but simply a restaurant." I bowed, and asked if he could tell me where to go, as I could not return to the waggon. "If you step into my private room," he said, "I will send you some supper, and I will send round to the "Edinburgh" and "Royal" to know if they have a room to spare." I was only too glad of the offer. Jimmy went back to the waggons, and I had a nice little supper whilst I waited. But alas! there was not a room at either hotel; all were full. Mr. Carter (in this instance I give the real name of the individual) then said that all he could propose was this: there was a small room at a little distance from the hotel, whose usual occupant was absent. Mr. Carter had the key, and I could use it for that night. I forthwith started, with a coolie servant for a guide, and was taken to a small room in a stable yard behind a public house. There was a stable at one side, and I could hear men's voices in the room at the other side. It was a comfortable little room, and I observed a woman's dress hanging on a peg. Here my guide left me after he had lighted a candle. I proceeded to investigate the fastenings of the door and window. The former I could lock, but there was no way of fastening the other. It was not very pleasant, for the little I had seen of Pretoria that night had made me acquainted with the fact, which farther acquaintance only confirmed, that it is a very rowdy little village, and that a woman might better walk about late in London or Paris than in that place. I began to wish I had brought my pistol with me; however, there was no use wishing, and so I put a chair on the table that stood under the little window, so as to be sure of hearing if any one attempted to get in, and then turned into bed, and found it very comfortable.

The next morning I had nothing to do but to go to breakfast at the "European." The eating room was full of men, but Mr. Carter took me into it himself, and seated me at a little table; this he did at each meal as long as I stayed there, for which I am still grateful to him. That whole day I passed looking for a lodging, but could find none, and had to sleep once more in my little room. The next day was the same. In the morning a gentleman spoke to me as I was standing under the verandah of the "European." "You are looking for a lodging, I believe?" he said. I replied in the affirmative. "So am I," quoth he; "let us go together;" so off we started. Life is very free and easy out here, as will be observed, not only on this occasion but on various others throughout my story. The gentleman told me how he came to be in Pretoria—he was travelling to see the country; and I told him something of how I came to be in Pretoria. We walked about and called at various houses, but fruitlessly; at last, as we were walking along a grassy rose-hedged lane, which in Pretoria is called a street, we saw two fashionably dressed ladies standing under the verandah of a cottage with a strip of garden in front. "Let us ask them if they let lodgings," said my companion.

"I don't think it would do," responded I; but he evidently thought it would, for he went up and asked, and I thought I might as well go up too, under the circumstances. The ladies were very kind; they did not let lodgings, but they asked us in; my acquaintance soon left us to go in quest of some abode, but I was tired both of walking and of looking for a room, and I stayed and chatted, and had a cup of coffee.

In the afternoon, whilst standing under the "European" verandah, I was accosted by the volunteer officer we had met on the road, and shortly afterwards by the gentleman who had on the night of my arrival told me the way to the hotel. In conversation with them I mentioned my difficulties about finding a room, and also the fact that I had two letters of introduction to ladies in Pretoria, but that I was loath to present them so long as presenting them was tantamount to asking them to put me up. I mentioned the names of the ladies, and one of the gentlemen said he knew them; and with that he walked off, and presently reappeared bringing with him a gentleman, whom he introduced to me as Mr. Farquarson, the husband of one of the ladies, and the son-in-law of the other. Mr. Farquarson took me to see Mrs. Parker, whose house was not far from the hotel; but on the way he heard from some one that she was not at home, and hence I simply gave him my letters of introduction and returned to the hotel; but not immediately, for I took a solitary walk first on the outskirts of the village, and thereby missed seeing the two ladies, who called at the "European" whilst I was out.

Early the next morning I heard a knocking at the door, and the coolie's voice outside, saying I must get up at once and clear out, that the Newcastle post-cart had just come in, and brought the rightful owner of the room I was in. As may be supposed, I turned out pretty quickly. But my difficulties were to cease that day, for Mr. Farquarson came in the morning and carried me off to his cottage at the upper end of the town. Oh, how nice it did seem, with its carpets, and sofas, and nice little nicknacks, and, best of all, its pretty mistress, after travelling so long with rough men!

I went afterwards to Mrs. Parker's cottage, smaller but prettier; a very gem of a little cottage, with a small brilliant garden in front, and a well-filled kitchen-garden and orchard behind, and a verandah all overhung with beautiful creepers, and with ferns in pots, and easy chairs, under it, with graceful young trees standing all round it; and with a pretty setter who gave her paw, and a little spring-bok,[19] and a cross little prairie-dog, or meer-cat[20] as it is called here, as its inhabitants, without counting the mistress of all these nice things; mistress also of two of the smallest maid-servants I ever saw—two little Hottentot, or rather Bushman, sisters. They were mere children, but they looked like two pretty little baby monkeys, tripping about noiselessly with their little bare feet, and dressed in their clean little print frocks. The old lady was a relation of old friends of mine in England, and her house and that of her adopted daughter, Mrs. Farquarson, seemed veritable harbours of refuge to me.

Chapter 6

We remained a week in Pretoria, during which time all our things had to be removed from the waggons that had brought us from D'Urban, and packed on two others which were to convey us to Rustemberg. This was the destination of our party, and it had been arranged that I was to be lodged and boarded at the farmhouse of the farm they were to work on, and there to remain for a year, during which time I was to receive instruction in the superintendence of South African farming, while I intended to employ my spare time in learning Dutch—or what is called Dutch here, for the Dutch talked by the Boers is such a mere patois, with Kaffir, Hottentot, and even English words, mixed up in it, that a real Dutchman, or what they call here a Hollander, neither understands it nor is understood by the Boers.

When I saw the waggons which were to convey us to Rustemberg my heart sank within me. One was a buck-waggon, the other a long tent-waggon. The buck-waggon was provided with a buck-sail or tarpaulin, the tent of the other was supposed to keep out the rain without any tarpaulin; but as one could see daylight through it, it was not likely to be of much avail. It was so packed that it was impossible for any one to sit up in it, and only a space of about a foot and a half left at the back to allow of dressing, whilst the flap at the back was so ragged that it was easy to see through it, and impossible to fasten it tightly down. Then my tent, which I had lent to the party at their request during my stay in Pretoria, was lost by them during the loading-up process.

We started about the middle of the day; our oxen were a mixed lot—a very bad thing, for if oxen are to pull well, one must span them in their accustomed places and on their accustomed sides. Many oxen will never make either good fore or hind oxen. Our drivers were a half-caste of the name of William, and a Kaffir. William drove the tent-waggon. We were hardly out of Pretoria when, at a very small brook, we broke the "disselboom," or pole, of one of the waggons, I forget which. This caused a long delay, for William had to go back to Pretoria to get a new one. In the meantime we remained outspanned, in a valley about two miles broad and about sixty long. It runs between the Magaliesberg and the Wittwaters Randt; and if any one wants to know the positions of these big hills, or ranges of hills, let them look at the map. The next day William brought the disselboom in a donkey cart, and we started rather late in the afternoon. There are three high roads by which one can go from Pretoria to Rustemberg in a waggon. One goes over Mosilikats-nek, commonly called Silikats-nek, one over Commando-nek, and another over Oliphants-nek.[21] We were to go over Silikats-nek, and hence took the turn which leads to it. The tent-waggon was leading, and was well ahead of the other; and the Kaffir driver of the other went along the main road without troubling himself to look where the leading wagon was. Some of the men were with one, the rest with the other wagon. The blankets of the party were on one, the food all on the other. It was nearly dark by the time we outspanned, and the division of property made the evening and night [dis]agreeable for both divisions of our party.

The buck-waggon joined us the next morning, and we got as far as the foot of Silikats-nek by midday. The scenery here is fine. The wagon was outspanned under some trees in the middle of thick bush; above us rose the rugged sides of the Magaliesberg, now beginning to show what becomes its characteristic further down the valley, namely, a precipice of some hundred feet high crowning its wooded sides. This formation is here called, not inappropriately, a kranz, or crown. Creepers hung in festoons round the bushes, turning them into bowers or impenetrable barriers, as the case might be.

I rambled about in this refreshing maze of verdure until dinner was ready, and then I determined to walk on over the nek in front of the waggon [. . .] Leaving an apparently old road to my right, I kept along this pretty road until I saw another one turn off to the right. Here I hesitated, but my instruction having been to keep to the left, I did so. Presently a sudden thunderstorm caused me to take shelter under a thick bower of trees and creepers. This was, however, not thick enough to prevent my being wet through by the rain, which came down so quick and strong that it soon turned the road into a river. The storm passed, but no waggon was to be seen or heard, and I, although soaking wet, still wandered on, keeping in the grass by the side of the road [. . .]. Presently a small tax cart, drawn by two weedy looking ponies came along the road towards me. In it were two men, one an oldish man with a big beard, the other a sleek but dirty-looking little fellow in black clothes, with a sanctimonious look about him. The former said "Good evening!" as he passed, which made me stop and ask him if I were on the Rustemberg road. He asked where my wagon was; and I told him I had left it at Silikats-nek. "Then," he said, "I think you probably have passed the turn you should have taken, to the right." [. . .] I thanked him, and he drove on. I now considered that as it was near sunset, if the wagons had taken the other road I could easily pick them up, as they would be outspanned for the night, and that I should be able to know whether they had done so by the fresh marks of wheels and oxen's feet, and hence I determined to walk a little farther [. . .]. The thunder was beginning to growl once more, and bright flashes of lightning to light up the dark mass of cloud behind the precipice of the nek, whilst the nearer hills and the trees were burnished by the setting sun.

I stood and looked, then turned, but only to stop and look again, although in front of me when I turned the sky looked unpleasantly lowering. Presently, however, a tremendous crash of thunder, accompanied by some very large drops warned me to be moving. But I had waited too long; before many minutes the sky was as dark as night, the rain began to fall, though not very heavily, and when I reached the road I thought the wagon might have taken, I could only see it by the flashes of lightning. It was evident no wagon had passed there. It was now pitch dark, and I had some difficulty in finding the old road which I had remarked on my way out. By the flashes of lightning I again discovered that no wagon had been there. I now concluded that the wagon had had some mishap on the nek, and soon I heard voices, and came up to the party and to the tent-waggon, outspanned on the very top of the ascent. The buck-waggon with all the eatables in it had stuck half way up. The rain was coming down pretty sharp now. There was nothing to eat or to drink but some rum of which the men were partaking, and I, being still wet through, thought it best to follow their example before rolling myself up in my damp blankets, for the tent leaked as I expected. [. . .]

[After three days of additional mishaps including broken oxen leads and yokes, strayed animals, further storms, and difficulty in fording streams, Heckford strikes out on her own, trying to find a way to get to Rustenburg. She again meets the man who had tried to help her when she was lost.]

True to his word, my new acquaintance sent a Kaffir boy early the following morning to show me the way to his farm, where I was to have breakfast, and to find a cart and horse to take me to Rustemberg [. . .] The one I was to have, belonged to the sanctimonious-looking little man I had seen driving my acquaintance. He was a Dopper, i.e. belonged to a very sanctified sect of the Dutch Church. The sleek little man had shuddered with holy horror at the idea of his committing the impropriety of driving alone with any woman not related to him, neither would his conscience allow him to hire out his vehicle so as to facilitate any such inappropriate action on the part of his neighbour; at last, however, his scruples had been overcome to the extent of consenting to drive me to Rustemberg, provided his neighbour (my new acquaintance) acted *chaperon* to him.

We three, therefore, set forth in the dewy morning through a park-like country. The little Dopper sat in front, and said never a word. Mr. Deckbird,[22] on the contrary was very talkative. So was I at first, the relief from the dreadful wagon being so great that I really felt in high spirits; but gradually it began to dawn on me that my companion was mad, and I confess that I was very glad that the little Dopper was in the front seat driving that day's drive. As I say, I believe that man was mad, but he was very kind for all that; and although I was certainly afraid of him, I shall always remember his kindness with gratitude. We outspanned three times, once near a farmhouse, from whence Mr. Deckbird brought me a basketful of beautiful fruit; once at another farmhouse, where the women came out and insisted on my getting down, and where Mr. Deckbird introduced me in Dutch as his second wife, which, considering that I could not say anything to the contrary, owing to not knowing Dutch, although I understood what was said, and had to confine myself to shaking my head vigorously, was not pleasant. The good people all laughed at the joke, and gave me some very good coffee, and milk, and bread, and sat and looked at me. I, in return, looked at them, and once more observed to myself that many of these Boers, if dressed up in antique fashion, would look like the models from which Rembrandt and others of the old masters painted.

Our third outspann was in sight of pretty, diminutive Rustemberg, and was in the open veldt, near, I think, a quarry. The cause of this outspann was original.

"We must outspann here," said Mr. Deckbird. "I must change my trousers before I go into Rustemberg; I know some people there." And retiring to the quarry in mufti, he reappeared in magnificence.

Before we reached the little village I was introduced to a habit common to the Transvaal, and which is not a pleasing feature in the life here.

"You will be sure to meet Mr. Lestrange," said my companion. "A charming man; you will be delighted with him. But you must take care; don't trust him."

This was the first time I heard this; I have heard it now *ad nauseam*. Mr. A. tells you to beware of Mr. B., he is very nice and all that, but to be on your guard; Mr. B. says he sees you know Mr. A., that it is all very well to be friends with him, but that you must not trust him too much; both Mr. A. and Mr. B. caution you in a friendly spirit against Mr. C., and Mr. C. in the same manner cautions you against them; and this sometimes even when the people who speak thus appear to be on the most intimate terms.

Chapter 7

The village of Rustemberg, from which one can see the last place inhabited by white people, and through whose streets numbers of Kaffirs and Kaffir women troop daily, dressed in skins, and adorned with barbaric ornaments appeared to me to be a sort of *Ultima Thule*.[23] It had some little shops as stores, and a little prison, and a little post office, and three little churches—for even here the population is large enough for sects to exist; and it had also numerous rose hedges bounding its grassy streets, and a missionary station and a mill. Everything looked as if it were just winking between two sleeps [. . .]. Amongst other things that Rustemberg possessed was a little inn, kept by a big, jolly Dutch woman, a Mrs. Brown, by virtue of her marriage with an Englishman. In this worthy couple's house I spent a month, and if I never see Mrs. Brown again, yet shall I always remember her as the cheeriest, heartiest, most kindhearted, and sturdiest of housewives. Her heart was open to everybody, whether the body walked on two or four legs. Did she see a half-starved Kaffir dog look in at her kitchen door or crawl trembling towards the dresser, it was not "Furtseck," or "Get out," that she would cry, but "What a shame to starve that poor thing so!" and a piece of bread or meat was sure to be offered. Did she see an ox being ill-treated, she would rush out and interfere. The horses in her stable, whether her own or her lodgers', were well cared for; her oxen sleek, and dire was her anger if she saw marks of heavy stripes on their glossy backs. Her cows all knew her well; and a bevy of dogs, amongst which was one little spaniel she had rescued from a cruel master, sat round her every morning and at every meal, for her to give to each its portion.

Then, as to her own species, she had brought up and portioned one orphan girl, had opened her doors to another, whose mother was dead and whose stepmother was unkind to her, and was talking about the necessity of taking a third because she was so unkindly treated. Her husband was a carpenter; he left her the principal management of the hotel, but was fond of, and kind to, all her various *protégés;* whilst his special favorite was a large tom cat, who always sat by his side at table, and whom Mrs. Brown averred he spoiled by feeding it whilst he was eating himself. [. . .]

We had early coffee in our bedrooms, breakfast at eight, dinner at one, supper at six, and then a chat in the big sitting room till we went to our bedrooms. Often visitors for Mrs. Brown would drop in of an evening and then I heard Dutch talked. Mrs. Brown could not speak English at all perfectly, and was delighted to hear that I wanted to learn Dutch; she was, however, a dangerous preceptress, for she would teach me all sorts of phrases, assuring me that their signification was so and so, and then, upon my repeating them innocently, her ringing laugh and the wink she would give, showed me that she had been putting me up to say something very different from what I thought. Of course I soon made friends with her four-footed pets; and the little dog "Gip," which she had taken in compassion, got so fond of me that she made it a present to me. [. . .]

But with all Mrs. Brown's kindness and merriment the time at Rustemberg was very trying. On arriving there I soon found that what I had suspected for a long time was only too true. The scheme about the farm was a snare and a delusion; both the men who came out to work on it, and I, who had counted upon getting instruction there, had been utterly deceived. The party arrived some days after I did, and it was a week or so before the whole affair was quite shown up; but when it was so, two or three of the men, and Jimmy, went on to the farm, such as it was, the rest went as volunteers, and I had to shift for myself.

It was evident that I could do nothing in the farming line until I could understand and speak the Boer tongue; evident also that unless I were to earn more money somehow, my small stock would rapidly dwindle to next to nothing, for living at an hotel, or boarding, in the Transvaal, is frightfully expensive.

In this dilemma I was helped by Mr. Richardson, the clergyman of Rustemberg, to whom I had brought a letter of introduction from the rector of Pretoria. He asked me if I would go as a governess in a farmer's family; and on my answering in the affirmative, he said he would write to an English Africander farmer, who had two young daughters whom he was anxious to educate well. This farmer's name was Higgins,[24] he told me, and his farm was about thirty-five miles from Rustemberg, on the southern slope of the Magaliesberg. From all who spoke of Mr. Higgins I heard a good account of himself and his family; and his house, I was told was the finest farmhouse in the Transvaal. The post only goes out once a week from Rustemberg, and hence there was some delay before Mr. Higgins's reply came. It was to the effect that he would come in to fetch me as soon as he could. My engagement was that I was to be paid five pounds a month, with washing, and that I might take other pupils besides Mr. Higgins's two daughters at any terms I chose to make, while Mr. Higgins undertook to give any such pupils their dinner.

Several days passed, and I neither heard nor saw anything of Mr. Higgins. I used to pass my day in writing a story,[25] without which amusement I should have collapsed under the combined heat, dullness, and anxiety of that time at Rustemberg; but it is wonderful how one can forget oneself and one's own troubles in inventing the joys and woes of creatures of one's imagination! I used to sit up late writing, and as soon as day broke get up to write again. Little Gip was my constant companion now. He would not remain an instant away from me, and many a time his little paw scratching my dress would stop my pen, and call upon me to take the small beast up and give it the caress it wanted; for Gip never cared for being fed, but only for being coaxed and played with [. . .].

One beautiful evening, after a very hot day, I was standing at the door of my little room, enjoying the cool air, and admiring two fine grey horses that were cropping the grass in the street, watched by a mischievous-looking Kaffir boy of about nine. They were evidently fresh arrivals, for I had not seen them before. While I was standing thus and chatting to Mrs. Brown's *protégé*, a fine-looking man, dressed in a riding suit, with high boots and a wide-awake-hat, and with a sunburnt honest face, merry blue eyes, and a fine reddish-brown beard, sprang up the steps that led to my little door, and touching his hat said, "Mrs. Heckford, I think; I'm Higgins. I came while you were out," he went on; "those are my horses," pointing to the animals I had been admiring. We settled everything in five minutes. I told Mr. Higgins that he might inquire about me from Mr. Richardson, who would be able to tell him who I was, and what were my antecedents; but he said it was of no use, that he was quite satisfied with what he had seen and heard of me, and only wanted to know when I could start. I said I should be ready to start early next morning; and so my stay in little Rustemberg, and under the friendly roof of Mr. And Mrs. Brown, came to an end.

Chapter 8

Early the next morning I packed all the things I could into the tax cart with a canvas hood to it which was to convey me to my new home, the farm "Surprise;"[26] my heavy luggage I had to leave behind in Mrs. Brown's charge. Then after breakfast, and amidst much shaking of hands and many good wishes, I got into the cart, climbed on to the back seat—Mr. Higgins and the mischievous-looking Kaffir imp jumped up in front—little Gip was lifted up to me, and Mr. Higgins having said I might take him, I joyfully tucked him under my arm—and I was launched into my new life.

That asking whether I might take my dog seemed like the first plunge into a cold bath on a frosty morning; it was part of the part I had to play now, and I wondered how I should play it. I had always pitied governesses, and had also always objected to be an object of pity myself, even to myself. I never could see the use of self-commiseration, which to some seems to be so delectable. How I wondered what Mrs. Higgins would be like, what my pupils would be like, what the whole life would be like, and what sort of a governess I should make, as we bowled along the pretty road, over Oliphants-nek, and then along the southern side of the picturesque Magaliesberg once more, into the long valley, up and down which I had looked on the day of our breaking the disselboom a little outside of Pretoria, but distant about sixty miles from the spot. Mr. Higgins in the meantime chatted away pleasantly. He was not an educated man, as he said himself, but he was evidently a very good fellow. He said his children were respectively eleven and nine, the name of the older was Augusta, of the younger Sarah. He said they had had no teaching to speak of, but that their mother was very anxious they should have good schooling. Then he told me the names of the two greys that were drawing the cart were Sam and Dick, that they were brothers, and that he had another horse, a fine brown horse, called Free State, or, as a pet name, Baby; and then he talked about other horses he had had, and about a little dog his youngest daughter had. We outspanned twice, and twice stopped for Mr. Higgins to pay a little visit at farms we passed, and on each occasion he piled my lap and filled his pockets and handkerchief with peaches. At last, just as the sun was setting, and as we were turning round a spur of the hill all wooded with thorn trees, Mr. Higgins said, "Now you'll see the house;" and in a few minutes I saw a good-sized red-brick house with a verandah, standing in the middle of the grassy slope, the wooded sides of the mountain and its high kranz[27] rising behind it, an orchard of large fruit trees and a fine stretch of cultivated land lying below it, and a background of mountain range and wooded slope running down into the long valley beneath it.

At the same moment Mr. Higgins said, "There are Mrs. Higgins and the children;" and I saw two tall black-robed figures and one small one (the family were in mourning for the youngest child), and a little black and white dog, coming to meet the cart. It was alongside of them in a minute; and Mr. Higgins jumping out, little Sarah was lifted up and took the reins, whilst her dog Fido, who jumped up with her, went through a series of frantic antics ending by nearly tumbling out, all meant for demonstrations of joy at her master's return.

Let me introduce my employer's wife and children. Mrs. Higgins was a very tall, fine-looking woman, with a stately grace about her movements and manners; she talked bad grammar, and misplaced her "h's," but I felt at and from the first that I was in the presence of a lady. Augusta, a child of eleven, was as tall as most girls of fifteen, and looked almost grown up. Slight, with beautiful fine brown hair hanging over her shoulders and down to her waist, with soft almond-shaped blue eyes fringed by long dark lashes and over-arched by pencilled eyebrows, with a sweet but haughty little mouth, and with a white and rose-pink complexion, with long, slender, refined hands too, I thought I had rarely seen such a lovely girl. Everything about her breathed of refinement and indolence; you would have sworn she had been bred in some luxurious drawing room, and waited on by obsequious servants.

Little Sarah was a contrast to her sister. Small for her age, and with a baby chubbiness still clinging to her; with mischief, wilfulness, and bright intelligence sparkling in her eyes and ringing in her voice; with an expression ever changing, with still unformed features, and with a shock of wild-looking hair hanging about her face, in some ways she reminded me of an unbroken Shetland pony, and in my mind I installed her as my pet.

We were soon at the front of the house—a house not after the Boer model, but built on Mr. Higgins's own plan [. . . .]

We had supper in the dining room, and then we went to the drawing room—a prettily-furnished apartment, with a fairly good piano, and a nice harmonium in it. I got the children to play on the former. They performed a duet from ear—for they did not know their notes—and kept exact time. Then I was asked to play. I had no music with me, the little I had, having been left behind with my heavy luggage, and I had not touched a piano for months, nor practised on one for years. They particularly wanted to hear me play a piece called "The Battle of Waterloo." It was one of those pieces that sound more difficult than they are, and I read it easily enough. Then followed "Shells of Ocean" with variations, and "Home, Sweet Home," and some others with variations, all arrangements new to me, but with which I did my best. It was very encouraging to hear that I gave great satisfaction—I was so dreadfully afraid I should not; but it was evident that the pleasure caused by my playing was genuine. Then an old copy of the entire opera of "Norma" was brought out. The family did not much care for "Norma;" but, oh! how strange it did seem to listen to that well-known music, which carried one back to the gorgeous Italian opera, and recalled faces and voices—some of them passed away, some of them never probably to be seen or heard again—in that little drawing room of the farmhouse on the Magaliesberg, with listeners around to whom the very names that were household words to me, were utterly unknown!

Life is a wonderful romance for many of us. It never struck me more forcibly that it had been so, and was still for me, than on that evening, when, having bid the family goodnight, and having been kissed by the children with heartiness that showed they were prepared to like me, I stood for a while at the open window, with the dark outline of the mountains before my material eyes, but with visions of all that had passed since I had first listened to "Casta Diva,"[28] shutting out the present, and substituting for a short while scenes widely different. Before I went to sleep, however, the present reasserted itself in the shape of Gip. Gip was determined to sleep with his little head touching my shoulder. He had not been accustomed to do so, but I suppose he felt strange in the new house, and wanted a sense of protection. At any rate he was determined on this point. It was useless putting him off the bed; and he would patter on the floor, and scratch at the side of the bed, and make little springs, and whine in a manner that rendered sleep impossible, and I felt that sleep was necessary; so at last I took him up and let him have his own way, although I wondered in my mind what Mrs. Higgins would think of a dog sleeping on her nice white counterpane.

Chapter 9

I woke early the next morning, and took a survey of my new abode, and a stroll towards a wooded spur of the mountain, where I was told Mr. Higgins's father and mother and two young sisters lived, in a little cottage. The road, if road it could be called, passed along the top of some upper cultivated lands, on which a fine crop of Indian corn was standing, and which were shut in partly by a low stone wall, partly by a rose hedge at the top and sides; whilst an orchard of big orange, lemon, peach, almond, apricot, and fig trees separated these, the upper lands, from the lower lands, which were much larger. At the bottom of the upper lands stood an old thatched house, used as a stable and outhouse, with two enormous syringe trees overshadowing it. This was the oldest house in the Transvaal, and had been built by old Potchieter,[29] who was afterwards made mincemeat of by the Kaffirs—in days not indeed far distant, but when elephants might be shot on the place where Mr. Higgins's house now stood, and when the cultivated valley beneath me was still covered with bush. A little farther on, the road passed over a broad stone bulwark, which served to dam up a rivulet, which, gushing out of the precipitous crown of the mountain, found its way down its side through a ravine overarched by trees, and carpeted with ferns, to a place at which it was compelled to form a big pond or dam. [. . .]

From the dam the road took me over a little rise, on which some Kaffir houses were built, and then down towards the valley. It was a pretty walk. As I was returning I observed that the house had a loft, but no outbuildings of any kind. It is the same with all the best farmhouses in the Transvaal. They are comfortable in many ways, but they lack what we consider the commonest conveniences of a dwelling; and this applies to some even of the houses on the outskirts of Pretoria.

The children came to meet me near the dam, and we went in to breakfast. This was Friday, and Mr. Higgins said I had better take it easy, and not begin lessons till Monday. My life now seemed settled for a time. I was to give the children what is called a good English education, and to teach them to play the piano, to draw, and to sing. Foreign languages are not much cared for in Africa.

Besides Augusta and Sarah, it was arranged that I was to have Mr. Higgins's two sisters—Alice, a girl of sixteen, and Ada, who was thirteen—as pupils. Their mother, a pleasant-looking old lady, came over from her cottage, and made the arrangement with me. Alice, a small, plump, and pretty girl, with something very sweet and yet determined in her look, and with activity stamped on her every movement, was engaged to be married to a young man who was half farmer and half trader. Ada, almost but not quite so tall as Augusta, was yet a tall girl for her age. She was slight and graceful, with hands as delicate as those of her niece. With a pretty impertinent nose, arched eyebrows, and eyes that could coax you, or calmly overlook you, according to the mood of their pretty owner, with a scornfully-turned upper lip, and a pouting under one—very rosy, and which could part into a delightful smile when she was pleased, or wanted to please—with a prettily disdainful languor in all her movements (except, by the way, when she went in for a romp, at which she excelled), Miss Ada Higgins looked like a little princess in disguise. Like her niece, she had masses of brown hair hanging from her well-set-on head, but her hair was even heavier in its flow than Augusta's.

I had to begin with the very simplest lessons. Even Alice had to learn to spell monosyllables, and be taught the meaning of words which a child of eight in England would laugh at you for asking her to explain. They had no idea of the points of the compass, and had never heard of an article; but they were on the whole very good pupils, and only Sarah was wilful and idle at times, making up for this afterwards by the greatest attention and intelligent comprehension. It was a terrible trial to this small girl to be kept at lessons—she who, up to the time I came, had been allowed to run wild, and romp all day with the Kaffir children on the property. Many an excuse would she make to escape from the schoolroom, and forthwith perform a dance with Maikee or Vittaree, or have a sparring match with Fiervaree, the Kaffir imp who was supposed to look after Sam and Dick. Many a day would she pretend to be ill until she persuaded her mamma to let her off school, and then set to, with gleeful enjoyment, to help Sannee, the Kaffir girl who assisted in the housework, to clean the pots and pans; or turning up her sleeves, and tying her doll on behind her back as the Kaffir mothers tie their babies when at work, she would get a pailful of cow dung and water, and proceed to smear the floor of the little lumber room with it, pretending that it was her house. This smearing operation, unpleasant to English ears, is a necessary part of house keeping here, where most of the floors are made of mud or rather, of a mixture of ant-heap and water, stamped and levelled down, and where, without the aid of cow dung, one would be stifled with dust and eaten alive by fleas.

The life was monotonous, but not unpleasant. Breakfast at between seven and eight, then lessons till one (dinner time), then lessons again till about five, when there was afternoon tea, then supper at about seven, a chat or a little music, and to bed. I worked my pupils pretty hard, but I tried to make them fond of me, and I think I succeeded. I certainly became fond of them, but little Sarah was always my pet, though I used to make her cry about four days out of the seven. There was a great difficulty in getting books, &c., for them, Pretoria, the nearest town, being forty miles distant, and it was often difficult to explain common things to them, owing to their experience being so very, small. It is not easy to convey the idea of a bridge even, to a child who has never seen any nearer approach to it than the wall of a dam with a road over it, or a piece of plank stretched across a furrow; or to convey the idea of a steam engine, or a steamboat, to one who has never seen anything of the sort; or to create an idea of a large town in one who looks upon a tiny village as a very imposing place. However, all things considered, the children got on well, and their parents were satisfied. Mr. Higgins let me ride "Free State" occasionally, on one occasion taking me to a small Kaffir kraal that was on his property, where I went into the neat huts and admired the cement-like mud floors.

The Kaffirs living in the kraal were what is called raw Kaffirs, the men indeed being in some sort clothed in old European garments, but the women wearing skins, and the children being naked. Mr. Higgins, as landlord, had the right to their services for taking the crops off the land, without paying them; and also of commanding their services at other times, for the wage of a shilling a day, at most, to the men, and of something much less to the boys. He also had the right to order the women to weed or to scoffle, as it is called here, giving them a basket of peaches in return, during the fruit season, or without payment if there was no fruit. Besides these, he had several families of what are called Urlams, or civilized Kaffirs, living in mud houses on his property. These families dressed like Europeans, and had food like Europeans, even to the drinking of early coffee. They also went to school to the missionary station at Rustemberg periodically, and learned a little reading and singing of hymns. I don't think the school did them much good. I heard of one Kaffir woman saying, that when she came back from school and had been made a Christian, she would sit on a chair and eat with a knife and fork, and not let the raw Kaffirs eat with her, for that then she would be better than they.

Sannee, the girl who helped in the house, after her return from school refused to help her mistress, who was very ill at the time, saying that the missionary had told her that she must not work for some months, only study. Mr. Higgins was a very kind, indulgent master, partly from good nature, partly from indolence. He could get Kaffirs to come to squat on his farm when other farmers could not get any; but then they squatted and did little else, except when a sudden fancy to do a little work seized them.

I also rode to old Mr. Higgins's little cottage, a small structure stuck on a very picturesque spur of the mountain, with a big wild fig tree in front of it. It was simply a mud and stone cabin, with the bare rafters and thatch showing overhead, its one long room divided into three by rude canvas partitions, without a trace of paper on the walls, and with planks supported on the rafters doing duty as shelves. Outside, a straw house did duty as outhouse, stable, cow-house, or anything else, a conical straw hut, with a hole at the top, was the kitchen, and another small straw structure close to the sheep kraal served for a fowl-house. There was an old piano, however, in this funny little building, and on it Alice and Ada practised their music. Old Mrs. Higgins kept no servant; she and Alice cleaned the house, cooked, washed in a washing machine, ironed, and made the dresses of the family. Ada, the princess, did nothing, not even mend her own clothes. How Alice managed to do the work she did and learn her lessons I don't know, but she did manage it.

There were no windows to this odd little building, only square holes in the wall, with movable frames stretched over with calico fitted to them, and there was no chimney. Old Mr. Higgins, who had been a great hunter when younger, was now a victim to chronic bronchitis of a very bad type, and how he managed to live in that cabin I do not know. He had not even the convenience of an armchair. He was a small grey-bearded man, much bent, but with a keen look about the eyes that spoke of his hunting days, and with a still easy seat in the saddle—a thorough old gentleman too in all his ways and thoughts, and with a fund of queerly assorted information. Often he has startled me by the things he know of, having been all his life a great reader, and given to buying books in lots on sales.

Mrs. Higgins the younger did the principal part of her housework herself, and wonderful was the amount of needlework, or rather machine-work, she would get through in the day besides; yet she never seemed in a fuss or a hurry, never spoke loudly or crossly, but was always stately and ladylike, even with her dress turned up, her arms bared, and a broom in her hand. Augusta, like Ada, did nothing but look ornamental. This was what the two girls were meant for by nature, and they could not, I believe, be useful if they tried; but they didn't try. Little Sarah was already a famous housekeeper, but she scolded the servants well.

There was a wonderful old Hottentot maid, "Khrid," the second wife of a certain Jonas who squatted on the farm—a good sort of creature, who was very helpful in the house, and of whom Sarah was a special pet and persecutor. Sometimes she would spring on the woman's back, and tightening her legs round her waist, pinch her and beat her—in fun it is true, but pretty hard for all that—until the old woman would lie down and roll, to get her off.

In this family I was treated not like a governess, but like a welcome guest. The best of everything was at my disposal without my asking for or even thinking of having it. Whatever there was unavoidably rough in the life, Mrs. Higgins did her best to shelter me from. A stranger would, I am sure, have thought that I was there teaching the children as a friend, not as one paid for it. When poor little Gip got ill and became troublesomely dirty at night, Mrs. Higgins expostulated with me for having cleaned and washed up the things myself; and when my poor little dog died, she got a Kaffir to dig a grave for it, and in no way objected to lessons being interrupted to attend to it before its death, or to see it buried afterwards. I was dreadfully sorry for the little dog that had been so fond of me when I was a stranger in the land, and it was true kindness to me to indulge me as she did. But it was not to me alone that she showed tact and delicacy of feeling. It was the same with even a raw Kaffir. The true politeness of quick sympathy and unselfishness, was always there, for the benefit of any one coming within her sphere of influence.

It must be remembered that all this time the Boer scare was going on. Horrible tales used to be told at meal times and in the evening as to what the Boers meant to do to the English, or any of the Africanders who held with the English; and the Higginses were very loyal. There was even talk of its being as well for the family to go into the Free State. This being the case, I began to feel unhappy about Jimmy, who was away on a farm with three or four other English. This farm was about thirty miles from Surprise, and I had no horse or any other means of conveyance to take me to him. I therefore began to be very anxious to buy a horse, but it was not easy to get one.

The scare had for a time subsided, when one day, while I was in the schoolroom, one of the children cried out, "Oh! there is Uncle Walter," and of course they all wanted to go out to see Uncle Walter—an unmarried uncle who, with a bachelor brother, kept a store at Marico. I remained in the schoolroom. Presently Mr. Higgins called me, and said he wanted me to meet his brother. I went out, and saw a fine-looking man standing by the side of a handsome dun horse, and with another horse standing close to him with a rein in its mouth for leading it by.

"That's a nice little horse" said Mr. Higgins; "what do you think of it?"

"It does not look bad," I said, not much prepossessed by the lean animal with a draggly tail, that I was looking down on from the stoop.

"Do you think it would suit you?" he asked.

I looked closer at it then. It was a good horse at all points, with a little head, taper neck, and fine ears, which spoke of good blood, better than generally seen. It had been roughly treated, evidently, not over well fed, and ridden hard, and was very dirty, but that time would cure. It was a light-red roan—what is here called a red grey—with white stockings, a white streak down its face, and chestnut mane and tail. The eyes were full, but a little mischievous-looking, in spite of the otherwise very mild appearance of the creature.

"I think it might," I replied, "if the price be not high."

"Would you give twenty pounds?" asked Mr. Higgins.

"Yes, but not more," I answered.

He inquired of his brother whether the horse, which was his, and which he had had for some time, was sound and fit for a lady to ride. He said it was so; and the bargain being struck, my new acquisition, "Eclipse" the grandson of a famous old colony racer, and himself the winner of two races in the colony, was turned loose to graze, whilst Walter Higgins rode off on his handsome dun—a horse whom everybody said was thoroughly "salted,"[30] and for whom he had refused sixty pounds, but who died a few days after, it was said from "horse sickness," but I rather fancy from the bots.

Not long after, a neighbour came in. "Have you bought that red-grey horse?" he asked. "Yes."

"Are you a very good horsewoman?"

"No."

"Then take care; he'll break your neck. Why, he bucked Walter Higgins off him—and Arthur Sturton—and he nearly threw me, only I jumped off. I never saw a horse buck so cleverly as he does."

This was pleasant, the more so as before a day was over I heard further confirmation of it. However, the thing was done, and I had to make the best of it.

Mr. Higgins allowed me forage for my animal, and I groomed him, fed him, and bedded him up myself. No hand but mine touched him. He was stabled in the stable with Dick, Sam, and Free State, and I now saw how the Kaffir boys who had charge of these horses neglected them. Anticipating buying a horse, I had brought all the articles necessary for one with me, and Eclipse soon showed his change of owners. At first he was troublesome to groom, but he soon got accustomed to it and fond of me, nor, though a very lively horse, did he ever attempt more than a little playful jump with me; but his character was bad. The Dutch farmers seeing me ride him would exclaim; and even men who had ridden him could never account for the change in him, although it was easily enough accounted for.

Eclipse knew as well as most horses how to distinguish between a master who treated him well and never punished him except when he deserved it, and one who neglected him and spurred him to make him show off. I certainly felt much happier after getting my horse, although I had to be up early to groom him, and had trouble about his bedding; and although I had no time to ride much—for it is not good during the summer months here to have a horse out of the stable early in the morning or late in the evening—and I was occupied during the day on weekdays. Still many a ride I had, generally with one of the children with me on Dick, and I felt now that if there were danger I could get hold of Jimmy [. . . .]

The Boer scare now set in again. Plans used to be discussed as to what was to be done in case of an attack, and at last even Mr. Higgins, who generally took things quietly, began to look serious, and to check me when I laughed at the idea of danger—for I thought there was too much talk for anything to come of it. One day a neighbour rode up to say that there was a Kaffir commando marching on Pretoria, that a son of Cetewayo[31] had ridden through the valley and over the mountain to Rustemberg the night before—that he had told the farmers from whom he had commanded a horse and money, that a great outbreak of the Kaffirs was close at hand, and that all who did not wish to be murdered had best go into lagers.[32] The veldt-cornet[33] had ridden late at night to warn some people in his district; all was authenticated beautifully. Surprise was alarmed: no shame for it, for Pretoria trembled in its shoes at the same rumour. I can't say that I felt frightened, but then it is difficult for any one accustomed to profound peace, and a civilized country, to bring his mind to realize the possibility of a sudden outbreak of savages. The Higginses knew what it was from practical experience, old Mrs. Higgins having had to fly with a child under one arm, and a money box under the other, alongside of her husband, who was laden with another child and the powder bag. My employer had seen his parents' property swept away more than once in the old colony by Kaffirs, and hence it is no wonder that he felt more concern than I.

It was the most absurd hoax, that ever was practised, and the Kaffir who personated Cetewayo's son, and ordered the terrified Boers to give him horses and money must have had a laugh at the success of his piece of fun. Their having obeyed the dictates of a half tipsy Kaffir was a sore point with the Boers afterwards, and this absurd escapade did not serve to raise my opinion of their courage. But hardly had this blown over, than the Boer scare broke out again. Mr. Higgins wanted to take loads down to Natal, and ride transport up—transport was very high then—but waited and waited for the Beeinkommste,[34] which was then sitting, to break up. Terrible threats were current as to what was to happen to the dwellers on outstanding farms, if the demands of the committee were not listened to, still worse was it to go with us if the English Government attempted to lay hands on the leaders.

Time went by, and at last Mr. Higgins said he could wait no longer, or that he should have too cold weather on his return journey for the oxen; so he loaded a big pistol for his wife, and hung it up in the hall, told her she must do the best she could in case of any disturbance, and on a fine April morning he started off the waggons loaded with wool bags, and prepared to follow them on horseback. Great had been the preparations for starting the waggons, biscuits having to be baked for the road and other provisions provided. A Mr. King, a small farmer and a great friend of Mr. Higgins, went with the waggons, he came to breakfast before he started, and a starved-looking rough black and white terrier with big beseeching eyes all covered by his long hair came with him. The dog did not belong to him, but was loafing about, and came to Surprise for something to do, I suppose. We all turned out to see the waggons start. The one with a splendid span of eighteen black oxen in it—their sleek skins shining in the sun, and with their driver, a Kaffir called Saul, alongside, looking proud of his beasts, and glad of the change—made a great impression on me, and I said to myself, "I will never go down to the coast till I can go with such a span as that." Soon after Mr. Higgins saddled up, and bidding us good bye, took a short cut after the waggons. We all felt very flat as the last flick of Freestate's tail was seen through the long grass; how I did envy Mr. Higgins to be sure, but we soon settled down, and I began to like being alone with Mrs. Higgins and the children. The rough black and white dog stayed behind, and in process of time came to be my dog, and developed into a very pretty playful little animal, up to any amount of fun, and a good watchdog, but with a terror of being lost or stolen from me. He would often go off visiting on his own account, but his dread of being taken hold of by any one strange, and the way he would struggle and bite, were amusing; a terrible dog for fighting too was this little animal, whom we christened "Rough."

Winter was now beginning, and though I regretted the summer in some ways, I was glad it was gone; for the dreaded "horse-sickness" goes with it. It is strange that no one has ever found out exactly what the "horse-sickness" is; the only thing certain about it is that horses that eat the grass after the sun is set, or before the dew is off, are more liable to it than others. Opinions vary as to whether mere exposure to the night air affects horses in the matter. It is averred that horses that have once had the "horse-sickness" rarely have it again, and if they do get it, have it very mildly; one is told many other things regarding this curious disease, but authorities disagree. I believe that numbers of horses are said to die of "horse-sickness" when in reality they die of bots and of neglect. In this country, where horses are so seldom kept decently clean, the bots make terrible ravages amongst them. I have frequently been told, and that, too, by people who ought to have known better, that it was impossible to clean the bot-eggs off horses that were roughing it in the veldt, and it stands to reason that if the eggs are left on the animals for them to lick off, they will soon be full of bots. I speak now of horses that are ridden. In the case of a herd of mares and colts, it would of course be impossible to prevent harm, grooming in such cases being out of the question [. . . .]

The great thing, therefore, is, if possible, to prevent a horse from getting the disease, and I was as careful about Eclipse not being exposed to the early or late air as a mother with a delicate baby.

Chapter 10

Not long after Mr. Higgins's departure we were all startled one day by Arthur Sturton's riding up from his farm in the valley to tell us that a neighbouring farmer—an English Africander—had just come back from Pretoria, and had brought the news that Sir Bartle Frere[35] had met the Committee of the Boers—that there had been much angry discussion, and that at last the Boers had leapt from their seats, overturning the chairs and crying, "War! war! We give you notice that we will march on Pretoria tomorrow." He had told Arthur Sturton that every waggon was being pressed into Government service, and that his own had been seized; so that but for a chance he should have had to walk all the way from Pretoria, whither he had gone with a load. Arthur Sturton said that he had sent a Kaffir to his father's farm (which is halfway between Surprise and Pretoria), there to wait for further intelligence; Moyplas, as it is called, being on the high road, and any one coming from Pretoria being likely to call there. He said that when the Kaffir returned he would send news to us.

Mrs. Higgins and I held a council of war on the verandah that afternoon, and it was resolved that if the Boers came to Surprise, we would receive them civilly, but when we saw them coming, we would put the girls into the bedroom and lock it. The invaders were to be allowed to take what they liked, but if they wanted to enter that room we would first expostulate, saying we had put the girls in there to prevent their being more frightened than necessary, and that if the men insisted on forcing an entrance, we would use our pistols and knives; also that we would do the same if they attempted any liberties with either of us. Mrs. Higgins had told me that many of the Boers around had said that they would not kill the women of their enemies; but that they would strip them, and make laughing-stocks of them.

Two days passed, and we heard nothing; the third morning, very early, I was half awake, when I heard what sounded like a very distant cannon shot. I thought sleepily, "I suppose that is at Pretoria," but roused up when I heard a second and similar sound. I meant to lie awake, but sleepiness overcame me, and I was just dropping off, when I heard a third sound of the same character, after which I went fast asleep. In the morning, however, I told what I fancied at breakfast, and proposed that in the afternoon I should ride down to the valley in search of news. When Alice heard that I was going, she said she would go too. We did get news of rather a surprising character, to the effect that all the inventive young farmer had narrated was pure fiction. My heavy guns have been a laugh against me ever since!

We really felt quite dull after the Boer excitement was over; of the story we had heard, so much alone was true that the Beeinkommste had broken up after Sir Bartle Frere met the Committee. It seemed to me quite stupid to settle down to commonplace life again, after talking of pistols and knives; and I know the children had the same feeling in a different way. They quite enjoyed the Boer scare, and once Ada dressed herself in my mackintosh, and girding on my belt with knife and pistol, blackening her eyebrows, and putting on a cork moustache, she gave the Kaffirs in the kitchen a fine start. Mrs. Higgins and I were still sitting at the tea table talking after tea, when we heard a violent knocking at the back door of the kitchen; Sannee, the maid, opened it rather reluctantly, being dreadfully afraid of the Boers, when a gruff voice exclaimed,—

"Var is Bob Higgins?" and presented a pistol in her face.

Sannee and two little Kaffir children uttered a succession of unearthly yells, and rushed into the dining room, where they clung to Mrs. Higgins's dress, hiding their faces, whilst the Boer dashed past, pistol in hand, to search the rooms. We had a good laugh, and Ada was delighted at the success of her scheme.

Winter now came on in earnest, and soon great grass fires were to be seen every evening on the opposite randt.[36] One day Mrs. Higgins came into the schoolroom and said she smelt that there was a fire coming our way across the Magaliesberg, and that she had sent some Kaffirs to see. It did not, however, come close, greatly to my relief.

In the beginning of June, Mr. Higgins came home. For days before, the children, Mrs. Higgins, and the Kaffirs had been on the lookout for him, and at last a Kaffir ran in just as we finished dinner, to say that the "boss" was coming. We all went quickly out on the stoop, and saw a mounted Kaffir-boy with a led horse, and Mr. Higgins with another led horse, coming up the short way from the valley. Of course there was great excitement. The new horses were two handsome young black stallions (brothers), for whom Mr. Higgins had exchanged a farm in the bush-veldt, and a bay pony for old Mr. Higgins. Freestate had come, too, but so changed that none of us knew him at first. Eclipse was grazing close by as Mr. Higgins dismounted, and I remember his first remark to me: "Eclipse is looking well. I see you *have* kept him clear of bot's eggs;" for Mr. Higgins had asserted his conviction that I should not do so. I had already remarked that his horses were thickly covered with them.

I had forgotten to say that during Mr. Higgins' absence, Mrs. Higgins had kindly sent in a waggon to Rustemberg for my heavy luggage, and had allowed it also to call at the farm where Jimmy was, to bring him over to Surprise, with whatever luggage he had—the whole affair of the farm, &c., having come to complete squash—and Arthur Sturton having offered to take him on his farm, where he could learn and make himself useful, in return for his board and lodging.

A few days after Mr. Higgins's arrival, he rode to Pretoria, and on his return rather late in the evening, he said he did not know what was the matter with Freestate; he had seemed so tired on the road. Mrs. Higgins and I were alone when he came in; all the girls and Harriet Sturton, who was paying them a visit, having gone off on horseback and in the cart with Sam, and Dick to Fahl-plas, the farm of James and John Higgins. They were escorted by Alfred Sturton and Alice's intended. Alfred was a younger brother of Arthur. The occasion of this festivity was little Sarah's birthday, and there had been great excitement among the young people, for they were to have a dance.

The next day Freestate seemed very ill, standing about listlessly and eating but little, and Mr. Higgins said he ought to have a bran mash, but the Kaffir never gave it to him. At about two o'clock we were startled by seeing the cart with Ada and Alfred in it, and Alice and Harriet on horseback. I shall never forget the sharp ring of terror in Mrs. Higgins's voice as she greeted them with, "Where are my children?" Little Sarah, they told us, was very ill with sore throat—diphtheria had been fatal in the family—and Augusta was ill too. It was decided to start at once for Fahl-plas, Mr. and Mrs. Higgins in the cart, and I riding, for Mrs. Higgins said she would like me to go to see the children. The two greys did their return journey well. We got in before dark. Little Sarah was very ill with high fever, and her throat dreadfully inflamed—she was almost delirious at times. Augusta had simply a bad cold.

Then, for the first time, did I see the misery of illness in this country. The two houses at Fahl-plas could muster but eight rooms together, counting the kitchens. Into these eight rooms, or rather six rooms, had to be stowed four men, five babies, or children little more than babies, two little girls, and four women—fifteen people! Mrs. Higgins, Augusta, Sarah and I were all in one small room, and its one window had to be kept shut! Its door opened into the dining room where two of the men slept and it had no chimney to admit air. Then the impossibility of keeping the small children quiet! I remember two little boys inventing a dreadful species of drum made out of an old biscuit tin, which could be heard for miles off, and when it was taken away, their shrieks were worse than the drum itself.

Augusta was well enough in a day to be driven over to Surprise; the rest of us stayed with little Sarah. Her throat ulcerated and was dreadfully bad, but finally the ulcers broke, and she began to mend. Before this, however, Mrs. Higgins expressed a wish that I should return to Surprise, to be with Augusta and Harriet, and great was their astonishment at my appearance just as it got dark one evening. Poor Freestate was dead—killed by the bots [. . .].

Harriet Sturton was a very pleasant addition to our party, and except for my anxiety about little Sarah, I should have quite enjoyed this time, but I now felt how fond of the child, and still more of her mother, I had grown. I could have cried for joy the day she was brought home.

Mr. Higgins now prepared to leave home for the bush-veldt, and here I must explain what the bush-veldt is.

Lying towards the northern borders of the Transvaal are large tracts of land, unfitted for cultivation except in parts, owing to there not being much water, and hence given over to nature, and such trees as nature causes to grow there. There are not many parts of this bush-veldt where the trees are fine, owing to the constantly recurring bush-fires; but the bush-veldt of Zoutspansberg, which is called the Wood-bush, produces fine timber, and steam sawmills have been established there lately. Along that part of the Crocodile river which runs through the bush-veldt there are some large trees, and I believe in the bush-veldt, bordering the Swazee [Swazi] country, trees of good size are also plentiful. The bush-veldt generally has few Boer houses in it, although it is divided into farms, whose proprietors live elsewhere in summer, leaving their possessions there either tenantless or tenanted only by Kaffirs. In winter, however, they trek there with their flocks and herds, also generally with their families, and then the bush-veldt is full of waggons and tents. The Boers greatly enjoy this annual picnic; the men hunting, the women and children sitting and playing about under the trees, and enjoying the verdure, which, to those who live on what is called the high or Ur-veldt, a barren but healthy tract of the Transvaal, is a luxury. The bush-veldt is fatal to horses during the summer, but is safe for them in winter; and the grass there remaining, as a rule, green under the bushes all through the winter, the oxen, and sheep have nice feeding, whereas in the other parts of the Transvaal the grass is either long, hard, and dry, or burnt off by the grass fires. There are, however, great drawbacks to going every year to the bush-veldt. Poisonous herbs grow there, one of which is fatal to sheep, the other to oxen. It is easy to lose animals in the thick bush, and when lost they are liable to fall a prey to wild beasts. It is also difficult to keep the herds of different owners separate, and hence the disease called "lung-sick" (which is contagious amongst cattle) often does much damage; whilst a long pod which grows on one sort of thorn tree has a poisonous effect on cattle that eat it, lowering their condition, and sometimes even killing them. Many also of the farmers live at a great distance from the bush-veldt, and the long journey tells against their animals. On the other hand, if cattle and sheep are to be kept in the higher parts of the Transvaal in the winter, good shelter for them must be erected, and hay and other food laid by for them. This would necessitate outlay and trouble, both things that a Boer detests. He and his wife are so accustomed to the detestable jolting and discomfort of a waggon that they think nothing of the long journey; so much accustomed to the higgledy-piggledy arrangements in their cabins, or small houses, that a tent is far preferable—and indeed a tent can be most comfortable. But the idea of cutting grass for winter fodder, or growing turnips or mangel-wurzel![37] They would stand and laugh a broad he-haw at such an idea in most cases, only a few being sufficiently enlightened to confess it might be well to carry it out. Their plan is to put a match in the grass when it is dry, to burn it and get rid of it, so that the fresh grass may sprout, and trek to the bush-veldt. Grass fires are very dangerous. Waggons, stock, and dwelling houses are sometimes destroyed by them; but then it is only sometimes, so what does it matter? The result of this treking to the bush-veldt is, that for about six months in the year milk cannot be got except in the bush-veldt; and the same may be said of butter, for the Boers make butter so badly that it will not keep. They do not, besides, make much, and cheese they never make. In Pretoria milk sells readily at a shilling a bottle in the winter, and butter sometimes runs up to four, or even five shillings a pound; three shillings is considered a moderate price.

Even at the best of times, in this great pasture country (for, as a whole, the Transvaal is that) the cows give very little milk. I have seen over twenty cows give about two buckets when they were in full milk! It is usually said that the cows of this country are bad milkers, and only good for breeding oxen; but it strikes me that even good cows, treated as they are here, would soon become bad. Exposed constantly to the weather, whatever it may be, every night driven into an open kraal, sometimes knee-deep in mud, with their calves left close to them all night, only kept from sucking by a barrier of thorn bushes, or a few poles, or at best a stone wall, by which a division is made in the big kraal; sometimes trying all night to break through to them; never given any food but grass—what can be expected from them? Boers, too, will assure you that no cow will give milk unless her calf is first allowed to suck, and that if the calf dies she will run dry. Like many other things in this country, a little good management would set it to rights.

Why Mr. Higgins sent his cattle to the bush-veldt I really don't know, for he said himself the journey was bad for them, and that they could get as good eating in the kloofs (or ravines) on his property as they could anywhere, instancing the fact that the cattle belonging to his kraal-Kaffirs, that grazed about the mountains in the winter, looked better than his did when they returned from the bush-veldt. However, he had sent them under the care of the Nell family as soon as his waggons came up from Natal, leaving only one span of oxen to do the farm work, and one fine ox that was too sick to walk, at Surprise, and now he prepared to follow them. His father and mother had gone before, leaving Alice and Ada at Surprise, and we once more settled down in our quiet life.

Before going farther, allow me to introduce the Nell family. It consisted of a hulking black-bearded father; of a stout garrulous mother, who had unlimited powers of invention, and who could speak a little English; then followed two big sons, and a whole bevy of little boys and girls, ending with an infant in arms. Krishian (I spell as pronounced—I believe his name is Christian) was a young gentleman who wished to be elegant. Whenever he got any money by working—an occupation he objected to—he spent it in making himself lovely in velvet coats, &c., occasionally investing in that most perilous possession in the Transvaal, a horse, but when he had one he took no care of it. As may be imagined, the ups and downs of this young man were frequent. The second son, Dahl—I don't know what his real name was, Dahl being, I heard, his mother's abbreviation of darling—was a big hulking fellow with a baby's face, and the most wonderful talent for romancing I ever met with or heard of, except in Lever's creation of "Potts" in "A Day's Ride."[38] He was a better fellow by far than Krishian, although dirtier, and worse to shake hands with. Of the younger members of the family I have no distinct knowledge; to hear their names, you would have thought they were a family of pups. There were Tic, and Tol, and Toss, besides others. The father and mother had come from the old colony, where they had had, and lost, money, and in consequence considered themselves something better than those of their neighbours who were as poor as they, but they let their children, big and little, be on terms of equality with the Urlams Kaffirs.

There was a small one-roomed cabin, situated at the lower end of Mr. Higgins's property, originally built by William Sturton, who, like his brother Arthur, had married a Miss Higgins. He had built it for himself and his wife, before he hired a farm in the valley near to his brother, and since then the cabin had remained tenantless. Just before Mr. Higgins went to Natal, Krishian and Dahl had asked to be allowed to occupy this eligible residence, and to till some ground near to it, in return for their services on the farm. Mr. Higgins had consented, saying, however, that they must come alone! He had had previous and disagreeable knowledge of the whole family as tenants.

"You will see that the whole troop will come so soon as you go away," Mrs. Higgins had said.

"Then I will send them packing, when I come back," replied her husband, causing Mrs. Higgins to laugh in a way that told me she doubted his ferocity. True enough, two days after Mr. Higgins's departure, a waggon was seen depositing the whole family and their baggage at the cabin. How they all managed to pack into that diminutive abode, Heaven only knows! but houses here are wonderfully elastic. They commenced tilling some adjoining ground in a leisurely manner, made themselves very much at home at Surprise in a cringing sort of way, and did as little as possible. On Mr. Higgins's return no change was made; he, an over-easy master for Kaffirs, was not likely to be less so for people of white race. Mrs. Nell would sometimes pay a day's visit at Surprise, where her conversation was a mixture of flattery and gossip; she knew everything about everybody, and her curiosity was unbounded. She would follow Mrs. Higgins about as she did her household work, sitting down in the nearest chair and pouring forth a stream of talk. She and her husband were very anxious for Mr. Higgins to adopt one of their small fry, a diminutive but perfect specimen of a Dutchman—chubby, stolid, with little knickerbockers, short jacket, and broad hat, all complete, only wanting a pipe to be quite perfect. I don't know whether he was Tic, Toss, or Tol but anyhow his parents, whilst giving him an excellent character, were anxious to part with him, partly, they averred on account of his own surprising attachment to Mr. Higgins; Mrs. Higgins, however, resolutely rejected this handsome present. Dahl Nell often favoured Surprise by a short visit, generally asking for a loan of something, which it was difficult to get back again, and enlivening his conversation by stories of doubtful veracity. Once he gave a touching description of the death of an acquaintance of the Higginses, who was in robust health at the time; but his grandest flight of fancy, that I ever heard of, was reserved for a farmer who lived at some distance. Chancing to meet this individual, the babyfaced Dahl recounted to him that he had been fortunate enough to obtain from old Mr. Higgins the loan of his span of oxen, that he had also got a waggon, and was prepared to ride transport to the Diamond Fields, familiarly called the "Fields." High prices were being given for produce there at the time, and transport was also high, and many a young man's dream was to be able to get a span and a waggon to take loads there. I suppose Dahl as he had trudged along on foot to where he met the farmer, had dreamed a pleasant daydream of how at some future time he might make enough money to afford himself a horse. The farmer pricked up his ears, and the affair ended by a bargain being struck for Dahl to take a load for him to the Fields. How Master Nell got out of his contract I don't know, but as he had no means of fulfilling it he must have got out of it somehow, probably scathlessly, for the Nell family seemed to have a knack of wriggling out of difficulties in safety.

Why Mr. Higgins trusted his valuable cattle to go to the bush-veldt under the care of these people I can't say, but the Nell family were delighted to be so trusted. They would have milk all the winter, could make butter, and sell it afterwards if they chose to take the trouble of putting it in jars, or if not eat it themselves; they could have meat too, which was a luxury to them, for they could easily invent a story to account for the death of an animal; and then they were paid into the bargain. They had got an old tent-waggon and departed happy, and by the time Mr. Higgins came up to them had killed a cow. They said she had gone blind! they swore she had—so blind that she could not see where to walk; but it was strange that the Kaffirs with them had been unable to detect her inability to distinguish surrounding objects. I forgot to mention that amongst other talents Mrs. Nell possessed that great female accomplishment of being able to weep to order, and this always settled the matter with Mr. Higgins.

Chapter 11

I have a pleasant remembrance of winter at Surprise—the bright crisp morning air as I walked through the hoar-frost to the stable, there to warm my hands by cleaning Eclipse; the cheery breakfast of bread, and mutton, or sometimes eggs, occasionally pleasantly diversified by hot scones, and which my exercise always caused me to enjoy, although I confess I missed the milk; then lessons. I don't maintain that they were always pleasant—that would be impossible; and the schoolroom—a bare room, with the rafters showing overhead, a mud floor, and with a big deal table, two forms, one chair, and a big packing-case for furniture—was sometimes bitterly cold; but Mrs. Higgins would bring, or send us in, little iron dishes of hot embers to warm our toes, and we wrapped ourselves up in all sorts of jackets and shawls. Rough would curl up in my lap and act muff; and so we pulled through, and except when little Sarah's grief at not being able to have a good romp instead of saying lessons, became overwhelming, we used to be quite merry over our spelling books, geography, &c. Dinner of mutton, pumpkin, potatoes, and sometimes crushed mealies,[39] made a diversion; and then afternoon tea, when Mrs. Higgins generally managed to get an egg to beat up in my tea, and make a substitute for milk. I used to enjoy that tea, I lolling on the table—having been sitting too long for standing not to appear preferable to sitting to me; Mrs. Higgins, always with some work in her hands, sitting on the sofa; and the children running about the room chattering, as children always do when let out of school. The singing lesson generally came after; and then I hastened off to catch Eclipse (for although he would let himself be driven up towards the house by the little Kaffirs, he would not let himself be caught except by me) and take him to the stable, to give him his evening feed and bed him up.

Just before starting for the bush-veldt, Mr. Higgins (having sent the Kaffir Jonas away) had given me his house as a stable for Eclipse, but before that, I used to feed him outside the old stable under the big syringa trees of an evening, and many a pretty Rembrandt-looking group have I seen of the Kaffirs, little and big, sitting round this evening fire, which threw fitful lights on the trunks of the surrounding bushes and trees, and on the long grass, also on elf-like little figures dancing some uncouth Kaffir dance, and chanting some equally uncouth Boer ditty, interrupted by peals of ringing laughter as one or the other played some trick off on his or her companions. Great amongst the trick players were little Sarah (who, free from school, was wild with spirits) and Fiervaree, the small groom. Then to walk to the house, and see the light of the bright wood fire in the drawing room gleaming through the darkness, and know how cosy it would be that evening after our supper of bread and tea, when we would all draw round the fire, and with the three youngest girls curled up on the ground, or sitting in the big fireplace, a petition would be put up by a chorus of young voices for a story, and I had to recall old German "Marchen" and eastern "Arabian Nights" and make De la Motte Fouque's charming "Undine"[40] come forth from the treasury of my memory, to delight these pretty little Africanders, who hung on my words as if I had been a veritable Scheherazade. There were two additions to our family always in the room; these I had forgotten to mention. One was a dassy,[41] or rock rabbit, a round furry little beast, guiltless of a tail, and with the brightest eyes, and the sharpest of white teeth, which it was not slow to use [. . .]. At mealtimes Dassy was great. He would make one spring from the sofa to the table, and once there he would put one little paw on the side of a dish, and tilt up the cover with his little snub nose, look what was inside, and if he liked it nibble a little, if not put down the cover and go to another dish. I have often looked at him sitting in the middle of the table eating alternately from four dishes. If he was interfered with, he would charge at the offender, barking, and showing his teeth, and if he could not bite his enemy, he would at least fasten on and worry his sleeve. If there was nothing else to eat he would nibble hair or wool mats, and window blinds, sometimes even he would sit on my shoulder and nibble my hair. He and Rough were great friends, and he would curl up on Rough's back, or between his paws, and look exquisitely comfortable. Dassy was a Sybarite. His slumbers were not to be disturbed with impunity. He generally slept in his master and mistress's bed, and would bite them if they, in moving, interfered with him. In the morning he would have his early coffee, and if it were not given quickly to him in a saucer, he would jump up and upset the cup; then he would hop up to the window, and pop his nose through a hole in one of the panes to try what the temperature was, and if it was cold he would retreat to bed [. . .].

The meer-cat, an animal I had often seen in the Zoological Gardens, was even funnier than the dassy. With its long black bushy tail, long sharp nose, and bead-like eyes, it looked as if it would be the more active of the two. But the dassy beat it hollow in jumping. Meer-cat, however, would canter along as quick as a horse, and many a time has he even outrun Eclipse as he cantered; when, jumping up on a convenient ant-heap, this little piece of absurdity would stand bolt upright, balancing himself on his tail, and with his fore paws crossed, and his head turning from side to side, would survey his surroundings with the greatest complacency, until the horse, being abreast of him, he would jump down, and with his tail erect make off to the next nearest ant heap [. . .]. He was as mischievous as Dassy, only in a different way, and having been accustomed in his early youth to follow the fashion of meer-cats and live in a hole, he was never tired of grubbing, either in or out of doors.

Sometimes our evening's amusements were diversified by making pancakes, or by playing games, such as magic music and friar's ground,[42] and sometimes the children would give me a good laugh by chasing old Khrid as she went about her duties in the kitchen, carrying a lighted candle in a pewter candlestick poised on her head.

Occasionally a chance visitor from the outer world would drop in unexpectedly—strangers travelling through the country for the first time, or people out for a day or two from Pretoria, or sometimes people of the country travelling on business. Whatever or whoever they were, they met with genial hospitality at Surprise. Then, at other times, Jimmy would come up to pay a visit on Sunday, one of the girls and I would ride down to the valley, or I would ride over to the farmhouse where the post was left, for letters.

One hideous episode alone, broke the pleasant monotony of this time. One night I was awakened by a loud tapping at my door and Mrs. Higgins's voice calling me. I jumped up in a fright, thinking that one of the children must be ill, but was glad to hear that it was only a Kaffir child, the little daughter of a certain Andreas, who lived in a small separate kraal on Mr. Higgins's estate. Andreas affected to be something better than the usual kraal Kaffirs, but his wife was a mere savage, dressed in skins and blankets, and his children ran about either naked or with only a narrow girdle on. Mrs. Higgins took me into the kitchen, where I saw Andreas with the little girl squatted on the floor, and the mother with a baby in her arms standing close by. After examining the child I felt convinced that she had taken poison—some vegetable poison; I could not say what. The history told by her father, and which, owing to my still imperfect knowledge of Dutch, had to be interpreted to me by an old Englishman who was building a stone cattle-kraal at Surprise, and who had been aroused from his sleep in the lumber room by these late visitors, was this. The mother had gone a short time before to a neighbouring kraal where the family of Andreas's brother's wife lived. She had taken the girl with her, and from the day she returned she had been ailing. The father seemed greatly distressed; the mother did not seem in the least interested. After doing what I could for the child and leaving the kitchen, I communicated my opinion as to the cause of the illness to Mrs. Higgins. She then reminded me that this very Andreas, shortly after my arrival at Surprise, had been accused of poisoning his brother, Roykraal by name, having administered a certain poison to him which had caused him to go mad. That Roykraal, a fine lad not long married, had gone raving mad for a time, and had since remained in a half mad state, whilst he looked quite old, was certain. He had deserted his wife, and generally wandered about talking nonsense to himself. Andreas had been accused before the captain or chief of his tribe, but the charge had fallen through in some way. I remembered too that Mrs. Higgins had, at the time, said that Roykraal's people would take revenge. I also remembered that a short time before, Andreas and his wife had had a desperate disagreement, ending by Mrs. Andreas running away to her father across the mountain. This is a usual form of husband-bullying among the Kaffirs. Girls are sold high amongst these people, an attractive and active girl fetching a considerable price in cattle for a wife. She has to work hard afterwards, for the cultivation of the fields is done principally by the women; but if her husband displeases her she walks off to her old home; and as it is considered a great disgrace to a man for his wife to be in her father's kraal, he generally buys her back, paying the father one or more head of cattle to restore her. Andreas had bought his better half back again, after grieving over her departure for some days; but shortly after she had betaken herself for a visit to the kraal of the father of Roykraal's wife, and the eldest of Andreas's children, and his favourite, was ill since then. It struck me as strange that Mrs. Andreas, who was of course well aware of the vindictiveness of her own race, should have chosen Mrs. Roykraal's kraal as a place to make an excursion to with her children. I watched the child until early morning, then went to have some sleep. When I saw her later, although still weak and at times lightheaded, she could eat with relish; and as it is not pleasant to nurse any one, especially a dirty Kaffir, in one's kitchen, I agreed with Mrs. Higgins that the child might be taken to her home. We cautioned the parents that they must not leave her alone a minute.

The day passed as usual. I was very sleepy in the evening and went to bed early. I always slept with my window open, and Rough always lay curled up at the foot of my bed. Some way on in the night I was startled by his furious barking, and jumping up, I saw a black head protruded inside of my window, whilst its owner said, in a frightened voice, that Andreas's child was dying, and that he had brought it. I let the people into the kitchen, and called Mrs, Higgins. It was a frightful scene. The child was in the most raving delirium I ever saw, convulsed in a most horrible manner, and her howls were unearthly, interrupted, every now and then, by the most touching appeals to her father— touching because of the sound of her voice and her action. Her own father could not understand what she said. He had brought her tied on his back, which she had lacerated with her nails and teeth. The poor fellow had no thought for himself, but with anguish in his face and voice he besought me to save his child. I asked if he had remained all day with the girl; he answered that he had been obliged to go away once or twice, but that the mother had remained with her. That more poison had been administered was, however, certain. I looked at the mother; she was squatted in the chimney corner, rolled up in two blankets, and was looking at her daughter's writhings with a stolid curiosity. Then a horrid suspicion crossed my mind.

The child, after taking some medicine, became quiet, but soon began to get deadly cold. We got all the blankets we could to roll round her, and put hot bricks to her feet and the calves of her legs. The mother never moved. At last, the child still being cold, I ordered Andreas to take one of the blankets off his wife, as she was warm enough with one, sitting as she was by the fire. The patient was just getting a little warmer, and I had turned away from her for a few minutes, when I noticed that the mother moved and began to arrange the blankets round her child. I watched her to see what she was going to do, and was horrified to see that she pulled her own blanket out, uncovering the child, and proceeded to roll it round herself, saying, it was explained to me, that she was sure the girl was dying, and that she could not remain, but was going home. It struck me that Andreas was afraid of the woman; but I pulled her blanket off somewhat urgently, and again rolled it round the child, telling the woman that she might go without it if she chose; but she crouched up again by the fire. The father again made a passionate appeal to me to save the little girl's life; and Mrs. Higgins having come into the kitchen, I asked her to tell him that I was doing all I could, but that I was combating no disease, but poison, and that it was a poison which I had not the proper means at hand to combat successfully. The wretched man wrung his hands. "Oh!" he exclaimed wildly, "if I could but get to (mentioning a Kaffir name) behind the mountain, he would save her." Saul, the driver, who was standing close by Mrs. Higgins and me, whispered, "That's the man he got the poison for Roykraal from."

I shall never forget that night—the almost dark kitchen, the awe-struck group standing round the child with her father kneeling by her, the witch-like figure of the mother crouched in one corner of the large fireplace, with an impish-looking boy of about twelve—the shepherd—crouched in the opposite one, with a grin on his face, and with his lanky bare arms and legs looking more like a hideous spider than anything else, and the sickening conviction that was growing upon me that the mother was an accomplice to the poisoning!

Towards morning I had so far succeeded that the child was warm, and appeared to be sleeping naturally. I felt quite worn out, and not wishing to disturb the children's routine by sleeping the next day, I told the father to call me so soon as the little girl should awake, and then I lay down on my bed in my clothes. It was already dawning, and it was still very early morning when I awoke. I got up and hastened to the kitchen. All but the elf-like Kaffir boy were gone; he, as usual, was making early coffee. He told me that at break of day, the mother had insisted upon removing the child to the old stable near the garden. He said the child had seemed to him better. I drank the coffee, and Mrs. Higgins sent a boy to ask how the patient was. The answer came back that the child was again in convulsions; but on seeing me preparing to go, the boy said it was useless—that as he left, the woman, regardless of Andreas, had rolled her child tight up in a blanket, and had started for her kraal with her burden on her back. It was evidently a hopeless case. In the afternoon I rode down to the kraal, two small huts in a little yard enclosed with reeds. The yard was lined with women, squatting on the ground and talking, the mother amongst them. In the principal hut Andreas was seated on the ground, holding his little girl in his arms. She was in a stupor, which I saw at once was the precursor of death; several kraal Kaffirs were squatted round; one of them, called Old Jas, a relation of Roykraal, with a most diabolical grin on his face. The child died that evening, and amidst much shrieking of the women, amongst whom the mother distinguished herself, was buried in her father's little cattle-kraal—the place of honour amongst Kaffirs—and the huts were deserted as being ill-omened, Andreas and his family going to the big kraal.

No farther notice was taken of the matter, but I heard various stories of Kaffirs having poisoned even white people's children in revenge, which, together with what I had seen, finished the disgust which I already felt for Kaffirs as a nation. The men who knew the Kaffirs best, and to whom I mentioned my conviction of the woman's guilt, said they had no doubt that I was right in my conclusions; that Kaffir women were quite capable of poisoning their own children in revenge upon their husbands.

Chapter 12

Mr. Higgins returned from the bush-veldt ill-content with the management of the Nell family, but thinking that he had set them on the right path. We had hoped for a little butter, but none was sent. Things went on in much the same way after his return, with the exception that the storytelling came to an end, except when one of the children did not feel well and went to bed early, getting me to sit by the bedside, or on the bed, and recount tales. I rather think there was a good deal of "foxing,"[43] done on little Sarah's part: Augusta never "foxed" about anything.

It was midwinter, and the grass fires were wonderful and terrible to look at, as they swept along before the wind. Of course it depends on the strength of the wind whether they are dangerous or not, and it has always appeared strange to me how little the knowledge that the wind may rise or veer in a minute seems to trouble the farmers. One evening I was going to bed, when I observed the whole sky ablaze from an evidently large fire at the other side of that part of the mountain which formed a spur in front of my window. The trees clothing the mountain side, and the magnificent precipice at its top, stood out in effective relief against the flame-coloured masses of smoke which were rolling, not towards Surprise, but, driven by the south wind northward over the mountain. The danger, so long as the wind remained steady, was not to us, for although the lurid light seemed near, I knew the fire could not even have reached the confines of Mr. Higgins's property. However, I called him—he had not yet gone to bed—and showed him the fire. "It is far off," he said; "don't be frightened, the wind is not blowing this way." "But suppose it changes in the night?" said I. "Oh, it won't change," he answered, laughing, and returned quietly to his rest.

I was convinced Mr. Higgins was not infallible about the wind, and I knew that Eclipse was shut up in a house surrounded by such long grass that it nearly reached to the thatched roof, so I opened my window wide, and resolved to wake several times during the night; this I can do when I choose. The first time I awoke the fire was no closer, it was being slowly driven northward; the second time the wind had changed, evidently only a short time before I awoke (it is possible its change woke me, for there was a slight breeze blowing into my room), and the smoke was pouring over the spur in the direction of the house. I had lain down in some of my clothes in case of emergency, and I immediately hastened through the dressing room to Mr. Higgins's room, and tapping at the door told him of the change of wind. I had awakened and startled Harriet Sturton and the children, who were sleeping on the floor in the drawing room. By the time I regained my room the flames could be seen, dancing amongst the foliage along the top of the spur. I now dressed; and taking a bridle in my hand, I went down to Eclipse's stable, so that in case of the wind rising I might be able to get him out of it and into safety quickly. I did not go in, but waited and watched the scene. It was impressive. The moon was a little past the full, and shed her light on all around; to the northwest she was eclipsed by the fire, that came steadily on, curling round the foot of the precipice, whose projecting crags it lit up fitfully, with its many tongues licking up the long grass, and shooting along the stems of the trees and amongst their branches, until they, instead of standing out black against a lurid background, looked like enormous torches. It came closer and closer, till I could not only feel its hot breath, but could hear the roar of the flames and the crackling of the grass and bushes; then at last some Kaffirs came from the houses beyond the dam, and extinguished the fire by beating it down with big branches. It broke out again during the day, however; and the; next evening, as I was riding back alone from a visit to the valley, I saw its red serpent-like track creeping up and across the mountain. [. . .]

I was beginning to think that it was time for me to look about for a farm, as I had not intended to remain more than one year as a governess. I had learned a good deal in various ways, too, during the past months, as much as, without neglecting my duties, I should ever learn, and hence, having seen some advertisements in the *Volkstem* and *Argus*[44] which looked promising, and hearing that Arthur Sturton with his wife and Jimmy were going to Pretoria for the races in September, and would take their waggon, I asked leave to go too, as I should be able to send up a dress in their waggon and not be entirely dependent on my habit, as I must be in the event of riding up alone. Mr. Higgins was going to the races also, and upon my getting the desired permission, it was agreed that Mrs. Higgins and the children should accompany him.

Only two events that occurred between Mr. Higgins's return and our going to Pretoria have left any particular impression on my mind, in addition to that made by the fire: The first was the return of the cattle from the bush-veldt in the early spring, very shortly before we started. It was a beautiful afternoon when the little Kaffirs came running with the news that the herd was in sight, but a long way off. We all turned out, lessons being hurried on in honour of the occasion, to see them come up. And a pretty sight it was; the cows, with their calves, born in the bush-veldt, trotting beside them, the sturdy oxen, and the frisky young cattle, all coming in, a long line across the fresh young grass of the hillside and under the thorn trees, bellowing a welcome to their old home, and the evening sun throwing their shadows far along the ground. [. . .]

The second event was the visit of the Bishop of Pretoria, who came and went on a jolly and evidently petted pony. He confirmed the three eldest girls, also old Mr. and Mrs. Higgins; and I shall never forget the singularly impressive sight of this world-worn couple, kneeling beside their two young daughters and their fair-haired grandchild in the drawing room at Surprise, and answering from their careworn hearts that they steadfastly believed in that religion from which they had drawn comfort in all their many troubles, whilst the children's fresh lips repeated the same words, without even an idea of what steadfast belief meant.

We used to have occasional religious services in the drawing room, Mr. Richardson coming from Rustemberg twice, riding; and then a young Englishman (not in holy orders), who was tutor to the children of an English Africander farmer at some distance, being entrusted by the bishop with the spiritual care of the district in which Surprise was the largest farmhouse. On these occasions old Mr. and Mrs. Higgins and the Sturtons, who lived in the valley, and sometimes John or James Higgins and family, would be our guests, also Jimmy; and while I played the piano (for owing to my lameness I could not play the harmonium), the young people sang the hymns. The young amateur clergyman was a very amusing person, and used to convulse us with laughter at his absurd anecdotes of his life at a Boer's where he had at first been tutor. He certainly did not seem to have slept on roses there. Besides being tutor in the English Africander's family, he had to help with a store and mill; at last he found his duties too onerous, and all attempt at church services ceased.

Chapter 13

There were many preparations to be made for going to Pretoria—dresses to be made for the children, and biscuits baked for us all, for we were to live in the waggon whilst there—and the children were in great glee. At last the morning came; the waggon was packed; bedding, and boxes, and provisions, were all put in, and lastly Mrs. Higgins and her children. Then the waggon started, leaving Mr. Higgins and me to follow on horseback. We gave them a fair start; and, leaving the old Englishman who had been building the new stone kraal, in charge of the place, and of the dogs and other pet beasts, who all had to be shut up until we were gone, and having locked up the front part of the house, we mounted our horses and followed.

We came up with the waggon about half way to Moy-plas, outspanned just across a deep spruit. The travellers were having a tea-dinner, so we off-saddled and enjoyed it with them; then leaving them once more, we rode on. For some distance the road was uninteresting, its chief advantage being that it was good for cantering; but as we neared Moy-plas and crossed the tributary of the Crocodile river, which I had previously crossed when riding to Fahl-plas, we came to a farm which made a great impression upon me. Stretching right across the valley and to the top of the ranges on either side, with water from two tributaries of the Crocodile irrigating it, with its broad lands, magnificent orchard, its outbuildings, and its small but trim farmhouse, it looked the perfection of a Boer farm, and made one picture to oneself what it might be if it were an English one. The owner of this fine property—a tall, gaunt woman with a pleasant face, the widow of three husbands—was standing by the gate of the little yard in front of her house, a yard trim as a room, with oleander and other trees round it, and shut in by a low whitewashed wall. She received us cheerily, looked inquisitively at me when Mr. Higgins introduced me as his children's schoolmistress, told us that Arthur Sturton's waggon had passed, that he had paid her a visit with Jimmy, and that she thought Jimmy was rude because he did not shake hands all round, but she was delighted at my attempts to talk Dutch, and told me I must pay her another visit. She was surrounded by children of various ages, and all related to her in some way, whose parents lived in some of the buildings which looked like barns. This old lady was a remarkable woman. Hospitable and freehanded to all, of whatever nation they might be, she was yet a frugal manager. She and her first husband had started in life with a waggon and a span of oxen. I don't know what sort of man he was, but she was a host in herself. If her oxen stuck in a difficult drift, she would tuck up her petticoats, pull off her boots, and leaping from the waggon take the whip from her Kaffir and drive the team through herself. If labour was scarce at harvest time, or when water had to be led on the lands, she thought nothing of doing the necessary work, but she attended to her household duties withal. She had never allowed her children to take any part in politics, and I don't think any one exactly knew what she thought of British rule. Like all Boer women and men, she regarded husbands and wives as articles so necessary to household comfort that no time must be lost in replacing them when lost; still she was of opinion that there was some limitation as to age in the matter, and I heard a delightful story about her reception of a suitor after the demise of No. 3.

Mr. Higgins was riding home from Pretoria one day when he met a young Boer, so magnificently got up that he knew he must be going a-courting; for Boers array themselves splendidly, and pay great attention on such occasions to the quality and colour of their saddle-cloths, a very favourite sort being a large-patterned drugget[45] with much green and red in it, and with a broad yellow woollen fringe. The young Boer seemed disconcerted when Mr. Higgins asked him where he was going, and still more so when Mr. Higgins playfully inquired whether the fair one was Lettie Matersen. This aroused Mr. Higgins's suspicions. Shortly after he had occasion to pass by Mrs. Matersen's farm, and, as usual, went in to pay a visit. He asked if she had lately seen (mentioning the young man's name). "Yes," she said, "he had been there;" and then went on to tell how the unfortunate individual had been dealt with by her. He had come to pay a visit, and the old lady instantly saw through his motives. She tormented him with questions as to whom he was going a-courting to, and as she knew all her neighbours, soon forced him into a corner by making him confess it was to none of them he was bound. She was deaf to his assertion that he was searching for a lost ox (a favourite excuse with a would-be suitor), although he described all its marks; and at last when she extorted from him that she was the object of his hopes and fears, she turned sharp on him with "Ah, ah! You young idiot. You have come a-courting of my farm, have you," &c., &c., until she drove him frantic from the house.

We reached Moy-plas as the sun was beginning to get low, and found the Sturtons' and old Mr. Higgins's waggons there already—for Alice and Ada had persuaded the old people to take them to the races.

I must try to describe Moy-plas. It was a large, irregular-shaped cottage, whitewashed and thatched, and it looked more like an English farmhouse than any place I had seen in the Transvaal. It was approached by a road branching a little off the highway to Pretoria, and the back of the house was turned to this road and to the outbuildings, which partially enclosed the sheep and goat kraal. At each side of these were sheds for protecting the animals in bad weather. The front of the house opened on a verandah, from which a step led to a yard like Mrs. Matersen's, this in its turn opened on a strip of grass, with a well-kept path leading to a little bridge across the broad water-furrow (like a rivulet), and into a trim garden and orchard, where you might walk under rows of big orange and lemon trees, and along hedges of figs, pomegranates, and quinces. There were vines, too, kept low and trim, and lots of brandy was made at Moy-plas. Inside, the idea of an English farmhouse was suggested by the wooden ceilings, with their supporting rafters, painted and polished, and the ample cupboards. One apartment, the dining room, was papered with prints cut from the *Illustrated News*;[46] many of them recalled the ghosts of former days to me, in a manner that was almost pleasant from the sense of strangeness that it awakened in me.

Old Mr. and Mrs. Sturton were already at Pretoria, having gone there on account of Mr. Sturton's illness, and Harriet with her elder sister Maria, and her younger Clara, were to follow them in Arthur Sturton's waggon. The youngest girl, Lettie, was at Pretoria. Two sons—Percy, a jolly young fellow with a ferocious beard, and Augustus, who was still a child—were to be left in charge of the farm, which, like Mrs. Matersen's, stretched from the top of the Magaliesberg across the valley to the top of the opposite range. William and Alfred, the two remaining sons, were the one on his farm, the other at school near Fahl-plas, his tutor being the amateur clergyman.

During the afternoon two rakish-looking men rode up, and were introduced to me as I sat under the verandah: they, too, were going to the races. One was an Englishman I had often heard of, Charlie Harris; the other, a Boer, whom, however, I took for an Englishman, as he spoke English perfectly, and I did not catch his name, Van der Veen, when he was introduced. I must here remark that it is far more the custom to talk of people by their Christian and surname together, than to use the term "Mr." It is very common, indeed, to use the Christian name alone. These individuals did not stay long, not even off-saddling. The Sturtons made me have my meals in the house, but the others cooked beside their waggons, and I had a picnic tea by old Mrs. Higgins's camp fire.

Our waggon came in late, and in the very early dawn it and its occupants, together with Arthur Sturton's and old Mr. Higgins's waggons, and many accompanying waggons laden with forage for the Pretoria market, were got under way. They were to outspann for breakfast immediately after they had crossed the Crocodile. Mr. Higgins, Arthur Sturton, and I, waited for early coffee, and then started after them on horseback, Percy Sturton riding with us so far as the first outspann.

Very pretty the wooded drift of the Crocodile looked that morning, the river flowing past it towards the deep cleft through which it winds its way to the back of the Magaliesberg. All but one of the waggons were already outspanned on the opposite side, and the camp fires alight, the ladies and children standing in groups looking down at the one forage waggon which had stuck in the drift. I rode on, and Mr. Higgins and Percy Sturton, dismounting and taking the whips, soon drove it through.

We outspanned that evening close to Dasspoort, and within two miles of Pretoria, which lies on the other side of it. The name is derived from the number of dassies that used to live in the rocks at either side; none are to be seen now, but the name remains.

The next morning we inspanned early, and Mr. Higgins rode on before the waggons so as to be early on the market with samples of his forage. We all followed in the waggon, Eclipse being led. I thought Dasspoort looked very pretty in the early morning light, the road being cut out of the face of the rock a few feet above the course of the Apis river; and even before we outspanned on the outskirts of the village, I remarked that it had greatly increased in size since I had seen it last, and that a great deal of building was going on.

Chapter 14

The great excitement during our stay at Pretoria was the races, but other things, too, made an impression on my mind. First of all, the sleeping in the waggon; Mr. and Mrs. Higgins slept in the back part with little Sarah; a curtain divided them from Augusta and myself; and Sannee made up a sort of bed for herself on a box which stood, across the fore part of the waggon, called the waggon-box, from which she had a tendency to roll down on my head in the night. Our washing arrangements were very limited; and camp life, though jolly in its proper place, is a bore on the outskirts of a village, particularly when the village calls itself a city. However, we rubbed along. We found old Mr. Sturton very ill, and the arrangements for taking care of him were such as made my hair stand on end. A bare room had been hired at an enormous rent, in a house whose owners did not trouble themselves much about the illness of their tenant. A few things had been put in hastily, and there he lay, in danger of his life, with the cooking having to be done in his room, or outside, in a sort of yard, into which the refuse from all the neighbouring houses was thrown. There were no means of keeping the rooms fresh and clean—no comfort which an invalid requires. On the arrival of his daughters another small room (also bare) was hired, and here the girls slept, and sometimes sat, on mattresses spread on the ground; all this discomfort was not caused by want of money, but because the necessary accommodation was not to be had.

I, of course, saw my kind acquaintances again at Pretoria, and then there were the races. These were much better than I expected. The horses looked more up to the mark than I thought they would—the jockeys, also—and the running was not at all bad. Eclipse, remembering his old racing days, I suppose, was in a great state of mind at the first start. I rode with Mr. Higgins to see that, and then we separated, and I presently fell in with Mr. Van-der-Veen at the Higgins's waggon, which was drawn up in a line with many other waggons. The scene was characteristic of South Africa—the ox-waggon element predominating—but there were also traps of various kinds drawn up in line, a little grandstand, with the ring close to it—refreshment and other tents, a number of men on horseback, and two women besides myself. Mr. Van-der-Veen proposed to go with me to see another start, and told me that one of the horses in this particular race belonged to an old Boer who believed greatly in him. He said he was glad to see Boers doing this sort of thing—it approached somewhat to civilization—in short, he talked altogether so much as if he had nothing to do with the Boers in general, that I was much surprised when I heard afterwards that he was the son of a Boer. He and I then went to the Edinburgh Hotel, where I had put up my horse during my stay at Pretoria; there we had lunch while the horses had a feed. I had been rather amused at Mr. Van-der-Veen proposing this proceeding, although I thought it a very good one.

By the end of the day the male portion of the community were getting very lively,[47] and rows were plentiful. Poor old Mr. Sturton participated unpleasantly in this part of the day's programme, for while the noise outside his window was unceasing, his hosts favoured him with snatches from "Bonnie Dundee,"[48] and other ballads, until a late hour; and Mrs. Sturton would not interfere, or allow me to interfere, because she thought it likely that if we did the invalid would be told to march the next morning, in spite both of his illness and the high rent he was paying.

The next day I did not go to the races, as I thought the surroundings of the course would be too lively; and on the third the waggons started on their homeward way. I remained behind, having affairs at Pretoria which, owing to all places of business being shut during the first two days of the races, I had been unable to get through before. I picked up the waggons at their first outspann, and had tea. Mr. Higgins had already arrived on horseback from Pretoria, and before we started James Higgins and his wife, with Alice and Harriet Sturton, in his covered-top cart, drawn by two good horses, came up; and, after a short rest, I started for Moy-plas in their company, but on horseback. Halfway we stopped at a Boer's house, where I was asked to prescribe for the children, who were very ill with whooping cough; and by nightfall we reached Moy-plas once more. The waggons came in the next morning; and in the afternoon Mr. Higgins, Arthur Sturton, and I started for home, leaving the rest to follow.

Two events had taken place during our absence, both of them unpleasant. A neighbouring farmer, Do Kruger—brother of the well-known Paul[49]—had been murdered by one of his Kaffirs; and a tremendous grass fire had swept up to within a yard or so of the house Surprise, and to within about three feet of Eclipse's stable; it had even destroyed part of the rose hedge bordering the upper lands.

The circumstances of Do Kruger's (pronounced Kreer) death were singular. He had an old quarrel going on with some Kaffirs, who lived in a little kraal just where his property touched Mr. Higgins's. Of late the quarrel had been getting worse, the Kaffirs being very disobedient. They had lands given them to cultivate for their own use in lieu of payment (a common arrangement in the Transvaal), and the natural consequence was that they wanted to work on their own lands when their master wanted them to work on his. The letting of water was the immediate cause of dispute. Do wanted water let on his lands, whilst the Kaffirs persisted in spending their time letting it on theirs. At last Do, having made up his mind to go to the bush-veldt to see how his cattle were getting on there, thought he would make an example. He called on some of his neighbours, amongst others on William Sturton, to ask them to accompany him to the little kraal, as he meant to give the Kaffirs a good lesson. This was a common practice amongst the Boers before English rule. William Sturton declined, but several Boers agreed; and the next day, saddling his horse and bidding goodbye to his wife, he started for the bush-veldt, intending to settle his quarrel with the Kaffirs *en route*. His friends joined him at his own house, and having all reached the little kraal, Do called the Kaffirs. One only came out of the hut, to whom Do said that he must immediately let on water to the land. The Kaffir replied, that he would do so after he had watered his own, no doubt speaking disrespectfully as well as disobediently. Upon this the Boers leapt off their horses and made a rush for the huts, forced their way in, overturning a small child, and seized the man who was particularly obnoxious to them; but just as Do entered the house, a man of the name of Manell hit him over the head with a stick with a heavy knob at the end of it, here called a "knob-kirrie," and felled him. His friends were intent on belabouring the man they had caught; but Do called out, "Leave him alone and help me out—they have killed me." He walked a short way towards his house and crossed a spruit, then he said he must sit down. A large blood tumour had already formed behind the ear where he had been struck. He soon became unconscious, and died shortly after he was carried home. Strange to say, he received his deathblow on the very spot where his father had cruelly killed a Kaffir. His wife, a very fat woman, had seen her former husband brought home dead, killed by lightning. She went into convulsions and wept unceasingly, and did all the proper things to testify to the intensity of her grief on the occasion of Do's demise, and married for the third time six months after. The two men—Manell, the one who killed him, and Paul, the one who was going to be beaten—on hearing he was dead, ran away to Pretoria. They got there whilst we were there, and were caught whilst sitting by Mr. Higgins's campfire. After a long imprisonment Manell was hanged.

The pretty farm of Surprise was a mass of black, with the ashes still lying on part, and the whitish effect they gave to the otherwise black prospect made it almost ghastly. Fido and the other animals were all right, except Rough—he was gone. It appears that he had got into one of the rooms when we were locking up the house, and had been shut in. The Kaffirs hearing him whining had, after two days, forced a window open and let him out, when he immediately rushed off to Eclipse's stable, and then down towards the valley, the way I used to ride. I therefore concluded that he had gone back to Mr. King's, whom he had left to come to me, and this was the case. Mr. King came up the next day, and told us that he had seen Rough sneaking about his cottage; but I had not time to go down for him. The day after Mr. King came again, and brought his big dog. This dog knew me, and must have told Rough on returning home that I was at Surprise, for that very evening Roughy came running in at the door, and up to me.

The old life began again, disturbed only by my constant inquiries about farms. There were, of course, plenty of people willing to sell if they could induce me to pay exorbitantly; but none of the Boers in the vicinity, who had good farms, were disposed to part with them at all. At Pretoria I had not been able to arrange anything.

Shortly after our return the dreaded "lung-sickness" broke out among the cattle. Investigation proved that an ox had died of lung-sickness in the bush-veldt, but the fact had been hushed up by the Nell family, who swore it died of what they call here "heart-water," in order to save themselves trouble; for it is of the utmost importance when a case of "lung-sickness" occurs, to innoculate the grown cattle, and to drench the young ones. They take the disease after these operations, but have it slightly and become "salted," that is, are not liable to have it again; whereas if they take the disease naturally (and if it once breaks out in a herd it is sure to run through it) they are most likely to die of it. It was also found that the Nells had let some of Mr. Higgins's cattle get into the kraal of a man whose bush-veldt farm touched Mr. Higgins's, and had let them remain there a whole night, although it was well known that there was lung-sickness in it. The worst part of the whole was, that when the disease broke out at Surprise they said it must have been caused by the malice of this very man (who was on bad terms with Mr. Higgins), for that he had buried the intestines of the cattle he had lost by "lung-sickness" close to the place where Mr. Higgins's cattle went to water. At first Mr. Higgins believed the story, but subsequently found it to be untrue [. . . .]

[A description of the inoculation of cattle against "lung-sickness" follows.]

Chapter 15

In the beginning of November I at last decided to accept an offer Mr. Higgins had made me of buying half his farm, including the small house his father had hitherto occupied. I need not enter into the various reasons which induced me to do this, but need merely say that, all things considered, it appeared the best thing I could do, and that I bought the farm conditionally. I was not to pay the purchase money for some months, and was to be free to leave the farm, if I chose to do so, before that time. I was to take Jimmy to live with me, as he and I had agreed; and besides, I had engaged the services of a young Englishman who, with another, had come to Mr. Higgins's place looking for work. It was much to be suspected that they were deserters; however, the one had evidently been a working farmer, and the other a groom; so Mr. Higgins arranged to take the former, and I the latter.

Before I left Surprise I was called upon to doctor one of William Sturton's children, the baby, who was dangerously ill with inflammation of the lungs. It had been ailing for some time, but not much notice was taken of its illness until one day, when, having ridden over to see the sick wife of a neighbouring Boer, I took William Sturton's [house in] on my way home, and was shown the child. It was very ill then, but before two days were over it was so bad that I remained with it and Alice, and, later on, Mrs. Higgins came to nurse it. That was not my first experience of the misery of illness in this country, but yet I must revert to it, it made so painful an impression on me. A small house, consisting of two rooms and a kitchen; one of the rooms used as a store and general sitting room; a father, mother, and three young children; no servant but a dirty, more than half-savage Kaffir; no convenience of any sort! Fancy nursing a baby, choking with inflamed lungs, in a room where, if the window was opened, the draught could not do otherwise than come on the bed; where the door into a draughty passage was being perpetually opened by the two elder children, who, when not quarrelling, were always crying, and both of whom had sore eyes and no one to look after them. If the window were kept shut the heat was stifling; and so it became necessary to open a window at the top of the gable, which had been intended as the door of a loft, but which, owing to the ceiling not being put in, still opened into the room. I remember this was decided upon late in the evening when we were all suffocating, and to do it an enormous, roughly-made ladder had to be brought in by William Sturton and the Kaffir, and left in the room, so that we might be able to get up to shut the window if necessary. Even with this window open the heat was dreadful, and I felt the fever I had had badly in India, and the approach of which I was only too well acquainted with, creeping over me and prostrating me. After two days of incessant care, the baby so far recovered that it was out of immediate danger; but I was obliged to lie by for a day or two—and even then I felt weak.

On the 19th November, I at last moved into my new abode, old Mr. Higgins and his family going to live at Pretoria. I bought his flock of sheep, and old Mrs. Higgins's fowls and two pigs; and Ada, much to her regret, had to leave me her two cats, for the good reason that they positively refused to be put into the waggon. One was a fine grey-and-white tom, the other, tom's mother, was a very ancient specimen of the feline race, with a crooked eye, and the most surprising voice a cat was ever gifted with. I was not able to afford as yet to buy a waggon or oxen, wishing first to feel my way, and there not being any immediate necessity for oxen, as it was not time for ploughing. I also tried to do with as little furniture as possible, and as few servants. A small bed and a dressing table and washing stand, made of old cases, together with a chair and a box, made up the furniture of my bedroom. The bed was lent by Mrs. Higgins. A deal table, three old chairs, and a horizontal piano, which had been old Mr. Higgins's, and which I used as a table, adorned the sitting room; while planks, supported on the rafters, gave standing room to various articles, and others of a very miscellaneous character were hung on nails and lines round the walls. The third little apartment, partitioned off like the others with canvas, was a lumber and forage room, and here Barrie the groom slept—Jimmy sleeping sometimes in it, sometimes in the sitting room. As I mentioned before, doors there were none, except the outer one. A curtain hung over the entrance into my room alone; windows also there were none, only large square holes in the wall which could be closed at will by shutters of stretched canvas. Goat and sheep skins did the duty of carpets, and the skins of two tiger cats and one wild cat which had been killed at Surprise, hung on an old folding armchair, completed the Robinson Crusoe look of the place. After experience of the same, I think a Robinson Crusoe cabin is nicer to read about than to live in; and yet sometimes of an evening, with the light of a dip made from the fat of my own sheep, lighting up, in the feeble manner of dips in general, the motley ornaments of bridles, saddles, bits, firearms, tools of various sorts hanging on the walls, and faintly showing the dogs crouching on the floor and the cats' heads peering from off the rafters overhead, I used to think that it would not make a bad picture of an African-squatter's "interior." It will be observed that I say "dogs," for besides my own Rough I generally had two visitors; one was a half-bred brown pointer left behind by old Mr. Higgins—a dog of an undecided character, who never could make up his mind to whom he would belong. He was not one of those independent dogs who decline to belong to any one—but go on visits to their friends; on the contrary, he was a very slavish, poor brute, addicted to yowling piteously if any one raised a hand to him; but he was always running away from one place to another, and kept in a circle between my place, "Grünfontein," the Nells, and the Kaffir kraal. The other visitor looked like a half-bred turnspit. He had belonged to James Higgins, at whose house I had first made his acquaintance, and bestowed on him the name of "Moustache"—for he had a ferocious pair at the time. He was afterwards presented to a Kaffir of the name of Mangwan, who in his turn made him a present to his son and heir, called Magaliesberg. This young gentleman and his father valued the dog highly, in spite of his preternaturally long back, nose and tail, the shortness and crookedness of his legs, and his generally ridiculous appearance. The only thing Magaliesberg objected to was his moustache, and that he cut off. They failed, however, in awakening corresponding sentiments in the ugly quadruped's breast, for he always ran away to me whenever he could, and had to be fetched home again, looking the picture of dejection. Considering that he got next to nothing to eat, and that the deficiencies in his feeding were made up by plenty of beating, it is perhaps natural that Moustache preferred Grünfontein to his master's kraal [. . . .]

I must give a little description of the property I now called my own. It was perhaps as pretty a property as one could see in the Transvaal. It was bounded to the north by the precipices of the Magaliesberg, jutting out in bold bluffs and receding into clefts, which rendered it very picturesque; the ground, at first broken and covered with trees, ran abruptly downwards, then up again, forming a sort of upland valley, and then sloped sharply down to the valley, having reached some little way across which, my property ended. A sharp wooded spur ran out from the mountain side, about halfway down the incline, and here the cabin and funny little outhouses had been built between masses of rock and tangled brushwood, while the water, diverted from a rivulet, came babbling down to the tiny dam near the house, making a path for itself sometimes between the rocks, and, until I made a drain and bridge, occasionally made a swamp quite close to the cabin. A rough road led from the cabin round the lands to Surprise, but the shorter way was by a narrow path through the orchard, and across a piece of ground that I afterwards cleared and tilled, and which then went by the name of the Upper Lands, to where it suddenly dipped into a deep and rugged ravine, down which a rivulet from the side of the rock high up, gurgled pleasantly beneath tall ferns and overhanging trees. Some stepping stones lay in the water to help passersby, and then the path, climbing up the opposite side of the ravine, brought one to a grassy and partially wooded slope, which, being passed, the boundary of Grünfontein was also passed, and that of Surprise entered. A pretty scrambling path it was, which, if you took it on horseback, necessitated much bending of the head, and putting aside of boughs, and gave the rider the chance of picking luscious figs and soft peaches without dismounting, by merely stretching out his hand; and many a time Eclipse has been startled by the birds he himself had startled from feasting on the fruit. And oh! what a quantity of fruit there was. How it lay in heaps under the trees that still were overladen! Kaffir girls came in troops to gather it in for me to dry and make vinegar of it; little Kaffirs from Surprise came to steal it; any and all who came to Grünfontein might eat as much as they cared for; the Nell family sent their children daily to pull a big basket full; the pigs ate of what fell to such an extent that they waxed ridiculously fat without getting any other food; and still such quantities went to waste before it could be gathered or eaten off the ground, that one trod on masses of fruit when walking through many parts of the orchard.

The boundary of the other side of Grünfontein was another deep and wooded ravine, even prettier than the one near the garden; but the prettiest spot in the whole property was just below where the cabin had been built. Here the spur of the mountain terminated in a small, level platform, round whose outer edge the rocks formed a sort of low wall, breaking off suddenly, and falling in jagged masses first to another smaller and lower platform, then in all manner of rough grotesque shapes into the sloping valley beneath. On the upper platform stood a beautiful syringa tree; the rockery below was thickly interspersed with shrubs of different sorts intertwined with the beautiful wild clematis [....]

The high road from Pretoria ran through the valley portion of my property, and I used to think how I should point out the house when it first came in sight, and so on, like a great many dreams a great many people have doubtless dreamed in wild homes, which they are trying to shape into civilized ones.

In the meantime it was rough work at Grünfontein. Besides Jimmy and Barrie I had only a Kaffir woman, called Reva (Manell's wife) to help during the day—she went away early in the evening and came late in the morning—and a little Kaffir boy to mind the sheep. I rose at early dawn, called the little shepherd, who slept in the straw kitchen, to light the fire, roused Jimmy and Barrie, and generally got to work before the sun shot his first rays upwards behind Wittwaters Randt, where it intercepted the eastern horizon. As I wanted to push on with the work as fast as I could, I did as much as I could myself, so that Jimmy and Barrie could get on with what I could not do. The cleaning of the horse and stable, the looking after the sheep that were lame or sick, often the skinning and cutting up of one of them, fell to my share, at times also cooking, and cleaning the house, and other domestic duties—when Reva gave herself a holiday—besides superintending the work. Then there was the fruit-drying; and this was an important business, for dried fruit, besides being useful for one's own winter use, sells well in the Free State.

Parties of Kaffir girls used to come from different kraals, some thirty miles distant, to pull the fruit and spread it on things made of wood and reeds, called stellassees,[50] that look something like stretchers. Each girl would bring a large conical-shaped basket on her head; into this she would pull the fruit, and she expected to be allowed to fill it once for her own benefit as payment. These young savages looked very picturesque, with their necks and arms and ankles ornamented with beads, gay handkerchiefs, or a gay strip of cloth bound round their heads, skins or blankets loosely hanging from their often shapely shoulders, walking in single file, with their baskets poised on their heads, or sitting in a circle cutting the fruit up and spreading it on the stellassees; but they had to be kept in order, or they would eat more than they plucked or cut up, and would talk their time away instead of working. Once or twice I had even to threaten them with my whip. The peaches and apricots alone have to be cut up; the figs have to be peeled, and gradually flattened out as they dry. When the fruit is all settled on the stellassees, they are placed on poles fixed in the ground, and the fruit left to dry in the sun. It has to be continually turned, and some experience is required to know when it is dry enough to put in a sack. Of course it must not be let get wet, and many a time the stellassees had to be brought into the house, and piled on the rafters or wherever a place could be got for them. Then there is another way of preserving peaches and apricots without sugar, when they are too ripe to dry well. They are squeezed in the hand to a pulp, and the skins and stones being thrown away, the remainder is spread upon a plank previously smeared with fat. The paste dries quickly in the sun, and can then be folded up like thick paper, and is very nice to eat. I made a quantity of dried fruit, and in consequence I was kept hard at work, for the turning, and flattening, and squeezing, and the hunting away of the fowls—they would flutter up and oftentimes upset a stellassee, if not watched—devolved of course on me, although in the last-mentioned part of my duty Rough and Moustache were valuable coadjutors, making sorties from where they would be lying in the shade, at my cry of "Sah! Sah!" accompanied by much barking and whisking of tails, to the confusion of the assembled fowls, who would rush off in dire confusion for a few yards, then stop and begin picking about in an apparently innocent manner, but with a tendency to come stealthily closer and closer to the stellassees. I have often amused myself watching their tactics. There was one hen of a more enterprising turn of mind than the rest. She used to go on picking away, keeping her eye on me all the while, always coming nearer and nearer. I used sometimes to pretend not to see her; for an instant she would stand, with head erect and a little on one side, looking at me, and then come picking along in a straight line for the stellassees. If I moved she would at once turn and take a circuitous route; but if she caught my eye she would give a frightened cackle, and make off as if the dogs were behind her, but only to commence operations again. Those fowls were altogether rather a nuisance, for they insisted on coming into the cabin, showing as great pertinacity about that as about the fruit, and when in, they would get on the table. This was particularly agreeable, if, dinner being laid, I had just gone out to call to Reva to go for Jimmy and Barrie, and on returning found a party of fowls picking in the dish; or if the dough for the bread was left uncovered for a moment whilst Reva and I went out, and the result was, its being all trodden upon and picked. Jimmy used to take their disregard of our wishes as something personal, and call them "insulting creatures," and throw broom handles, brushes, and boots after them.

Having but one servant, it was impossible in such an establishment as mine to keep up the usual distinctions between master and man. Barrie had his meals with us and passed the evening in the common sitting room.

He was not either a bad-looking or a badly-educated young fellow this Barrie (not that Barrie was his name; I don't know what his name was), that is to say, if by education one understands book-learning. He wrote a very good hand, read fluently, and was fond of improving himself, reading history by preference in his leisure hours. But I am afraid he was but a bad sort of a fellow, or was on the road to become one. He had a great talent for deception, and gloried in it; he had a favourite theory that dishonesty was the best policy; he was very sharp, very lazy, very noisy, very violent, but a good-humoured, merry fellow nevertheless. He never showed his violence to me or to my animals, except by a vicious look, but the look told of what was going on within; and one evening, when Eclipse, who hated him, made him run about three miles to catch him, and then had to be caught with Mrs. Higgins's assistance, I heard that he confided to the latter that if he had been his horse he would have shot him had a rifle been handy, "but that the missus was that particular as he daren't touch the brute." On the whole Barrie restrained himself creditably, for his language, although certainly inelegant, never became intolerable while he was in my company; and this must have cost him an effort. If he kept up a certain respect of manner towards me, he was inclined to be the reverse of respectful in his manner of talking of, and even to, the Higginses and Sturtons, and had to be periodically checked about it.

It is certainly demoralizing for English servants to come to this country. They may begin fairly; but even serving under one whom they acknowledge as undeniably their social superior, their ideas of master and man are liable to become confused after a time. The master cannot refuse to associate, on what appears to be terms of equality to the man, with Africander farmers both of English and Dutch origin, many of whom are in no way superior to the servant, whilst many are his inferiors, and only a few his superiors. They may be rich people, but the English servant knows well enough when they belong to the two first classes; but often when he remarks that those of the last class have no more "book-learning" than he has, he classes them with the former, although in their breeding they may be infinitely far removed from him. It is not easy to keep up the proper distance between master and servant when the very people whom he is called upon to bring in coffee to whilst they sit on a visit to his master, and behind whom he is expected to ride as long as his master rides by their side, are ready to drop into familiar conversation with him the next moment, or if they do not do so with him, will be on familiar terms with some one who is on familiar terms with him. For this reason, and others also, after many trials, I have come to the conclusion that it is more comfortable, and better in all ways, to have coloured servants than white ones. The Kaffirs are bad as a rule; but there is a class of half-castes between white and Hottentot blood, here called "bastards,"[51] in which very excellent servants may be found.

To return to Grünfontein. My sheep caused me a good deal of trouble, the tick tormenting them terribly, and several catching a sort of fever which is very fatal in this part of the Transvaal. My neighbours lost largely by both causes; but I took great care of my sheep, often working for two hours in the kraal with them, and I lost hardly any. I became quite an expert sheep-doctor, and could throw a good sized lamb alone [. . .]. Of horse-disease, as long as Eclipse grazed on my own property or that of Mr. Higgins, I was not much afraid, these farms forming a sort of healthy oasis in the midst of an unhealthy country although all along the southern side of the Magaliesberg the mountain grazing is pretty safe; besides, I heard from several people that Eclipse had marks about him of being surely salted, and I began to suspect that I had got him cheap on account of his viciousness, although, as I said before, he was gentle enough with me.

Chapter 16

Shortly before Christmas the Boer scare broke out again, and Mr. Higgins and Arthur Sturton determined to go into Pretoria. The morning the waggon left Surprise, Mr. Higgins rode up to my cabin from the high road. "Goodbye!" he said, shaking hands as he stood by his handsome black horse Wellington. "Don't be frightened; no one will hurt you." I laughed, and thought it was a very needless piece of advice. I was not at all frightened. A day or two after, Jimmy had occasion to go to the valley; he came back full of the news he had heard from William Sturton and Mr. King. The Boers had declared war; they were going to break out on the outstanding farms, and every Englishman, woman, and child was to be killed. There were all sorts of circumstantial proofs of the truth of this piece of news, which interested me too little for me to remember it. However, Jimmy and Barrie seemed impressed. A waggon was going up from the Sturtons to Pretoria, and I told them if they liked they might go up with it. However, they said they would stay; but they were not altogether comfortable. I think it was two days after, while I was busy about the stellassees, I heard an exclamation from both of them as they wore working at a little distance from me at the small dam and bridge.

"Look there! What's that?" And then Jimmy cried out, "There is a commando riding to burn Surprise" (an old threat amongst our Boer neighbours).

"Nonsense," said I.

"But you should go and look," persisted Jimmy. "Barrie says too that he can see a party of horsemen riding over the veldt to Surprise; they must be going to burn it."

Barrie thereupon expressed his belief that such was really the case. Now in my heart I believed Barrie to be a deserter, so I thought he might know something about what mounted men looked like, and I said, "You're sure they're not oxen, Barrie?" Barrie was sure they were not; so I went to look—but they were oxen nevertheless.

I think it was the next day that a young man, a brother of Alice's future husband, rode over from Fahlbank, to ask me to ride back with him to see John Higgins's baby, who was ill. Giving Barrie many instructions as to the proper carrying out of the bridge he was making, we started so soon as the sun began to decline a little. We had to call at Mr. King's, in the valley, for some medicine which he had, and which I had run out of; and as we saw that a storm was brewing we pushed along briskly, but it caught us just as we touched the top of the randt. How it did come down! In a few minutes the horses could with difficulty keep their feet in many places where the nature of the soil rendered it slippery. I had forgotten my waterproof, and was soon wet through, and before long it was pitch dark. Fortunately my companion knew the country well, and by a detour saved crossing the river at the deepest drift. It does not sound pleasant, does it? but I was getting sick of the monotony of Grünfontein, and the slowness with which the work seemed to progress, my feeling of weariness being increased by the fever, which kept hanging on, and I enjoyed it. The baby was not very ill after all. I slept in the room with the child, its mamma, and its little sisters, and the next day rode back alone to Grünfontein. The bridge was finished, and Barrie was triumphant at its fine appearance.

"If it is as good under as it is above, Barrie," said I, "it will do nicely." I rather doubted the fact in my heart.

"You may trust to me, missus," said Barrie. But the trust would have been misplaced had I done so, for a few days after Mr. Higgins's return, Wellington put his foot right through the bridge, and it had all to be pulled to pieces, and made again under my own inspection.

The new year came, and with it talk of the Higginses going on a visit to the old colony, where Mrs. Higgins's relations still lived. The weather was intensely hot, and there was a great deal of sickness about. The fever was steadily taking hold of me, and Jimmy was laid up with a slight attack; but everything went on much as usual, until one day we learned, through the paper that used to come to Surprise, that Pretorius (called Pretors) had been arrested at Potchefstrom [Potchefstroom].[52] The next day Mr. Higgins started on horseback for Marico, where he had some business; he was to take [in] Fahl-plas *en route*. Before leaving, he rode over to ask me to go to Surprise, as Augusta was ailing, and her mother felt anxious about her. I found the child not only ailing, but very seriously ill. Mrs, Higgins and I sat up all night with her. The next day we were surprised at Mr. Higgins's return. This time the

Boers had fairly broken out, he told us. He had met numbers the day before, riding through the pouring rain to Potchefstrom, armed. He had spoken to many of them. They all said one thing. Pretorius must be given up to them, or they would fight—aye, if they had to die for it. They would rather die than leave their leader under English arrest. Mr. Higgins said he felt sure they were in earnest now. He would like to put Mrs. Higgins and the children into the waggon and trek quickly into the Free State; he had turned back on purpose. They would have gone, had it not been that pretty Augusta lay dangerously ill; such being the case, they had perforce to stay. That there was a general ferment this time among the Boers was certain. There was great saddling in haste to ride to Potchefstrom, although when those who saddled in haste got to Potchefstrom they began to repent at leisure. Many Boers who had not horses talked about the desirability of having them, and some suggested borrowing them from those who had, but did not, on this occasion, use them. The next day Augusta was better, and I returned to Grünfontein in the morning, but rode over again to Surprise early in the afternoon. I had not been there long before a sound something like a cannon shot was heard. Of course everybody cried out "What's that?" and everybody but myself said it was a cannon shot. We heard it three or four times. Mr. Higgins stood on the stoop with a field-glass in his hand. We were in quite a state of excitement, still I did not believe that it was a cannon shot. Presently a Kaffir appeared, who told us all about it, he knew even where the shots came from. Pretorius was being taken under heavy escort to Pretoria. The Boers had attacked—the fighting was sharp. He could not tell the result, but he knew the place of the battle exactly; as to how he knew it, he was a little hazy. Mr. Higgins brought Wellington up from the stable, and put him into the store for the night, fearful that under these exciting circumstances some enterprising Boer might steal him, or as they say here "jump" him at night. The same idea struck me with regard to Eclipse. I asked if I might put him too in the store; but hearing that if I did he would have to be left loose as well as Wellington, I desisted; for Wellington was very fond of biting and kicking other horses, was shod all round, and was a much bigger horse than Eclipse. When I left Surprise in the evening, Mr. Higgins was still on the lookout, field-glass in hand, and perched on the top of an old stump.

As I rode up to where Jimmy and Barrie were working at the upper dam I was making, I was greeted by "Did you hear the cannon?" I remarked that I did not believe they were cannon; and Jimmy scouted me. [. . .]

The next day was Sunday, and I was cleaning the stable, preparatory to getting dressed for going to dinner at Surprise, when a delicate, gentlemanly-looking man, in a sort of blue serge blouse, ran up the little broken pathway leading to the stable, and raising his wide-awake, said he had heard that I was looking for brickmakers, that he and his mates were brickmakers and builders, and would be glad of a job. I glanced at his slim fine-skinned hands, and putting his appearance and mode of speech together, I said to myself "You're not, whatever your mates may be." I said aloud that I was in want of bricks, and that I thought of building, and asked where his mates were. He pointed to the cabin, and then I saw a sturdy-looking man of about forty, who looked every inch a tradesman, and a rollicking-looking fellow with a lot of yellow hair about him, who looked anything chance might require him to be, provided it did not ask him to attempt anything polished. I descended from the stable, pitchfork in hand, to greet them, and invite them inside. The tradesman, whose name was Williams, told me they had been thinking of coming to the cottage late the preceding evening and asking for shelter, but that knowing of the Boer scare, they thought they might frighten me, and so slept in the veldt. Of course I knew they were very hungry, and I had eaten up the last bit of meat that very morning; the bread was nearly done; I had no milk, no eggs; Reva was away, and I did not know what to do. So, retiring for a minute, I set Barrie to work to make flat cakes, and despatched Jimmy to get some milk and meat at Surprise, if he could, and to ask Mr. Higgins to come over after dinner. The result was that I engaged the men to make bricks at the rate of fifteen shillings a thousand, burnt out, and that they were to cut the wood themselves, and with the agreement that I was to get the brick-moulds made as soon as possible by a carpenter who lived at Fahlbank, and that until their completion the three men were to work at the dam at the rate of half-a-crown a day; I was to feed them into the bargain, and they were to sleep in the outhouse.

The next morning early the three men went to work at the dam, and I, leaving Jimmy and Barrie to settle the stellassees, which had been taken in during the night, was walking up through the long dewy grass to see how they were getting on, when I saw Mr. Higgins and a man in a white mackintosh and cork helmet, push aside the branches of the fig hedge of the orchard and ride through. They were some distance from me, but I perceived in a minute from his seat that the man was an officer, and his horse I knew to be an English-bred and groomed horse. A momentary thought that it might be some old acquaintance come to look me up, struck me, but in a minute I felt sure that it was for Barrie the officer had come.

"Where is Barrie?" asked Mr. Higgins, after a short "Good morning." "At the house." "Well, I am afraid you must lose him," said Mr. Higgins. "I thought so," said I; and continuing my walk up to the dam, I left them to carry out their disagreeable duty. It seems that Barrie swore to the last that he was no deserter, and became so violent that the officer had to draw his pistol. It was all over in a minute or so; when I returned to the cabin, in ten minutes, they were already gone. Mr. Higgins's servant was also captured, and from that day to this I have never heard more of them.

It appears that the party of soldiers accompanying the officer had struck terror into hearts of many a Boer on the road they passed along. It had been generally known the day before that the great Potchefstrom demonstration had come to naught, and the Boers thought this was a party sent out to catch other members of the committee, some of whom lived close to us. [. . .]

The first day's work at the dam showed me that the man who had first accosted me was not worth half-a-crown a day at such work. I told him so, politely, the next morning. He said that he had been on the point of speaking to me much to the same effect, and asked me whether I would allow him to help me in such ways as he could, without payment, until the brick-moulds were made. To this I agreed. On the second day the rollicking-looking man sprained his back, and had to have poultices applied, and to lie by. This was not very pleasant. However I made Mr. Letheby useful in the fruit-gathering and drying business, and soon learned that he was the son of a manufacturer in the north of England, had been a clerk in the office, had had a disagreement with his father, and had come out here. He had not got on—met with his present mates in Pretoria—could do lots of things a little—didn't mind what he did. It was the old story, that of hundreds out here. I could not call him Letheby, he was an educated man; so I called him Mr. Letheby, and then had to call the others "Mr." too, to prevent envy, hatred, and malice. These soon showed themselves without any extra incitement. The two workmen hated and despised their social superior after their manner, and he reciprocated the feeling after his; but they made a butt of him, and he was too yielding, and not sharp enough to be able to reciprocate; besides, they were coarse, and he was not. He used to amuse me by his *naiveté*. I think after his many struggles he had quite made up his mind to the advisability of marrying a rich Boeress if he could; he told me so, in fact, more than once, candidly admitting that all he should absolutely require was money; youth and beauty he should like if they could be got. He did not, I must say, assert that he was ready to take this course, but he used to discuss its advisability in a manner so personal to himself that it was hard for me to keep from laughing, At last, after Williams had been more rough than usual to him, and just when the brick-moulds arrived, he determined to break his ill-assorted partnership, and departed with a letter of introduction from me, which got him a place as tutor in a neighbouring Boer's family. There, I heard, he got on very well [. . .].

In the meantime Mr. Higgins and his family were getting ready to go to the colony. It was to be a great emigration, for they took a large number of cattle with them, some to sell, and also spare oxen. I felt that it would be very desolate after Mrs. Higgins and the children went away, and the increasing fever did not raise my spirits. Most of my fruit was dried, and packed away in sacks, ready for my friends to take with them to sell in the Free State; but a peculiar sort of yellow peach—a fruit unknown in England but common in Italy—had yet to be dried, and I was hard at work gathering it in, and spreading it on the stellassees. The weather had now become dry again, and the heat was very great—greater than usual. I sometimes felt as if I should break down unless I could have either entire rest or some violent excitement.

One day Mr. Higgins rode over early to my place, and said that he was off to Fahl-plas, and proposed that I should go with him, so as to reply quickly to a letter of interest to both him and me, which I expected to find there—the post being fetched at that time from the distant farm where it was left by John Higgins. I jumped at the idea; it would be a change.

"You look too ill to do it, though," said Mr. Higgins. "You won't stand the ride."

But I knew better, the programme being only so far changed by Mr. Higgins, that instead of riding there and back in one day, I was to dine at Surprise, start immediately after dinner for Fahl-plas, sleep there, and return early on the following day.

It was a very pleasant ride; the day was not too warm, and we got in just in time for a pleasant supper with the James Higginses. The next morning we idled about and talked, and did not saddle up until late, when a fearful storm soon drove us back. We saddled up after early coffee on the next day, and got to Surprise a little after breakfast—so we had our breakfast alone and as we were talking about how things would go on with me while the Higginses were away, Mr. Higgins said if I chose he would sell me his black span and the old waggon. The span, that had been of eighteen, had now dwindled to fourteen, but it had been twice down the dreaded Natal road, and all that remained were, I knew, salted with both red water and lung sickness. The sum asked was twelve pounds apiece, but I knew the oxen were worth it, and clenched the bargain. I felt perfectly delighted at getting possession of those oxen.

The Higgins family were to start in the early days of February, which wore now quite near and as I was anxious to see the last of them, I arranged to go with them as far as Fahl-plas, going in the waggon with Mrs. Higgins. Mr. Higgins was to lead Eclipse, who would carry me back. The day before they started I turned out all my dry fruit in the sun, and sorted it well. The weather was frightfully hot, but I knew a great deal depended upon the fruit being perfectly dry and free from insects before it was put in the waggon. I slept at Surprise that night, and felt very ill—I was not quite sure whether from fever or from the anxiety I felt at being left quite alone; and yet in a certain sense I was glad, for I knew that I depended a great deal on Mr. Higgins, and I knew too that I should never really succeed so long as I was not completely self-dependent. I should be so by the time the Higginses came back. We started the next morning; it was very hot, and by the time I got to Fahl-bank my bones ached so severely that I had to go to bed, or at least to lie down on the bed the whole afternoon. The next day, Sunday, I was better, but that evening [. . .], I felt the premonitory shiver of the real set-in of fever. [. . . Heckford has a major attack of fever and the Higginses do not leave her.] All this time I was being nursed with the utmost kindness in James Higgins's drawing room. John Higgins and his family were away, but they came back; and then Mrs. Robert Higgins carried me into their sitting room which was more adapted for a sick room than the other. I remember how everyone laughed at a suggestion made by Mrs. John Higgins as to how I could be moved, for walking was impossible and I objected to being carried. "Do you think you could carry me?" said I to Mrs. Robert Higgins. "Well, if she can't," said her sister-in-law, "at the worst there's the perambulator."[53] This suggestion conveyed such a comical appreciation of my smallness that I laughed heartily, in spite of my weakness. Two days afterwards I was so much better that I induced the Robert Higginses to start. It was very hard to part with them—in my then weak state it was quite a wrench—but the Higginses of Fahl-plas did all they could to make me comfortable; if I had been their own sister they could not have done more, and although it is a dreadful feeling to be ill away from home, still I admitted to myself that it was well for me that I was with them—not at Grünfontein. [. . . Heckford is forced to fire incompetent workers she calls the "Philistines."]

It seemed destined that the work at Grünfontein was not to make progress; but the next evening a note was, brought to me by an Englishman, who said he had come from Pretoria. It was from old Mr. Higgins, and told me that this man's name was Richard Hall, that he was the discharged soldier who had spoken to Robert Higgins about coming to work on his farm; and that old Mr. Higgins thought, if his son was gone by the time the man reached Surprise, I might like to engage him. I remembered to have heard of this man from Mr. Higgins, who said he had reason to believe he thoroughly understood farming, and that he bore an excellent character. Mr. Higgins had greatly hoped that he would come; and now he was there, and I could engage him, at least for a time, I felt very glad. It had been arranged that James Higgins was to drive me to Grünfontein on the following day; the difficulty had been as to how Eclipse was to be got there, but now I determined to let this man ride him over. In the meantime Richard Hall was taken into the dining room, and given something to eat. He was a fine, stalwart young fellow, and had a mongrel pointer puppy with him, of which he seemed very fond; but he was too free-and-easy in his manner towards the Higgins, for me not to see there would be the old difficulty there.

We started the next morning. Eclipse was rather disposed to tricks when the man mounted him, but quieted down when I spoke to him and petted him, and we all reached Grünfontein safely, passing the Philistines dead drunk at the canteen. Jimmy and Williams welcomed me back heartily, and little Roughy was overjoyed to see me; but the fruit I had taken such pains to get settled on the stellassees before I left was all spoiled or destroyed. The horses of Hermans Potchieter had come over one night when the stellassees had been left out, and had knocked many of them down and eaten the fruit, the rest Jimmy had piled one on another during the rain and covered with a waterproof. He had not uncovered them for days, and even the stellassees they were on had rotted in consequence; the fruit was a mass of black corruption. Roughy, too, had been seriously hurt in some way, and was very ill; the cats looked miserable, and were wild and frightened. It was a damp evening, and the discomfort of the house sent a chill through me, in spite of my desire not to feel it. The truth is, I was still so weak that objects had a tendency to waver before my eyes, and Grünfontein was not a place for nursing oneself. Perhaps the worst part of this species of fever is, that so long as it hangs about one, painful sores are constantly making their appearance on different parts of the body; when one crop vanishes another appears; the least scratch turns into one of them, but if there be no scratch they will come of themselves. My hands, legs, and feet were particularly affected by them, and the pain almost crippled me. There was no use in lying by, however, and I began my usual routine next day.

Richard Hall said he would not remain for less pay than six pounds a month, and although Mr. Higgins had told me, when I was making my calculations about farming, that good European labour could be got much more cheaply, my own inquiries subsequently showed me that it could not. It was evident that I must have some one besides Jimmy and the shepherd boy—and none of the Kaffirs on the property could be induced to work—so I said I would engage Hall for a month on trial. He spoke very confidently as to his own knowledge of farming operations, and remembering what Mr. Higgins had said of him, I thought he might be worth the money. His first task was mere labourer's work: viz., finishing the dam which the Philistines had left unfinished, so I could not at once judge of his skill as a farmer.

Chapter 17

At this point I must digress to relate a Kaffir idyll. It concerns Mangwan, the father of Moustache's proprietor. Mangwan was the son and heir of the great and powerful Kaffir chief Mosilikatz,[54] who only a few years ago held sway as far south as the southern slopes of the Magaliesberg. The Higginses, then dashing young hunters, and their father, an experienced one, used to pursue their game in his territory for months, and were on friendly terms with the old chief, with whom they exchanged visits and presents. Mangwan, too, used often to come to their waggons, and his brother also. At last old Mosilikatz died. The Higginses' waggons were not far from the place at which he expired. The old chief had many wives, but one was his special favourite. She not only fascinated the father, but the son; and on his father's death Mangwan persuaded her to fly with him to the Higginses' waggons. By Kaffir law, a son who appropriates one of his father's wives, forfeits both her life and his own, and loses his inheritance, but Mangwan and the girl were ready to risk all for each other. Old Mr. Higgins hid them, and kept them hidden, until he brought them to a place of safety. The property at Fahl-plas was then his, and he settled them on it. For a time Mangwan kept up state. He did nothing himself, nor would he allow his wife to do anything; he had Kaffir slaves who attended on both (even to cutting and cleaning his nails), but now that his dependents no longer supplied him with food, skins, money, &c., his store rapidly diminished, and old Mr. Higgins pointed out to him that as he had determined to forego his rights as chief for the sake of the Kaffir girl, he must now work for his livelihood. To this Mosilikatz's son could not bend. His flocks and herds dwindled, but he would not work. A son was born, whom he called Magaliesberg, and who grow to be the prettiest Kaffir boy I have ever seen. Little by little the slaves of Mangwan became reduced in number until he had but one, a wretched little girl who was starved and beaten, and made to sleep outside the door of the kraal in all weathers. When the child was dying of privation Mrs. Higgins pointed out to Mangwan the wickedness of letting her sleep in the cold and wet, without even a covering "Surely," said Mangwan, "the place for a dog to sleep is outside his master's door."

The little two-legged dog did sleep there until she died, and then the wife had to begin to work in a lazy fashion. When Robert Higgins bought Surprise he asked his father to come and live at Grünfontein, and told Mangwan he might build himself a kraal in the valley beneath. Both invitations were accepted, and so when I bought Grünfontein, Mosilikatz's son became my tenant.

He was an old man then, and very skinny and ugly, and the woman he had given up his kingdom for was a hideous specimen of humanity; but Magaliesberg was a very pretty, active, and graceful boy—also a disobedient, idle, and mischievous urchin. He would order his father about instead of obeying him, and he was the apple of his father's eye. He was supposed to tend the cattle and goats, but he never did so. Mangwan never worked, and he was not above begging, yet, as he walked along with an old blanket thrown over his shoulders, there was a certain stateliness about him. He never mixed with other Kaffirs, and he always spoke Zulu. Dutch he did not understand. In spite of his poverty he managed to marry two other wives, but the youngest ran away from him, and he never got her back. I suppose she thought the magnificence of his kraal hardly corresponded with his rank. But although Mangwan took unto himself other wives, his first wife was the one he always clung to; and the only time I saw Mangwan's serenity disturbed, was when a coolie servant of mine, who understood Zulu, after enduring her taunts and shrieks, and the snapping of her fingers under his nose, for about an hour, endeavored to push her forcibly out of my domains—at my order be it understood, for I was fairly tired of the termagant's vociferation. Then Mangwan, who had previously been sitting quite unconcernedly on a heap of stones hard by, leapt up, and throwing his blanket from him with quite a tragic air, gave one yell, and sprang at the coolie. They both rolled down the hill together. Mangwan arose with his nose bleeding, and his old bones sadly shaken, but still looking defiance. Magaliesberg, however, strongly advised him and his mother to keep the peace and retire to their kraal, and this they did. The next day the Kaffir presented himself before me. His dignity as well as his nose had been injured. He was very sad: indeed, I always felt sorry for the old man.

Whether to a European or a Kaffir the sense of having to ask for favours when you once dispensed them, to obey where you once commanded—the feeling of dependence upon a stranger—must always be bitter. Mangwan, looking down from my little eirie on the cultivated valley below, which had once been a wild bush, and his own hunting country, must in a miserable blind sort of way have felt something of what the exiled French Princes[55] experienced when they looked across the channel to the distant shores of France. Mangwan, climbing from his wretched little kraal in the valley to sit down in front of the door of my cabin, hoping that I might give him a little coffee or the feet of a sheep, or let him pull some fruit out of my garden, must have felt also, in a blind sort of way, the bitterness of the great Italian poet's heart[56] when he climbed the stairs of others! I always treated Mangwan with respect, and the old man felt this, I know. On the occasion to which I refer I fortunately had Saul the driver with me when he arrived, and I made him translate into Zulu what I considered a neatly turned speech for Mangwan's benefit. I alluded to the fact of his being Mosilikatz's son, and of my wish to treat him with respect in consequence, but I distinctly forbade Mrs. Mangwan's reappearance near my cabin. I saw that the allusion to his illustrious birth pleased the old man, and his peace of mind was restored by a present of some carbolic oil wherewith to heal his nose. He proceeded to smear on the oil with great satisfaction, and I added the gift of half-a-crown! Mrs. Mangwan was thenceforth no more seen at Grünfontein.

Mangwan had a great liking for the possession of animals, although he never took care of them when he had them. When the Kaffir Jonas was sent away from Surprise he left his cat behind for Mangwan. But the cat preferred its liberty, and would not let itself be captured by Magaliesberg. Thereupon Mangwan undertook to catch it, and the way he carried out his undertaking was by every morning for about a fortnight, walking up in a stately manner to Surprise with a sack (destined to receive the cat) on his shoulder, and perambulating the vicinity of Jonas's hut for about an hour. He never looked for the cat—that would have been beneath his dignity—but held his head erect, and if he looked at anything it was at the sky. It is hardly necessary to remark that the cat retained its liberty.

On Moustache he set great value. Moved to compassion by the entreating looks the poor little beast used to cast at me when Magaliesberg would come to drag him away, I offered Mangwan two shillings for him. I thought it a handsome offer considering the dog's surpassing ugliness; but Mangwan shook his head, and ejaculated "Pond," by which he meant that a pound was the value he set on the animal. During the Higginses' absence, however, Mangwan began to feel the pangs of hunger, for he used to get subsidies from their kitchen, given, not stolen—I don't believe Mangwan would steal—then he would often come to me and say, "Bow-wow, bow-wow," and hold up his ten fingers. That meant that his price for the dog had come down to ten shillings. I thereupon shook my head and held up five fingers, intimating that I raised my offer to five shillings. At last, one day, when Mangwan was very hungry, we struck a bargain for six shillings, and the absurd antics whereby Moustache testified his delight when Mangwan and Magaliesberg went off without him, quite repaid me for my extravagance. And so Moustache became a member of my household, much to Roughy's disgust, who, although much the smaller dog of the two, maintained his supremacy in a most lordly manner—flying at his rival and shaking him by his long drooping ears, until they bled profusely, whenever he thought his right of precedence was in any way interfered with.

Mrs. Mangwan never forgave me, but used to scowl in a most vicious way whenever she saw me. She was a terrible virago; and it was impossible to imagine in what her fascinations had consisted. Dressed in skins not more shrivelled and brown than her own skin, she used to inspire Augusta with horror, when she insisted upon kissing the girl's hand, on the occasions of her visits to Surprise. I have seen my pretty pupil run round and round the table, the old witchlike-looking creature pursuing her until she caught and mumbled over the fair soft hand that formed a curious contrast to the brown, skinny paw of Mrs. Mangwan.

The old savage always called Mr. Higgins "Bob," the name by which she had learned to call him when he used to hunt in Mosilikatz's territory. Her great delight was to be taken through the rooms at Surprise. She was never tired of admiring their splendour, and would clap her hands from time to time, and cry out, "Oh, Bob, Bob!" inclining thereby to convey an idea of her appreciation of what a wonderful man Mr. Higgins was, to have been able to amass such treasures.

Chapter 18

Shortly after Hall's arrival, Jimmy informed me that he was going to seek his fortune elsewhere, and departed, with his saddle-bag slung over his shoulder, by a bridle-path which led over the mountain to Rustemberg. [. . . After more labor troubles and Jimmy's departure to seek his fortune, Heckford hires Egerton.]

Hall had told me that there was a man of the name of Egerton, at Pretoria, who had expressed a wish to obtain work on a farm; he said he believed he knew something of farming, and that though he was drinking hard in Pretoria he might be steady on a farm. He had also told me that he knew a coolie[57]—a capital gardener, and accustomed to farm work—who would, he was sure, be glad to come. My meditations ended in my resolving to saddle up early next morning, and ride to Pretoria to look for workmen, for it was clear that workmen I must have, and at once too. [. . .] I put up at old Mr. Higgins's in Pretoria. He had a little cottage on the outskirts—a miserable-looking place outside, but snug inside; and he had a little stable, into which he kindly let me put Eclipse. Hall arrived late at night, very cross. The next day he found Sam and a brother of his, Mosamma—he was doubtful about finding Egerton—and these two I engaged. I could not get them to come for less than four pounds a month. In the afternoon I was riding towards the market square, and Hall was walking beside me, when, just as we passed a public house, he turned and spoke to a man, then called to me, and presented the individual as Egerton. He was a man of apparently about five-and-thirty, with two black eyes, and a face whose general pallor betokened late heavy drinking and consequent illness. I did not want any more servants, having engaged the two coolies, and the man's appearance as he stood before me in a battered wide-awake, torn and dirty coat and trousers, and apologies for boots, was not prepossessing. I had, however, heard that Egerton had said, when Hall was leaving Pretoria, "I would to God I could get out of the place," and so I thought I would see about it.

"You would like to get employment on my farm?" said I. He answered in the affirmative without raising his eyes. "Can you do farm work: do you understand it?"

He answered he had worked on a farm for nine months; but, in reply to my questions as to whether he could drive oxen or plough, he said he could but try. It did not strike me that he would be a very valuable acquisition, but I saw that there was some sort of painful struggle going on in the man; and, although he answered almost monosyllabically, his voice sounded refined.

"What wages do you ask? "

He hesitated a little, then said six pounds a month.

"No, I could not give you that," said I. "I give it to Hall, because I got him with a character of being a steady man, and one who thoroughly understood farming; I should not give it to him otherwise."

"And I have no character, or a bad one—this," said Egerton, raising his hand to designate his black eyes. "Would you think five pounds too much for me to ask?"

What trifles one is sometimes swayed by. A moment before I had almost determined to let the man go, but there was something in his voice and manner as he said this, that reminded me of the voice of a friend, of the manner which, had misfortune and his own fault placed him in Egerton's position, would have been his; it was a very faint resemblance, but it told me that there was something better in Egerton than what appeared, and I said I would give him five pounds, and that he might walk down to Grünfontein the next day in company with Hall and the two coolies. I told him to call later in the day at Mr. Higgins's to sign his contract with me. He did so, and then went away. I was busy in the meantime getting offers for the contract for building my farmhouse and out offices. To my surprise I found that I was known by name to a great many people in Pretoria whom I did not know at all, was indeed a small celebrity as a rich and enterprising farmer. I, of course, knew that there were unexpressed additions to these two adjectives, viz., "inexperienced," "green," and "fair game." I could get no offer for the execution of my plan which did not enormously exceed Mr. Higgins's estimate. I also heard much talk as to the large price I had paid to Mr. Higgins for my farm; when I said that I had not paid for it at all, and that he would let me throw it up if I chose, people laughed, and said I "had better try him." Of course I was offered other farms, which were all described as far more desirable than the one I had.

The next day the rain poured down in torrents, and the third day also. On the first rainy day, Egerton, who, together with his companions, was unable on account of the rain to set out for Grünfontein, came to Mr. Higgins's house. I think he must have been there standing outside for some time before I happened to go to the door. "Could you ask Mr. Higgins if I might sleep in the stable," he said, "it is so very wet?" The question told a terrible story. He slept in the stable, and the Higginses gave him some food. I had been obliged to put Hall up at the Edinburgh at ten shillings a day, I could not get him boarded for less. The next day the men started; I had given them provisions for the road. Sam celebrated his exit from Pretoria by getting gloriously drunk. I remained behind for two days, partially on account of Mrs. James Higgins having come up to Pretoria for a fourth little baby's advent. Her husband had had to hire an unfurnished house, and bring up furniture for it in his waggon. She liked me to be with her, so I stayed. The fever was yet hanging about me, and I was still troubled with the fever sores, and did not much enjoy the idea of my ride home; however, on Saturday at about half-past three, I saddled up, having managed to get through my various engagements at last.

It was rather late to start on a twenty-four miles' ride in the early part of March; however, I was too anxious to get Eclipse away from unhealthy Pretoria, to wait longer than necessary, and although I felt very tired, having been walking all the morning, I cantered sharply until I reached the farm which is situated midway between Pretoria and Moy-plas. I had calculated that if I could do the distance in three hours and a half I should get in just before dark, for there was no moon. I had kept time so far, but I could not hold out. The pain of those dreadful sores was becoming unbearable when I cantered, and I felt almost too weak to sit in the saddle. Eclipse, on the contrary, was very gay and festive, and as the rays of the declining sun glanced on the sticks or stones he passed, he would pretend to be frightened, and shy in play. It is tedious as well as tiring to walk twelve miles on horseback. The last faint streaks of day lighted me across the Crocodile; then it became pitch dark. I could hardly see Eclipse's pretty little head as he tossed it up and down impatiently; as to guiding hint it was out of the question. But my little horse was quite able to take care of both of us.

Winding about, now down a steep and stony ravine, now up the other side, turning cleverly round bushes and trees, he brought me safe to near the backdoor of Moy-plas, where he was assailed by a troop of dogs, whose barks and yelps soon ceased at the sound of my voice, but who heralded my arrival to the supper party inside [. . . .]

After giving Eclipse his supper in an outhouse, I went in to my own. Very cosy the long, low room, with the well-spread supper table looked, after my dark and weary ride, very cheery were the familiar kind faces of those seated round it, and very pleasant was their hearty welcome. Little did we all think that evening, when, forgetting my fatigue under these varied influences, I sat telling the news from Pretoria, that before that day twelvemonths, all that would remain of that comfort—hard won comfort, too—would be the bare walls, which may perhaps even yet fall victims to the revenge of the Boers!

There was one unfamiliar face, however, amongst my listeners. It was that of a little man who sat back from the rest—for supper was just over when I entered—and who struck me as being a stranger to the Sturtons as well as to myself. He was apparently between fifty and sixty, chubby, self-possessed, apparently on very good terms with himself, and engaged in a close scrutiny of everybody present, with a way of putting his head a little on one side in order to assist his investigations. This little man was so strikingly like a little cock-sparrow, that when he made any observation it almost sounded like a chirp.

The next morning at breakfast there was talk about my intended buildings, about what had been asked by the contractors I had spoken to in Pretoria, about the servants I had engaged, and who had passed by Moy-plas the previous day. There was a general impression that Egerton would be found worth nothing, the coolies worth little, but Hall worth a great deal. Mr. Sturton had let him have Wellington to ride home on, much to my horror, for I knew that he was not fit to be trusted with a horse. Egerton had gone on alone, the coolies remaining half a day behind him to prepare and discuss a currie [curry], for which purpose they had bought a fowl from the Sturtons. Mr. Sparrow listened to all this with his head on one side. After breakfast I loitered about. I always feel lazy on Sunday mornings, and besides, I was tired. Harriet had got a little pig as a pet, a jolly fat little beast that trotted about everywhere after her, and was very good-tempered, except when any one but Harriet happened to inconvenience it, then it made furious onslaughts on the offender's legs. There was the garden to look at, but after a while I became interested in some remarks Mr. Sparrow made to me about farm buildings: they betokened that he knew something about such things, and we began to talk seriously. Presently he asked me whether I would show him my plan; I did so, and then he pointed out various faults in it, and I saw that he was right. He gave me several valuable hints, all in the way a benevolent sparrow might have done, and at last said, that if I would allow him, he would draw me a plan which would, he thought, please me better—quite disinterestedly—just because it was such a pleasure to see any one so enterprising—so energetic; he was engaged in carrying out another contract, for he was an architect; indeed, he was in such request, because of his superior knowledge, that he had no spare time, that his head—his head, and he shook it a little as he thought of his sad case—was overtaxed; still, for a lady, and such a praiseworthy energetic lady, he would put on the strain. All this, and much more that was eulogistic of himself and me, did this benevolent specimen of the sparrow tribe twitter forth, whilst I thought to myself what a sly old bird it was.

However, disinterested or not, Mr. Sparrow evidently was a great deal more advanced than any one else I was likely to meet with, in knowledge of the sort of building I was anxious to erect. In the midst of the abundance of his self-laudatory and adulatory twitters I could see that he was also an original, and he amused me greatly; so I accepted his offer, and we parted very good friends.

Chapter 19

I saddled up after dinner, but alas! my first short canter showed me that I should have to make Eclipse walk the eighteen miles home. It was a dreary lookout, but there was no help for it. Soon I saw a slight figure walking towards me, the figure of a young fellow dressed in coat, trousers, and wide-awake—a white youngster too. Who could he be? None of the young men at Lettie Matersen's farm, I knew; neither was he any of the Sturtons of Moy-plas; he was not one of the Nells: who could he be? It is unusual to see a Boer walking at any distance from his house, and the pedestrian was evidently of the well-to-do classes. The figure and I were diminishing the distance between us all this time, and then I saw with surprise that the youngster was Jimmy. He had terminated his wanderings by getting employment as tutor to two small Boers. The paternal Boer was going out trading, taking his youngsters in his waggon; Jimmy was going too. The waggon was outspanned for a short time at Mrs. Matersen's. Jimmy had been to Grünfontein; had heard of how his riding accoutrements had been dropped along the road; had picked up bridle and saddle at Grünfontein, whither Hall had taken them, and was now going to Moy-plas to pick up his stirrups. I wished him Godspeed in his new life, and we parted. I had yet to pass Cucumoor's dog. I saw the brute sitting on the top of the rise across which the road went, and no sooner did he spy me than he began to bark and wag his tail—in a fiendish manner it appeared to me. I had heard that the Cucumoors were adverse to the English, and that they would encourage the dog to assault any one belonging to our race; but I suddenly made up my mind to beard Cucumoor in his den (a mud hut), and turning Eclipse off the road I cantered towards the house, whereupon Mr. Dog did the same. Then I saw three small Cucumoors running towards me. The cause of their *empressement*[58] was that a baby related to some member of the Cucumoor family had the thrush. They expostulated with the dog, and introduced me to a wonderfully large family, of several men, still more women, a good many hobbledehoy[59] girls, a troop of small children, and a sprinkling of infants, all related in some inextricable manner, and all capable of being compressed when necessary, like "Alice in Wonderland," judging from the diminutive size of the house compared with the number of its occupants.

During the day they only enter it by relays, so the eyes of the uninitiated are not favoured with a view of them in a compressed condition. Cucumoor's household was no more surprising in this respect than many others, but the family was the largest, as compared to their house, I had yet seen. They were very friendly. They gave me coffee, and I gave them a prescription. They asked what they were to pay; and when I said, "Nothing," they beamed. They laughed at my absurd efforts to speak their dialect, and I laughed too; and we parted excellent friends, after I had learnt the name of the dog—or rather dogs, for there were two of them. The savage was a jolly dog when you had a personal introduction to him, and his name was "Docks." This was supposed to be an English name, and was derived from the English word "dog." I heard it was a favourite name for a dog amongst the Boers.

It was nearly dark when I reached Grünfontein. Williams was better (he went away soon after). Several sheep were missing, but I afterwards recovered them; and there were two English brickmakers awaiting my arrival, anxious to get the job to go on with the bricks—a desire in which I gratified them. I began work in earnest now. The next day I went for my oxen. I had a plough already. Mosamma was a very fair driver, and a splendid cook; he was also conceited, lazy, and good-for-nothing, but his curries were delicious! Sam was not a bad fellow, but he was for some unknown reason the bounden slave of his younger brother. Egerton worked hard and spoke little, and Hall continued to develop quickly; he also in a very short time showed clearly that he could not hold a plough properly, or drive a span—he was in short an agricultural Mr. Winkle.[60] He was greatly disgusted at my clear perception of his ignorance, and put on extra bumptiousness. Then I administered a rebuke, the result of which was that the next morning he said he wished to leave me, and as I had meant to send him away, we agreed perfectly. I had been lately in the habit of having my meals in my tiny bedroom, while Hall and Egerton had theirs in the sitting room, the coolies of course eating outside. I had often listened to

Hall's loud talk, and observed Egerton's reticence and different mode of speech. I had no doubt now that he was a gentleman by education and early association, although fallen from that estate. So on Hall's going away I took my meals with him.

I had one difficulty with respect to him. The coolies called him "Jack" as Hall had done. It was evidently out of the question for this to be allowed, if Egerton was to be treated as a gentleman by me, and after a few days of more intimate acquaintance with him, I saw that it would be unjust to treat him otherwise. I knew, however that the two bumptious coolies, though respectful enough to me, would rebel at this, and probably leave me at the end of the month. However, I took heart of grace, and with a regretful eye at the finishing of the dam, the ploughing, the cutting of poles for fencing in the land, &c, I told them that henceforth he was to be called Mr. Egerton. They looked glum, but obeyed. In the mean time, about a day after Hall's departure, as the sun was setting, and as I was getting the table ready for tea, a German, of the thorough good working German type, presented himself at my little cabin door. I knew my man at once, and engaged him on his own terms, six pounds a month, and he was worth even more. Quiet, quaint, like one of the figures in some German etching illustrative of German country life, doing everything he did thoroughly and unostentatiously, with a love for a quiet chat over a pipe when work was done, careful of any animal whether belonging to him or committed to his charge, shrewd, business-like, strictly respectful, but with a thoroughly good opinion of himself,—my new acquisition, in his respectable dress, his enormous flat hat, under which his kindly and merry blue eyes twinkled, with his rugged face and greyish moustache, and his talk about fatherland, conjured up pleasant visions of my childish days before me. He had been many years in Africa, but had fought in the Franco-Prussian war, and had also fought the Kaffirs as a volunteer. So had Mr. Egerton—in fact, as a rule every man you meet here has been a volunteer—and they had had some slight acquaintance with each other.

The men who were making the bricks—an old man, Joe, and a young man, Jim—had also been in the volunteers at Secocoonee's[61] and so all were more or less acquainted. They all called Mr. Egerton by his surname, and I left that alone. The work, all but the dam, now got on well; but I had to give up the idea of making the embankment of the dam until I could build it up properly, and for that I had no lime; a second attempt at an earthwork embankment failed also. Pigsties had to be built, for so soon as the crops began to come up, the pigs could no longer be left to wander about. A large water-furrow was taken out, leading through the large dam to the small dam, and thence down to the new lands below; the garden had to be got into order; the poles cut for the wire fencing which I intended to get fixed round the upper lands; and the ploughing and sowing had to be done. In the midst of all this, one evening Jimmy made his appearance. He had tired of teaching, but was going to help in the Higginses' store at Fahl-bank; until they were ready for him he had come to me. He had to sleep with Mr. Egerton in the sitting room. The German slept in the stable by preference, and of course he helped in various ways—Grünfontein was no place for idlers. Reva no longer came, except to do the washing, and the coolies cooked, so that we had much better dinners, a change which Jimmy appreciated. On the whole we were very jolly.

Mr. Sparrow appeared one morning with his plan—and a very good one it was, vastly superior to mine; and at last we arranged that he was to have the contract for the house, I was to find material, he labour. He said he would send me his partner shortly, who would give me a specification of what would be required, and of the probable cost. [. . . The "Sparrow"'s partner, Mr. O'Grady arrives.]

Mr. O'Grady was an Africander, and a very singular person. He had a perplexing habit of answering at random at times, like a person who is deaf or who is listening to a foreign language; yet he was not deaf, and he habitually spoke English. He was fond of using long words, and had a disposition to laugh in an unreasonable and unaccountable manner. He might have been taken to be very simple, or very deep. He affected rather to patronize Mr. Sparrow, who in his turn spoke of him in like manner. He was certainly very obliging and good natured. [. . . Because they are disrespectful to Jimmy, Heckford fires the two Indian workers, again letting herself in for labor problems.]

Chapter 20

It was evident that something must be done under the circumstances, and that quickly. The German said he knew where he could get good Kaffirs to work, at a missionary station. He told me the name. It was eight hours on horseback from Grünfontein. I sounded him a little as to whether he would walk there to get them; evidently he was not disposed to do so. I had no horse but Eclipse, and he was not well; besides, even without its being horse-sickness time, I had no fancy to trust Eclipse to a stranger; I knew he would make a battle of it between his rider and himself at some part of the journey, and if he were the conqueror, where should I get my Kaffirs? If the rider were the conqueror, it would only be after severe punishment had been inflicted, and I did not care for my horse to be punished by any one but me. However, the horse as it was could not go; he was still weak from his attack of colic. In this dilemma I bethought me of Mr. O'Grady, and of his horse—a sorry brute, but if there be any truth in the theory of salting, it certainly was salted. It had been through the Zulu war, had had horse-sickness, and had recovered. I asked him if he would lend me the animal, I of course taking all risks; and he very kindly consented. The German set forth on a Saturday, and the next morning Jimmy too bade me goodbye. So Mr. Egerton and I were left sole possessors of Grünfontein. There was plenty of work for him in the garden, and for me in various ways. I had no one to help me now, for Reva had gone, as I think I said before, and she only washed for me, and I had been unable to get any boy to mind the sheep. There were several who would have come, and played noisily all day near the house or in the garden with other little Kaffirs, whom they would have invited to spend the day and have dinner with them, but there was not one who would mind the sheep, so I preferred doing without them [. . . .]

Days went on, and the German did not return. On Friday, Jim came to the cottage to buy some meal.

"Strange that German not a coming back," said Jim.

"Yes," I said

"I'm a thinking he must a taken the wrong road," said Jim.

"Why what wrong road?" asked I; "he knew the road. I don't think he can have taken the wrong road."

Jim's eyes twinkled, "Well, I was a thinking as he might a taken it on purpose," said Jim.

"What!" I exclaimed.

"Well," continued Jim in a stolid sort of way, although with a twinkle in his eye, "I said to my mate when I saw him a ridin' off on that there horse, as how he'd never come back."

"Do you really think he has stolen the horse?" I asked.

"Lor bless you, ma'am, yes," said Jim, smiling at my simplicity. "I did say to my mate as how it would be well if we was to offer to let our Kaffir go for you to get boys from his kraal; but then, you see, I said it certainly was no business of ours."

"I wish you had warned me, Jim," I said. "I never thought of his stealing the horse!"

"You have to be very particular in these parts, ma'am," said Jim, "more especially with them furriners. I knew a Frenchman as jumped a horse"—and he paused reflectively. "No, ma'am, I've no manner of doubt as how he's in the Free State now with that there horse."

This was pleasant. I went down to Mr. O'Grady's little canvas house below the spur where the hut stood. Mr. O'Grady still believed in the German's honesty. So did Mr. Egerton. But days went on; Saturday came, and Sunday, and passed. Jim was triumphant; we had all given up the missing German. He had asked me to give him some money for the road, saying, he had none of his own and what I had given him amounted to his wages—the things he had left behind were of no value. I gave him up at last, and I told Mr. O'Grady that he must name his price for the horse. He said that there was a salted horse for sale, in the valley, for twenty-six or seven pounds, and that, if he liked it when he saw it, he would ask me to buy it for him. He was to see it on Tuesday.

On Monday evening Mr. Egerton and I had finished supper and were playing chess (Mr. O'Grady lived in his canvas house), when the dogs jumped up and barked, there was a sound of horses' hoofs and the German rode up, with three Kaffirs following him. He had been delayed owing to the difficulty of getting Kaffirs. He said he knew that we should all think he had jumped the horse. He was very good-humoured about it when we confessed we had thought so, made us each a present of a handkerchief he had bought at the missionary's store, and ate a hearty supper. Two days after, I engaged two other Kaffirs, and the work went on quickly and well. Jimmy used to come over of a Saturday to spend Sunday, when we used to be very merry, carrying our conversations on sometimes until after we were all in bed—at least if Mr. Egerton's and Jimmy's blankets could be called bed, the partition between my room and the sitting room not in any way impeding it. Mr. O'Grady, in the meantime, drew a multiplicity of plans and elevations and diagrams of doors and windows, and partitions of stalls, &c, but I could not get him to give me the specification I wanted; he said he must wait for his partner—and his partner was not forthcoming.

At last one afternoon he appeared. He was full of importance; he twittered and chirped, and said now everything would go on delightfully. I pressed him for the specification, and at last a very detailed one was offered for my inspection. I went over it carefully, and got Mr. Sparrow to give me estimates as to cost. It ran up much higher than he had led me to suppose it would. It was very hard to bring things to a clear understanding, for he twittered and chirped so much about his head, and how overtaxed his brain was, and made so many digressions about the society he was used to, and so many polite speeches to me, that time went by, and I was often obliged to interrupt our business talks, to go about necessary household duties; but at last I pointed out things I should wish cut out, as merely unnecessary luxuries, and the specification was taken back to be revised.

It was drawing near the time when the Higginses were to return, and at last I got a letter telling me when I might expect them. They had left me the key of Surprise, and sometimes on Sundays I would walk over there to air the house; or sometimes, if the moon was up, I would go after work was over, and play on the piano. On one of these occasions I remember being struck by Mr. Egerton's delight at seeing a carpet which I had stretched out in one of the rooms. He said he had not seen one for years, that it was quite refreshing. It was also refreshing to me to hear any one say, as he did, when by chance I happened to turn over a waltz and play it, "Oh, don't play that stupid thing; go on with Norma, or Mozart's Twelfth Mass."

Looking forward to the Higginses' return, I was often struck by the curious gulf that lies invariably between the European settlers in this country and those born in it—a gulf which is rendered wider, doubtless, when the European settler has been bred amongst all the refinements of European life, but which exists even when he is of the lower middle, or even of the labouring class. To the European, life here is an excitement—it is a race after wealth. There is something of the spirit of the gambler in all who try their fortunes out here. They may work in the fields sowing crops, or they may tend their herds and flocks—unexciting occupations you would say—but all this represents a portion of a game on which they have generally staked all they have; and to all, there must be something of excitement in such a game, whether it be dice or oxen, cards or seeds of corn, that are the counters. Then further; until a settler here becomes demoralized, he always looks forward to something beyond what he has—it may be to go home; it may be to bring some dear one out to him; it may be to become very rich for the mere sake of being very rich; but there is always something. How different are this man's thoughts, as he glances over his cultivated lands, and at his livestock, from those of the Africander farmer, who, standing perchance by his side, thinks of all his possessions as things that he has perhaps won by toil, but with which, now that he has them, he is contented, looking for nothing beyond. His crops will realize a price which will enable him to live as he is living. If they fetch a higher price than usual, he can perhaps get a new waggon, or indulge in a half-bred English horse; or perhaps, if he be a very enterprising character, he may think he will some time take his children to Natal, and let them behold the sea and the great ships that he would be afraid to trust himself on, though, may be, he has faced a lion in his day; his cows will calve, his ewes will lamb, and he will every year mark some of their little ones for his own little ones, so that when they are men and women they too will have flocks and herds, without having to take away from their old father. The two talk of the market prices, and of the oxen, &c., as if they had a common interest; but they are as far separated from each other as a gamester is from the man who plays a quiet rubber of whist for sweets, with his wife and children of an evening. Of course if, joined to this, there be in the one the existence of a remembrance of all the artistic culture—the refinement—the romance—the historic remains—which can be the portion only of him who has lived in old countries, and which is denied to one born and bred in South Africa, the gulf is enormously widened. Once this had struck me forcibly at Surprise, when Mr. Higgins, looking at a representation of an angel on the cover of a photograph-book that was lying on the table, said to me, "What a beautiful thing! I wonder if there can exist such beautiful things." "I don't think that is so very beautiful," I said. "One can easily imagine a more beautiful angel than that." I remember the look in his eyes as he said, "Yes, I dare say you can. But do you know, I don't think any of us Africanders can imagine much; we haven't got the training; we never see anything." I felt so sorry for what I had said, but his words were a commentary on what I said before as to the commonplaceness of the country. What training more than that which Nature gives him does an Italian, or a Swiss, or even many a German or Frenchman want, to render him capable of imagining things of beauty? What taught the Greeks to become masters of the beautiful to all succeeding ages? Mr. Higgins was a man capable of admiring nature; his wife had a most sensitive appreciation of natural beauties, but they had never seen beauty. The greatest beauty Mr. Higgins ever saw, by his own confession, was a sunset lighting up the valley that lay below Surprise. I remember, one evening, his asking me in good faith if I had ever seen anything to surpass it in all my wanderings.

The consciousness that this great gulf lay between the Higginses and myself, struck me painfully now. It was irremediable; but as I looked forward to their return, and felt how delighted I was that I should soon see them, I could not help lamenting in my heart, that our friendship should have this flaw in it.

One evening after dark, Fiervaree came to the door of the cabin to say that Mr. Higgins had come, and wanted the key of the house. The waggons were to come in next day. I had just got the specification from Mr. Sparrow, and he had brought me the contract to sign as well, but I declined signing it until I had gone to Pretoria to see about the prices of material [. . . .]

I had promised to see on my way to Moy-plas, where I meant to sleep, the wife of a certain Fenter, an old Boer, whose house was not far from Cucumoor's. Fenter had ridden over to Surprise that morning to beg of me to do so, and I had promised; but the little Sparrow and his partner had delayed me, and it was rather late when I started. Added to this, Mr. O'Grady's sorry little pony was not up to keeping to a quick canter, although his master insisted he was. He would not let me leave him and ride on alone; he said he was afraid of losing the road, and he protested that his horse was so fresh he absolutely had to hold him in; although, if I cantered fast for any time, I could hear the poor little animal blowing behind me, and hear a cut given to it every now and then; and once, when Eclipse got far before it, it lifted up its poor little voice and whinnied for him to stop. Of course after that I kept Eclipse at a very slow pace, and so by the time we had to take the turn for Fenter's house it was nearly dark.

The house was a very small one, built of unburnt brick, and, as is general with Boer, or even English Africanders' houses, stuck down in the veldt without any attempt at making its surroundings pretty. Hearing the horse's tramp, Fenter, a small, thin, delicate-looking old man, came out. He was surprised to see me so late, and surprised, too, to see me with a companion. I introduced Mr. O'Grady as a builder, which explained everything; and then I told how I had been delayed, and asked old Fenter whether he could give me stabling for Eclipse. He said "Yes, for both horses." I did not ask whether he could put O'Grady and me up, for, arriving late at a Boer's house on such an errand as mine, I knew that to be unnecessary; some sort of shakedown was sure to be provided. After I had cleaned Eclipse, and given him his forage, I adjourned to the house. There old Fenter introduced me to Mrs. Fenter. As is very often the case amongst the Boers, the lady's proportions made up for what was wanting in those of her lord and master. If old Mrs. Fenter had been asked to sit in a stall at the Italian Opera, I don't think she would have been able to get in. She was a jolly-looking woman by nature, but just then she looked somewhat woebegone, having erysipelas[62] in her face—not badly, but doubtless enough to be very uncomfortable. Old Fenter was deaf. Mrs. Fenter having tied up her head in numerous bandages, was so artificially. O'Grady sat on the edge of his chair, and grinned at nothing in particular, occasionally varying his amusement by a chuckle, also at nothing in particular. Old Fenter occasionally asked a question of me, or made remarks about O'Grady and myself to his wife—not offensively; personally I have seldom found Boers offensive—but from a sort of natural rudeness which is in the race, and with which, being natural, it would be absurd to get annoyed. A little girl who helped in the house, and who I suppose was some sort of relation, looked covertly at me, and when she caught my eye smiled pleasantly and rather shyly, whilst I endeavoured in bad Dutch, to converse—or rather, to hold a soliloquy. This was a thing I was getting accustomed to—not very amusing, but good as practice. My auditors were generally much what they were in this case, only the number of fat women and shy little girls with pleasant smiles was sometimes multiplied, and a hulking young man or two, or a young matron already running to fat, thrown in. The soliloquy always had the same headings—the big dam I was making (the biggest dam in that part of the country, some one would always remark parenthetically), the fine span of salted oxen I had bought from Mr. Higgins, at which some one would always say, "Are you sure they are salted?" and when I said I had been at Surprise when they salted, they would wag their heads and say, "Ah, yes, that is right," and ask the price, and wag their heads again, and say, "Ah, yes, that was not too much for salted oxen, real salted oxen—oxen that had had red-water and lung-sick." Then I would tell what crops I was going to put in, and ask advice about it (the Boers like an English person to ask advice from them); and then I would tell of how I thought I might get manure from Hermann Potchieter's old kraal, which would lead to a little discussion between members of the family I was talking to, and give me time to think what should be my next heading; and then I would tell how many sheep in my kraal had had fever; and when I was running very low, I knew I could always make the whole party laugh by saying how I had tried to make bread myself, and how bad it was. That point was always a success, and led to my being asked whether the Boer bread was not nice; and that led to my saying how very nice the Boer biscuits were, and that we did not know how to make them in England; and that was always a second success. I flatter myself that my Boer neighbours thought me rather agreeable. They certainly thought me cracked, but that did not matter in the least.

Supper on this occasion caused a pause in my soliloquy. It was the usual bread and mutton and coffee. Old Fenter said grace. Presently I saw preparations being made for a bed on the floor of the sitting room—there were only two rooms besides the little kitchen in the house. Then old Fenter signified to O'Grady that he was to sleep in the sitting room, and Mrs. Fenter lighted a candle and took me into the bedroom, which was door-less—a curtain doing duty as door. It was a small room, with a four-post bed at one side, nearly occupying the whole side. This bed had hangings of white calico, which shut it in and made a sort of box of it. At the other side of the room was a trestle bed. Mrs. Fenter pointed to this as mine. Now, as I had intended to sleep at Moy-plas I had taken no nightdress with me, for I knew I could get one there, and I had sent up all my small amount of luggage in the waggon to Pretoria. As Mrs. Fenter had not given me any garment of the sort, I simply removed my shoes, and lay down on the bed. I knew that Boers never undress at night, even in case of illness, so I was prepared for this; but what I was not prepared for was to see old Fenter toddle into the room. Mrs. Fenter had just removed her upper dress, and then rolled into bed, raising the curtain to do so. The little girl had lain down near the foot of the same bed. I lay quietly watching old Fenter's operations. I rather wondered what he was going to do. There was a light hung on the wall at the other side of the four-poster, and I could see the portly form of Mrs. Fenter cast in shadow against the white curtain. Old Fenter divested himself leisurely of his coat and of his feldt-schoons, or field-shoes, made of untanned leather; stockings he had none; and then (having apparently an idea that going to bed was a process which demanded a certain amount of privacy, although compatible with having a small girl in bed with Mrs. Fenter and himself, and a strange lady in the same room) he, instead of boldly raising the curtain, like Mrs. Fenter, proceeded to creep in from the bottom of the bed, very cautiously, on hands and knees. A few minutes after, portentous snores proclaimed that the three occupants of the couch were fast asleep. I went to sleep, too, and slept till dawn.

I cleaned Eclipse (I always carried his brush and comb with me), had early coffee, and O'Grady and I up-saddled in the still dewy morning, and departed.

We had breakfast at Moy-plas, where I found Harriet's pig still flourishing; and after a short rest, saddled-up once more.

I had postponed a little of my talk on business with O'Grady, until I should be taking this ride to Pretoria with him, for the Sparrow and he, being fond of frequent digressions from the main subject of discourse, were apt to take up a great deal of time before coming to the point, and time was precious at Grünfontein. O'Grady seemed troubled in his mind. He at last asked me whether I really meant to let him and his partner carry out the contract? I said, certainly I did; was I not going to Pretoria on purpose to get materials for them to work with? He then repeated the kind offer Mr. Sparrow had made in his name, to save me all trouble if I would only let him know where he might find me at any moment. I suggested that this would be difficult, as I had a great deal of business on hand, and should be here, there, and everywhere during the day. I asked if it would not do for me to tell him some particular hour when he would be sure to find me at some appointed place. O'Grady seemed surprised, he had not known that I had business in Pretoria.

"Not about getting estimates, &c, for material?" I asked.

O'Grady thought that *he* was going to Pretoria for that purpose. If I were going to do this business, what was the use of his going also? I suggested that two heads were better than one occasionally, as also proverbially; to which proposition O'Grady, with a look of thoughtfulness, agreed.

We off-saddled half way to Pretoria, against my usual custom, but I was sorry for O'Grady's pony, and we reached Pretoria late. [. . .]

In the ensuing days I found out satisfactorily that the cost of material would enormously exceed anything that it had been estimated to me at. I found out, too, that the German could be as thorough in getting drunk, as in doing anything else. This did not surprise me; the former discovery did. Of course, I heard the same talk about my purchase of Grünfontein as I had heard before. In the meantime, O'Grady seemed gradually getting excited, and at last one evening called on me, and after much beating about the bush told me that he found he and the Sparrow had been mistaken, that they could not execute the building for what they had said, and handed me an estimate for nearly double the stated amount. [. . .]

I left Pretoria early next morning, as early at least as the opening of the "European" stables (seven o'clock) would allow. The waggon had gone on a little in front, but I soon picked it up, and had breakfast at the first outspann. Then leaving it to follow, I rode on. I had much to think of, and not very pleasant thinking either. From the time when I arranged to buy Grünfontein, I had known that to make it pay a certain class of buildings would have to be erected on it. It was not a farm, to the best of my belief, that could be made [to] pay by working it in the hugger-mugger fashion of the country. I had been careful in making all my calculations before going in for it, believing that I was making them on trustworthy data; now I found that I had been grossly, although I do not mean wilfully, misled. The meaning of all this to me was, that I must give up Grünfontein or be ruined. Of course I chose the former alternative, but it was very painful. I dreaded parting from the Higginses, and going as it were out into the unknown again. I knew that Mr. Higgins would be greatly disappointed at my not buying the place. I had worked so hard to improve it; had counted labour and hardship as nothing if I could but push on the work there; it was such a pretty place for this country! However, the truth was too obvious; to me Grünfontein meant ruin. I was sorry about Mr. Egerton, too. I knew that breaking up Grünfontein would very likely throw him on his beam-ends again, and that meant probably ruin to him. Then what was I to do? Of course I had to look for another farm, but in the meantime what was I to do with my oxen, with my sheep, with little Roughy and Moustache? I found Moy-plas bright and home-like, and the usual cheery welcome awaiting me. I started after breakfast the next day, and it was early in the afternoon when I rode up to Grünfontein.

Mr. Egerton, who was working at a large new fowl-house that I was making, came to meet me. He had been expecting me, having heard I was coming from O'Grady, and had something ready for my tea. I had hardly finished telling him the result of my visit to Pretoria, when Mr. Higgins rode up on Wellington. I felt I was in for it, and I told him, too. I watched him anxiously. People in Pretoria had said I placed too great trust in his high-mindedness in money-matters; I was putting him to the test.

If this were not a history of mere facts, without embellishments of any sort, or any flights of imagination—if it, moreover, were written for the sake of amusing or merely making money, not with a further object of giving any one who reads it a truthful conception of this country, I should be much tempted to make Mr. Higgins what I had imagined him; but as it is, truth compels me to say that he fell a little short of my ideal. He did not oppose my leaving Grünfontein, but he did ask for compensation beyond the improvement of the crops, and the bricks that I left on it. If I had not received much kindness at his wife's and his hands—kindness which it is not likely I shall ever have it in my power to repay—I think my natural pugnacity would have asserted itself; as it was, I paid the compensation, feeling more sorry that he had asked for it than that I had to pay it, although I was hard up for money too. Only when I was leaving Grünfontein for Pretoria, there, as I well knew, to have the whole matter discussed, and to be forced into speaking of it myself, did I tell Mr. Higgins that I thought he had not acted quite rightly—told him exactly what I should say to any one who might force me to express an opinion on the matter, but told him, too, that I hoped we should ever remain friends. In truth, I believe there is not a man in the country who would have acted better than Mr. Higgins, and few who would have acted as well. South Africa is a bad training-school for high class morality in money matters—or indeed, in any matter whatever.

Chapter 21

Before I left Grünfontein various arrangements had to be made, amongst others the disposing of the wool of my sheep, which I had had lying by for some time. I arranged with James Higgins that he was to buy it, and I sent it over to Fahl-plas on the waggon, with the German in charge. I had discharged the brickmakers, Jim promising in case I wanted his services, in any capacity, to come to me, and I was only waiting for a few days before discharging all the Kaffirs but two, who were to act as driver and foreloper[63] to the waggon. I had determined upon going to the bush-veldt to trade amongst the Boers. The winter was drawing near again, and the migration to the bush-veldt was beginning. I thought I would go first to Pretoria and meet some goods that I expected would be soon there, as I had sent to England for them some time before—whatever was deficient I could buy wholesale there; that I would go to the bush-veldt, taking with me the German, Egerton, and the Kaffirs; that, if I were fortunate enough to get rid of the goods quickly, I could leave the German in charge of the waggon and oxen at some place where the grazing was good, and, with Mr. Egerton, could ride to Pretoria, and when there look out for a new farm. All I should require would be a third horse, to carry a blanket or two and the saddlebags.

Accordingly, I sent off the wool to Fahl-plas, telling the German that I would follow on horseback for I had other business there. I saddled Eclipse towards evening. He had been hurt by the saddle, and was not quite well, but I arranged the saddle on him so that it seemed not to touch the sore, before mounting. At the end of a sharp canter he seemed uneasy, and I stopped to see if anything had gone wrong. Alas! the sore on his back was bleeding. I had no choice but to return home. The question now was what was to be done? When I reached Grünfontein, it was too late for me to ride to Fahl-plas that evening on the brown pony, even if I could ride so far on him at all; but my saddle did not fit him, and I knew a long ride on him would give him sore withers. It was, however, necessary for me either to go to Fahl-plas myself or send a message. [. . .] Mr. Egerton came to my assistance by proposing to walk, saying he thought the German might dislike his riding the pony; however, I would not listen to this. The risk had to be taken, for I was absolutely obliged to send a message where I could not go myself. Egerton started on the pony the next morning early.

In the evening I saw the waggon coming along the road at the foot of the hill. The German was walking beside it, and even from a distance one could see that he was all bristling with rage. He hardly waited a moment after he saw me before his wrath found utterance. From living amongst Boers and English for so long, he always talked a mixture of German, Boer lingo, and English, difficult at times to understand; but when wrath quickened his utterance he became quite unintelligible. I never knew the immediate cause of this outburst, although I could easily divine it; but the outcome of it was, that he vowed he hated Egerton, couldn't—wouldn't bear with him—and that if Egerton were to stay he wouldn't remain another day—that I could keep the horse myself. Of course when any one tells you that you must send some one else away if you mean to retain the services of the speaker, it means either that there is a legitimate cause of complaint, or else that the speaker must go. There was no particular cause of complaint even by the German's own admission. His complaint was founded on generalities, and so, although he was a valuable servant, I said of course if he couldn't agree with Egerton he must go as he said, but that he couldn't go immediately, unless he wanted to forfeit his month's pay, as he was engaged by the month, and his time was not yet up. He saw this, like a practical man as he was, although he was in a rage.

Egerton came home on the pony soon after. It had been just as I said. If Jimmy had not been at Fahl-plas I dare say the German's pride might not have suffered so much, but the English-bred boy made a sharp distinction between the respectable servant and the gentleman's prodigal son. The former had been given brandy in the store, and had bought more drink. Farther than that he had been taken no particular notice of, as he had the waggon to sleep in, and his food and means of cooking with him. The latter had dined with the family, and had coffee under the verandah. Egerton was not a careful master for a horse—he was not very careful about anything, himself included—but on this occasion I afterwards heard from Jimmy that the pony had been treated just as I should have treated it myself; still, I dare say the idea of his prospective pony having been ridden by the man who was treated as his social superior, added to the German's anger.

I was now in a difficulty. Egerton could not manage oxen at all, to say nothing of driving, and it was necessary to have somebody besides the somewhat raw Kaffirs to manage the oxen, for I am physically incapable of working with such very unwieldy beasts. In this dilemma I bethought me of "Jim." He, I knew, could not only work somewhat with oxen, but could drive them fairly well. I sent him word that I wanted him. In the meantime I arranged with Mr. Higgins that my sheep should be herded with his until such time as I could send for them. I was sorry, for I knew how little he looked after his own sheep, and I could not expect anything better for mine. Still I could do nothing else. I had nowhere to leave my flock except with him. The German did whatever I wanted of him punctually, but I could see him talking a great deal to the two Kaffirs I had kept, and at last he came and told me confidentially that they had told him that they did not wish to stay. On questioning the boys myself, however, I found that they were quite willing to go with me to Pretoria, and they even said to the bush-veldt. I was content so long as they would go to Pretoria.

On Saturday Jimmy made his appearance as usual. Jim was with him, and had a little donkey, that he had bought and trained while with me, packed up with his various traps. As they came up I noticed that Jim had got himself up very smart, and I was disagreeably surprised by his putting out his hand to greet me in Boer fashion. I hate snubbing a man publicly, and the German and Egerton were near me when he came up to me, besides Jimmy, so I took the proffered hand, reflecting that he must have been getting spoiled since I had last seen him. It was drawing towards evening, and presently Jimmy, Egerton, and I had supper. The German had long before asked me to give him board-wages, and let him cook for himself. I then called Jim to supper, but he said he was going to have supper in Eclipse's anteroom with the German, and would make his bed there. Jimmy was eager to come with me on my trading expedition; but my prospects were too unsettled and uncertain for me to consent to this, as he had a very good berth at Fahl-plas: we sat up late, discussing plans for the future. The next morning we were having an early breakfast, when Jimmy, who was sitting so that he could see through the open door, said suddenly,—

"I say, you had better go and see what's up; there's Jim packing up his donkey."

I went out immediately. Jim and the German were standing under the wild fig tree with the donkey ready packed.

"Why, Jim" said I, "what's the matter? I was just going to call you in to breakfast."

Jim looked a little this way and a little that way. Then it came out. "He had heard—heard things—he saw he shouldn't get on," &c.; but I was determined to get to the bottom of it, and the bottom of it was that the German and he had been talking, and that he had heard that Egerton was treated differently from one of them, and that he wouldn't stand it. He admitted that he knew that Egerton was a gentleman by birth and education; he admitted that I made no difference between him and any other man while they were at work, but still he would not stand it. Once [. . .] I made him speak out—and spoke out myself—he was quite reasonable, and perfectly respectful. He took his own view of the matter; it was one I could understand. With Jimmy he said he would work side by side, and treat him as a young gentleman; but Egerton had brought himself down to his (Jim's) level, and there he should remain—he had lost his title to social superiority. Jim was very ignorant, and he expressed this in his own language, which is very different from mine; but that was the meaning of what he said.

I said that I could not take his view of the case; that Egerton was doing his best to work well, and to redeem himself; and that I was bound to stand by him, such being the case.

"I'm afraid, ma'am, as you'll be the loser by it," said Jim.

"I'm afraid I shall, Jim," said I; "but right is right, whatever comes of it."

"Yes," Jim assented. "You be right there, ma'am; but I couldn't work with him like that—it would be no use my trying; but I wishes you all success, ma'am, as I am sure you deserves it."

And with that Jim and I shook hands, and he and his donkey departed down the hill.

I had moved from under the tree to the bridge, as I spoke to him, so as to be out of Egerton's hearing. I took a stroll in the garden before I returned. That spiteful little German had determined to pay me out for discarding him rather than Egerton; and he was doing so.

When I returned to the cabin Mr. Egerton interrupted some remark I made as I opened the little half-door.

"Mrs. Heckford," he said, looking very pale, "I must leave you—I am ruining you."

I said, "Nonsense;" but I felt there was a good deal of truth in what he said.

"No," he went on, "you may say that; I knew you would; but as an honourable man I have no choice in the matter, and can leave you none. You must see this yourself."

There was more truth in this than even in his former remark, and yet it was but superficial truth after all—such truth as passes current in the world—but not real truth; for ruin can never come to any one through doing what is right, and it is undoubtedly right for one weak human being to stand firm against the tide of ignorance and selfishness which will always set in against any other weak human being, who having once fallen publicly, tries to rise, even though it may be by dint of hard labour, and though his efforts may be made in a spirit of all humility, as were Mr. Egerton's. Surely there can be no dictate of honour which should tell such a one that he must cast aside the help that is voluntarily held out to him by one, who, fully estimating the cost of what he does, is prepared to do it fearlessly. It cannot be honourable wilfully to throw away the chance of redeeming oneself; and if any one here is disposed to say that a man ought to be able to do so without some external help when he has once fallen, I would advise that person, before he is quite sure in the matter, to come out here and see whether, after studying life in Pretoria for a little, he will not change his mind.

It is not easy to make all this evident to a man of delicate susceptibilities, with the usual ideas about honour, which, however strong they may be, are in nine cases out of ten very vague in men's minds, and who is smarting from a severe and recently-inflicted wound. I almost despaired of dissuading Mr. Egerton from packing up his small stock of goods, and starting then and there for Pretoria; but I gained my point in the end.

Jimmy remained with me until I left Grünfontein. I could not let him go; it was hard enough to have to bid goodbye to him and to the Higginses at all, without dividing the goodbyes. I paid off the German, and let him go; packed the waggon, killed one pig, and sold the other; loaded up my fowls for the Pretoria market; counted my sheep, with poor Hans and my pretty little pet ram [going] to Mr. Higgins; commended Ada's cats to Augustus's mercy; and then, having bid goodbye to the Higginses and to Jimmy, and started the waggon off, Mr. Egerton and I mounted our horses, and left pretty Grünfontein with little Roughy and Moustache as our companions. Moustache cared not a pin, but Roughy evidently felt much as I did—that he was going away from what he knew into a dreary unknown region, where there would be no more little Kaffirs to bark at, as they danced on moonlight nights; no more fowls to chase, no more trots over to Surprise and games with Fido. Poor little dog! A presentiment of evil seemed to have taken possession of him. He could hardly be got to leave the place, and when he at length followed us, it was with a drooping tail, and with a little miserable yelp every now and then, as if he was crying for pretty Grünfontein and homelike Surprise. I could have cried as I turned my back on them, if crying had been of any use.

Chapter 22

It was a bright afternoon as Mr. Egerton and I rode towards Pretoria; and as I looked at the waggon with its indifferent driver, and utterly untutored forelooper, at Mr. Egerton, who knew as little about oxen and waggons as I did, and at the span of splendid oxen committed to our joint charge, I wondered in my heart whether I were not a great fool to go in for the undertaking I had just entered upon. But, as I have said, it was a bright afternoon, and if there was risk in what I was about to do, there was also the excitement that always attends risk; and before I was many miles from Surprise I felt that the whole thing was rather enjoyable. We outspanned for the night near to Cucumoor's farm. There was a new moon; and although it was chilly, it was still pleasant for sleeping out. The waggon was too full for me to be able to sleep in it, if I had wished to do so; but I dislike sleeping in a waggon when there are horses and oxen to be looked after, unless I have very trustworthy attendants. My Kaffirs were not trustworthy, I knew, and Mr. Egerton, when he was once asleep, was very hard to waken. I had my blankets spread near to where Eclipse was tied to the waggon—for he had an objection to being tied, and was accustomed to a loose stall, and I thought it probable he might require my ministration during the night, which, in fact, was the case. It was a long time since last I had slept in the open air, and I enjoyed it. The next day, early, we passed Moy-plas, where I paid a visit. John Higgins was there; he laughed as he bade me goodbye. "You'll be well salted by the time you come back from the bush-veldt," he said. I picked up the waggon and Mr. Egerton a little before we had to pass the Crocodile [river]. The oxen took the waggon through well; but I could see that the driver was not up to much. That evening we outspanned close to Dasspoort, so as to be able to get in early to market next morning.

I had forage and seed oats, pumpkins and fowls for sale. As I sat on Eclipse, close by the waggon, waiting for these various articles to be sold, two or three persons whom I did not know, spoke to me by name. Presently one man, who seemed to know me quite well, though I had not the least remembrance of him, was accosted by a very good-natured-looking man with a brown beard. I saw them both looking at me, and then heard the man with the beard ask who I was. "Oh!" said my unknown acquaintance, "don't you know? that's Mrs. Heckford; let me introduce you;" and so he did. The man with the beard was Mr. Hans Felman, and his introducer told me if I wanted to hear about farms he was the very man to tell me about them. Mr. Felman then spoke very politely, saying if he could be of any use to me he should be most happy. I asked where I could see him if I wanted information. He told me where he lived, and asked me to call on his wife. I had much to do, having after the market to deliver the things I had sold; then to find out where my English goods were, and to load them up (they had just come up to Pretoria, and were still on the waggon that brought them); then I had to select and buy other goods, so as to have a fair stock to take to the bush-veldt. Then I had to unpack all these goods, and write out a list of their selling prices; besides, I had to get a third horse. The packing out and pricing of the goods I did at a farm close to Pretoria, belonging to a young Englishman, where I had obtained leave to outspann. There was very little grass to be had; but on his farm the grazing was still pretty fair. I slept in the veldt, and we had our campfire, and cooked for ourselves, of course. Indeed, the house was at some distance from where my waggon was. It was a house of only two rooms, and a little kitchen outside. In it the young farmer with his young Boer wife and two little children lived.

I got through all I had to do at the end of a week. My new horse was a big, bony, unkempt colt, barely three years old, and only half-broken. He had excellent points: but one thing I saw would always spoil his beauty, he had a fiddle head, so I called him Violin. He was very thin, and rather depressed in spirits, as well as in condition, but he had a vicious way of rolling his eye back, and an equally vicious way of flicking his tail straight up and down, as if he had a hinge in the middle of it. Mr. Egerton hated him from the first, and prophecied that he would turn out badly; and Violin, I suppose in consequence, never liked him. He soon learnt to know me, and would let me handle him as I liked; but he was a troublesome beast with most other people. After some bargaining, I bought this animal for fifteen pounds, and I was now ready to start.

Mr. Egerton and I were eating our supper by the campfire; I had been showing him a photograph of myself, which I had had done in Pretoria at Mrs. Higgins's request. I had a presentiment of evil hanging over me, and the look of this photograph displeased me, and strengthened it. It was a very nice photograph—as a pleasing representation of myself I was more than satisfied with it—but the individual represented in it struck me, as I looked at her, to be absurdly unfitted for a "Smouse," as a trader in a waggon is called here. Looking at that picture, it struck me that I was not only doing a foolish thing, but a ridiculous thing. Mr. Egerton had told me that he had heard some talk between the boys about wanting their pay raised. In the midst of my meditations they broached the subject. They said if their pay was not raised they would not leave Pretoria. I knew their game. They had waited to tell me this till all was ready to start. The time for the bush-veldt trading was going by; other traders were getting in before me—they thought they could extort money—for drivers were scarce in Pretoria then—Kaffirs, as a rule, not liking to go away from their kraals in the winter. I told them plainly that I should not raise their wages a penny; and we all turned in for the night soon afterwards. The next morning my friends said they were going. They hung about, however, apparently waiting for something, I meanwhile saddled up to ride to Pretoria to look for another driver, leaving Mr. Egerton in charge of the waggon. Then they asked me to pay them their wages, but I pointed out to them, that when servants left one at a moment's notice, even though towards the end of their month, they forfeited all pay. They knew well enough that I could have them put in prison, so they held their peace, and I rode off on the brown pony, Dandy. I had arranged the saddle so as to fit him as well as Eclipse; and he was a better horse for work in Pretoria, Eclipse being too larky to be left standing alone if I had business indoors. Dandy was full of spirit; but although quite young, he was quietness itself.

All that day I hunted for a driver, and other people kindly hunted for me, but I could get none. Day after day passed; every morning I saddled up, and bade Mr. Egerton goodbye: every evening I rode back to the waggon, to see him waiting by the campfire, that showed me in the half-darkness where the waggon stood, as I cantered over the veldt, always to tell the same story. I rode over to neighbouring kraals: it was of no use.

I had got the gentleman on whose farm I was outspanned, to have my oxen herded with his oxen. Mr. Egerton and I slept by the loaded waggon; got up early; and while he lit the fire and made early coffee, I cleaned the horses alone, until, coffee being made, he took his share of the work. Then I saddled up for my hopeless search. It came on bitterly cold; every morning the grass was white with hoar frost, and so were our blankets. In the middle of all this, one evening I felt unwell, and the next day I was choking with a violent attack of bronchitis. I went on my quest as usual that day, and for several succeeding days—but I could hardly speak. The nights were very bad. I would have gone into town to sleep at a friend's house but for two reasons, one, that I had the horses to look after; I was afraid of leaving them altogether to Mr. Egerton's care. He had been so long in South Africa that he had acquired a good deal of South African carelessness as to horses; besides, I thought, as he must remain at the waggon, it was only right I should not shirk roughing it. I shall never forget that man's kindness at that time; how he would get up when he heard me coughing, and get me whatever he could to relieve me; and how jolly he was over it all, as if it was the pleasantest thing in the world to turn out of his bed and walk about in a bitter cold night. He did all this in such a perfectly natural and unaffected way, so that it seemed as if it were an everyday occurrence for him to have to act nurse to a bronchitic lady in the open veldt.

At last, after I had spent about a fortnight there, I determined to try to go into Pretoria, instead of remaining on the farm—I seemed no nearer than before to getting a driver. I got the gentleman on whose farm I was outspanned to lend me a driver; Mr. Egerton acted forelooper, and I led Violin and Dandy, and rode Eclipse.

I had, some days previously, called on Mrs. Hans Felman. She received me very kindly; and she and her husband did all they could to help me out of the dilemma I was in. Mr. Felman was a Boer from the old colony, his wife a Transvaal Boer. They had three children—two girls and a boy. Their house, on the outskirts of Pretoria, was built after the usual fashion of Boer farmhouses. It stood on a large piece of ground, or erf,[64] with fruit and other trees round it, and would have been a very pretty house and place only that numbers of Kaffirs were allowed to congregate there, in return for their doing a little work, and they kept the whole surroundings of the house in a mess with the heads of oxen, a favourite dinner with them, partly because it is rather a cheap dish, and partly, I think, because it gives them plenty of fiddle-faddle work to prepare it. I may mention, incidentally, that I have seen Kaffirs throw away the brains as nasty, although they will eat the intestines with the dung just pressed out! The horns of these numerous heads, old bones, and old rags, bestrewed the Felmans' otherwise pretty erf. One evening, by moonlight, I happened to walk across it: it looked like a charnel-house! In one corner of the erf, the farthest from the farmhouse, was a diminutive house of one room, measuring about nine feet by seven, but with a fireplace. As it was impossible for me to put up at any hotel in Pretoria, and desirable that I should have some place of abode (for the waggon was too full to accommodate me), I arranged to take this eligible domicile for thirty shillings a month. It was not a very inviting-looking residence. It had a small window, closed by a shutter, and the door opened directly upon a swampy sort of pond. It was a peculiarly damp and low-spirited-looking spot; one where, if you dug a hole for a stake, the chances were that a frog would hop out of it, and that a series of other reptiles of the same species would periodically make their appearance from it, whilst the stake would decline to become fixed. The liveliness of its general appearance was enhanced by a gap in a neighbouring quince-hedge having been filled up with the skulls of oxen. The fact that this place commanded a rent of thirty shillings a month, tells sufficiently plainly that house-rent in Pretoria was rather high. Its advantage to me was that the Felmans allowed me to bring my waggon into their enclosed erf; also to let my horses graze in it—and these were two things of great advantage to me, particularly as most audacious stealing goes on in Pretoria.

Of course there was no furniture in the room. Mr. Egerton and I rigged up a table, and made seats of packing cases. My bed was made on the floor. Mr. Egerton slept outside—and a funny picture it would have made of an evening, when Mr. Egerton was cooking our evening meal, whilst I lay on the blankets on the floor, playing with the dogs and talking. But coming to Pretoria did not seem to bring us any nearer to procuring a driver; neither could I hear of any farm likely to suit me; so at last, in despair, I began looking about for a house in Pretoria.

Houses of five or six rooms sometimes fetched more than that number of hundred pounds; and I know of one nice cottage of five rooms, standing, it is true, in a very large and productive garden, which, shortly before the war, fetched two thousand five hundred pounds. I did not find it easy to get a house to suit my taste and my pocket. At last I heard of one which had a stable attached, a thing I was particular about; and just at the same time a gentleman, previously unknown to me, called at my funny little abode, and told me that he heard that I was in want of a driver, and that he could recommend me a good one, a bastard or half-caste, who had served with him while he was the Government transport officer. I was really delighted. The man came to be inspected—a fine-looking man with a good face, and who spoke English: his name was Hendrick. I engaged him at the wages he had been receiving from his former employer, viz., half-a-crown a day. He brought me a Hottentot of the name of Hans, who, he said, was a good forelooper, and to whom I was obliged to give one-and-sixpence a day; and Hans besought me to engage a small Hottentot boy (also a Hendrick) who had been left to his charge. This I eventually did, at ten shillings a month. I was now ready to start [. . .].

It was a beautiful moonlight evening towards the end of June, when at last, after so many troubles, I started for the bush-veldt. I was more than a month later than I ought to have been: however, I was glad to be off late though it was. We outspanned for the night about three miles out of Pretoria, and I was wakened out of my first sleep by a lively riding party from the town going out to a farmhouse near. The next morning early we started again, and outspanned for breakfast at Derdepoort—a pass through the Magaliesberg—where we were almost cut in pieces by the sharp wind which seems to be always blowing in this spot. Here I met two men coming from Waterberg with waggons loaded up with leather. They bought some pipes and some sugar from me, and I remember them particularly as having been my first customers. We inspanned after breakfast, and a long trek brought us, towards evening, to a missionary station, where there was a good-sized kraal of Kafiirs, supposed to be Christianized. Whatever progress they may have made in Christianity, they had made but little in civilization in general. Their kraal was on a bare slope towards a small river. There was little shelter to be got from the cold wind—but we had a good supper, and were all soon asleep.

I started the next morning by the light of the setting moon for Pretoria. It was bitterly cold, but as long as the moon lasted I did not mind so much, for we could canter. At last, however, the moon failed us, and, as the dawn was yet about half-an-hour off, we had to walk. Just before the waning light of the moon failed altogether, I had felt my watch chain, which was tucked inside my habit, get loose, and before I had time to put it in again, it swung as I cantered, and seemed to catch on something. When at last the day broke sufficiently for me to be able to distinguish objects clearly, I found that it had broken, and that some keepsakes I had on a ring, through which the chain was passed, were lost. I suppose there is a lurking superstition in all of us; anyhow, I confess that I could not help feeling that the loss of these trinkets that I had carried with me for years, which had been my companions in many vicissitudes, and which, of no great value in themselves, were dear to me from the memories attached to them, was like a bad omen. I reached Pretoria just as the Felmans were going to breakfast. I was perished, and sat by the kitchen fire sipping some hot coffee with great gusto, whilst kind Mrs. Felman got me some bacon and eggs, which I thoroughly enjoyed. The treaty about the farm fell through, and I had only just time to leave word with an agent, that he might offer four hundred pounds for the house in Pretoria, which I previously mentioned, before I had to start out to the waggon. It was already late in the afternoon, but we pushed along sharply, and got to our destination about half-past nine, very cold indeed.

Mr. Egerton had shot a hare and had some hare soup awaiting me, which I, and Hendrick, also enjoyed; and so I was fairly in for my bush-veldt experience, for we were to start early next morning, and to get to the outskirts of the bush-veldt the day after.

Chapter 23

We made but one trek the next day, and outspanned by the Apis river, in a thick and rather pretty bush, near to the other waggons—one, the property of a Boer, going to Pretoria with a load of planks for sale; the other, belonging I think also to a Boer, but an Anglicized Boer. The former gentleman was very fat, and toddled about like a barrel on legs (a common thing with the Boers). He bought some trifle, I forget what, and told me that his wife was dead, and that he had always to take his little boy about with him. The said boy was a shy bright-eyed child, with a strongly developed taste for sweets, in which his fond parent somewhat sparingly indulged him; whilst I, prompted thereto by his motherless condition, indulged him freely. The other people outspanned at this place also came to the waggon and bought something; but I remember them chiefly because, later in the evening, a spanking pair of horses in a spider, brought the sheriff from Pretoria to serve a writ on them. The night was very dark, and I was almost startled as we sat round our campfire to see an individual suddenly illuminated by its ruddy light, who asked in English (and Hibernian English too) where was the nearest water. He and his companions, he told us, were old Australian gold-diggers—they were going to Zoutpansberg, gold prospecting; they were travelling alone, except for their donkeys, and none of them could speak Dutch or Kaffir. I sent one of my boys to show the way to the water, and afterwards this man sat and talked for a while, and had a cup of coffee.

Early in the morning we inspanned. We had to make a long trek that day to get as far as the Eland river for the evening outspann. Our gold-digging acquaintances were just putting the packs on their donkeys; they were going a different road from us. I was looking at the way that one of their packs was padded, so as to avoid any chance of the animal's back being hurt by it, when Mr. Egerton uttered an exclamation of delight, caused by his having discovered two birds, and, jumping off Dandy, he threw the reins to me, and before I had time to gather up the assembled reins of Eclipse and the two led horses, he fired, quite close to them. I certainly was greatly gratified at the manner they all stood fire, but, whether it was owing to his finding a report close to his ears disagreeable or not, I cannot say, but, after that Dandy never would stand still when his rider dismounted to fire, but would instantly trot away with his head well in the air to prevent his tripping over the bridle, and refuse to be caught. He had a comical way of looking behind him to see the exact time when he must quicken his pace so as to avoid being caught; and many a time after that, was poor Mr. Egerton's temper tried by Dandy's antics and my amusement thereat. After this we slightly lost our way, but coming to a farmhouse, were directed rightly, and crossing the Pinaar's river, on a very rickety bridge, we outspanned for breakfast. The bridge was made of logs and sods, and the Pinaar's river was only a small affair then, but, as I afterwards saw, could become a tremendous torrent in an hour.

When we started again we were fairly in the bush-veldt, and very uninteresting bush-veldt it was. Thick bush was on either side of our narrow road, but there was no fine timber; and as all the trees were thorn trees, the effect was infinitely monotonous. There was no game of any sort to be seen; once we heard a sound of an axe, and going in search of its proprietor, found a young Boer cutting firewood, with his horse browsing beside him. Of course he looked a little surprised at seeing a lady, and asked who we were, and was farther a little surprised at hearing that I was a "Smouse." He told us that there were a lot of traders on in front, and that trade in the bush-veldt was slack. We reached the Eland river about an hour after noon, much in advance of the wagon, and off-saddled. Mr. Egerton took his gun and went off; I lay down to watch the horses browsing, and to look at the view, there being nothing else to do. A long line of tall reeds marked the course of the river between high banks. The ground was clear of trees for about a hundred yards on the side where I was sitting, but on the other for much farther. On my side the ground soon began to undulate, but on the other the hills were a long way off. Sheltered amongst the scrubby trees on my side, and about a hundred and fifty yards off from where I lay, were tents of Boers, stationed there with their flocks and herds. The grass was very dry, and near where I lay it was much eaten off, it being the usual place for outspanning, being near to a drift, where the cattle could easily go down to water. After I had had two or three half-dozes, and had watched a large flock of sheep being driven towards the tents by a Kaffir, and when the sun was getting low, I saw the waggon emerging from the bush. This meant dinner, whereat my soul rejoiced. The next morning early, I made up my mind to ride over to the tents and inform their occupants that I was a "Smouse." I did not particularly enjoy the prospect of doing this, for novelty is not always charming, though it certainly was something quite new to me.

Moustache and Roughy of course announced my approach by a little skirmish with some of the Boers' dogs. Boers are not very demonstrative: they generally stand in a stolid manner near the tent, and say good day in an equally stolid manner, although they may be really dying of inquisitiveness about a stranger. The individuals in the first tent I went to did this exactly, and when I told them that I was a "Smouse," and asked if they wanted anything, they said "No," in a manner so completely exhaustive, that I felt it would be useless to attempt conversation, so I rode on to the farther tent. Here I found women and several children. Both the women were big, strapping, peasant-like women. They asked me into the tent. The men, they told me, were in Pretoria, and they expected them out next day. They gave me coffee, asked numbers of questions as to what had brought me out to this country; whether I was married; whether I had any children with me; whether I had ever had any children; who the white man with me was; and a great many others of a similar nature. They said they would come to the waggon and buy, and they displayed all that they had to display, namely, their little children and their pets—two little night-apes:[65] funny small beasts, all furry and soft, and with such big eyes and ears, and such long tails, that they remain on your mind as having eyes, ears, and tails, and nothing else. The night-apes are very agile, and the Boers are fond of them as pets; the orthodox way of displaying them to admiring friends being, to swing them about by a piece of string attached to a collar round the small beast's neck. The Boers say the animal has no objection to the proceeding—in fact, rather likes it—but perhaps they may be in error. The springs the little ape makes, whilst undergoing the process, are very surprising, considering that it has nothing to spring from.

I was very glad to perceive that I could make myself fairly understood by these women, and could understand them fairly. I was not only anxious to be able to do so because it was necessary for my success in trading, but also because I was desirous of knowing something of the people. Up to the time of which I am now writing, my knowledge of the Boers was small. I had seen numbers of them, and had even been kindly received at their houses, but our conversation had been necessarily very limited. I had been able to observe that most of them are dirty and untidy—even the relations of the famous Paul Kruger, living in a state of dirt and disorder that reminds one of an Irish hovel; while at the same time, I had heard many accounts of their absurd ignorance—of how they believed the earth to be flat, and that the sun and stars were made expressly as lamps for our benefit, &c.; and I had been amused to learn that Paul Kruger had privately expressed his opinion, that the footman of his noble English host was both a better dressed and better mannered man than his master! Horrible tales had also been told to me of the brutality this Paul Kruger and others were capable of, when left to themselves, by men who had, in the olden time, served under or with them against the Kaffirs: of how they had taken little babies, too young to be easily reared, away from their mothers, who had perhaps been slaughtered, and had thrown them all into a heap in a kraal, and, covering them with dry grass and bushes, had set fire to it; of how they had shot nursing mothers in cold blood, and let them linger in misery for days, if the shot had not proved immediately fatal; of how children had been dragged from their mothers' arms and taken away as slaves, the mothers being shot if they ventured to run after the capturers, and annoy them by their despairing wailing. I had heard that the Boers were a treacherous, lying, hypocritical people, with all the faults but with none of the virtues supposed to belong to rough peasants; and I had even spoken to a Boer who, a very few years ago, dragged a Kaffir to death tied to his horse. I thought I would now begin to learn a little of them from my own observation.

I had not long returned to the waggon, and I was sitting on the grass, when the two women came up. They sat down by my side, and asked me if I had some cotton of a particular size. I said I would look. Then they asked if I would take eggs in exchange. Having expressed my willingness to do so, they asked if I had needles of a particular size; and I said once more that I would look. Mr. Egerton had to do the looking, by-the-way, and did not much enjoy it; my department was the talking business! My customers now expressed their desire to see some "kommekies" (be it understood that a "kommeky" is a small bowl used by the Boers instead of a cup—handles being inconveniently given to breaking on trek); I said I had, and then they asked what was their price. I named it, but my visitors threw up their eyes in horror. "Oh!" they said, "that is more than we give in Pretoria." I ventured to remark that the bush-veldt was not Pretoria. Then they asked what would I give for eggs. I said a shilling a dozen. Once more they were seized with surprise and horror; they had never heard of such a low price; all traders gave more. But I was obdurate. How those women did haggle over a penny more or less in the price of a few "kommekies" and a few eggs; the penny having to be subtracted in the former and added in the latter case. At last, to get rid of them, I let them have the coveted little bowls at almost cost price, and got the eggs at my own. But my customers were aggrieved—they rose to depart, and, as they wished me farewell, the elder woman patted her pocket fondly.

"Ah!" she said, addressing her companion, "I have plenty of money in it—I wanted to buy—but the woman gives so little for eggs, and her things are so dear!"

Mr. Egerton and Hendrick were indignant, and I made them worse by laughing at them; but the best of the joke we had to find out afterwards—half of the eggs were addled!

Not long after this, two Boers, father and son apparently, rode up to the waggon and dismounted. The father held his hand out to me across the disselboom[66] evidently expecting me to get up to take it, but I was too comfortable lying down.

"I can't reach so far," said I.

"No more can I," quoth he. "Have you any boots? "

"Yes."

"What is their price?"

"Eighteen shillings."

"You must not tell lies," remarked my visitor.

I assured him I was adhering strictly to truth; upon which he said I might show him the boots; but they were not strong enough for his fancy; and he and his son rode on to another trader, who was, I heard, stationed not far off.

Then Mr. Egerton's wrath against the rudeness of Boers in general, and of this Boer in particular, burst forth, regardless of my endeavours to point out to him, that, as friends and relations, in Boer-land, constantly recommend each other (in a friendly spirit) not to lie, the expression was doubtless only a playful allusion to the fact that traders are in the habit of making as good bargains as they can.

Soon after we inspanned, and Mr. Egerton and I riding on in front, we presently came upon the encampment of the trader we had heard of. He was stationary there for a time, and had set himself up very comfortably. After a few words we rode on, following the right bank of the Eland river, towards its junction with the Elephant river. The bush was thick, and the banks were so steep, that although we were close to the river the whole time, we were not aware of it; and here I may remark that it requires to get one's eye accustomed to the bush-veldt before one can discover where the course of a river or the source of a spring lies, and also where a Boer encampment lies, for the Boers draw up their waggons and pitch their tents often in the midst of thick bush; and a trader's eye must often be as practised as a hunter's, to see the little white speck they present amongst the green foliage.

Mr. Egerton and I overshot many at our first outset, giving Hendrick a laugh at our want of experience when he came up with the waggon.

The next day brought us to a Kaffir kraal. The river ran between it and us, but I halted the waggon, and sent Hendrick over on Dandy to ask if I could get mealeas [mealies] for the horses, and whether the Kaffirs would care to buy. He soon returned, escorted by a troop of whooping and yelling children, all nearly, and many quite, naked, who evidently looked upon the arrival of a "Smouse" as a delightful interruption to the monotony of their existence. They were closely followed by numbers of men and women: the former dressed in every variety of attire, from a worn out European suit to a strip of rag round the loins; the latter wearing girdles of leather, fringed, and more or less ornamented with beads or brass buttons round their waists, without any other covering in the case of their being young girls; the married women had in addition skins thrown round their shoulders or passed under one arm and fastened over the opposite shoulder. Many carried baskets containing mealeas, pumpkins, &c., on their heads, and babies in their arms.

This motley crowd of men, women, and children, literally besieged the waggon, chattering and screaming like so many monkeys, and clambering up on the wheels, and jumping backwards and forwards across the disselboom in an ape-like manner. As their excitement abated, and as they fell into groups, the *coup d'oeil*[67] was effective—the women, in their quaint costumes, and with their arms and legs decorated with beads and bangles, being the leading feature in it. Many of the men spoke Dutch, but none of the women could speak that language, so that I lost the fun of hearing their observations. One of the women was very graceful and pretty, with a turn of the head and neck that reminded me of the hunting Diana in the Vatican. She was quite conscious of my admiring glances, and took advantage of the knowledge they conveyed to her, to wheedle me into buying a pumpkin at a preposterous price.

I never saw so grotesque a caricature as these Kaffirs presented of scenes I have observed at Swan and Edgar's, and Howell and James's.[68] Some absurd-looking savage in a blanket, would ask to see a shirt, or a coat, or a pair of trousers, or perhaps a hat. The assembled multitude would become all attention. He would be turned round and round, the critics would fall back a pace or two, and look at him with deep thoughtfulness, while he watched their faces anxiously: no, there was a bulge in the back! or the brim was a little too narrow—he must try another. Or perhaps when the critics were satisfied, the purchaser would screw himself round, and gazing down his own back, say, "Don't you think it would be better if it were a little more this or a little less that?" and his friends would discuss the matter, gravely walking round him with their heads on one side, until it was settled to general satisfaction. The trying on of boots was very fine—the would-be purchaser often having very little on him except the boots. After pulling them on, he would promenade backwards and forwards in them, trying how they felt. When the purchase, whatever it might be, was concluded, the purchaser frequently celebrated the event by a "breakdown,"[69] amid universal applause. I stayed at this amusing place until the next morning, and then continued my route along the Eland river.

We passed several Boer encampments, the tents being pitched a little away from the path, and close to the river. I rode over to them to ask if their inhabitants wished to buy anything, but none of them did. They were very civil to me, however. One gaunt old lady, at whose tent I dismounted and had some coffee, was much interested in politics, as well as in all my private concerns; and farther wished to induce me to buy an ox at an exorbitant price.

"Why," said I, "you are asking war prices; no one will give you ten pounds for an unsalted ox in peace times."

"Ah," said she cheerfully, "we all mean to keep our oxen until the Kaffirs break out again: they are sure to break out—quite sure."

We outspanned for breakfast near the encampment of an old infirm Boer of the name of Prinsloo, who had a very jolly-looking wife. Prinsloo himself looked like a gentleman, and they seemed nice people in their way. They came over to the waggon, after I had paid them a visit in their tent, and bought a bottle of brandy from my private store; for I had none for purposes of sale.

It was near this place, but I forget exactly where, that two waggons laden with planks from the wood bush came along while we were outspanned. With them was a tall young Boer, who evidently had a very good opinion of himself, and thought it the correct thing to swear most villainously in all the English he knew. This prepossessing specimen of young Boerdom halted his waggons, and, swaggering up to Mr. Egerton, asked him his name; then whether he was the owner of the waggon.

Mr. Egerton pointed to me, upon which my friend swaggered over to where I was sitting on the grass, and proceeded to survey me as if I were a curious animal of some unknown kind. Then he said,—

"So, you are a Smouse, are you? Well, you will howl."

(N.B. The same word "heul" is used in Dutch for either crying or howling.)

"Indeed," said I.

"I want some brandy," said he.

"I'm sorry for that," said I; "because I can't give you any."

This disconcerted him, and he called to his oxen, and departed, swearing at them in English as long as he was within hearing.

For the next few days nothing remarkable occurred. We passed several encampments and one trader—and once I was most agreeably surprised by finding Mrs. Farquarson in a tent instead of a Dutch woman. Her husband was surveying neighbouring farms, and she, with her baby, was enjoying the free bush-veldt life as a change from Pretoria. I kept along the Eland river still, but I found that trade was bad, a great many traders being just in front of me; and so I determined to change my route, and turned across, past Schildpotsfontein, towards Waterberg.

Schildpotsfontein is a very muddy fountain in the midst of a large Kaffir kraal or town. The chief is named Andreas Mayepee (I spell as the name would be pronounced in English), and the principal feature of the place is sand. I never saw such a sandy place; you waded through sand wherever you went, you were in constant danger of getting your waggon stuck fast in the sand, and had to pilot it in its course to the outspanning place, as carefully as if it were a ship amongst shoals. If there was a breath of wind you were choked with sand; but, although not otherwise an inviting place, it recommended itself to me by its inhabitants doing a good trade with me, although another trader came there a few hours after I did, and also did a good trade. The chief was but a poor specimen of a chief, and kept a general store. His subjects paid him scant respect, and said his store had not much in it, and what little there was, was dear. The Kaffirs here were not half so amusing as those at the Eland river, although laughable enough. There were Kaffirs in European dress, and Kaffirs in blankets, and Kaffirs in shirts. I don't remember any naked Kaffirs here, and the women, girls, and children, were attired, or not attired, like those at the Eland River. The men mostly spoke Dutch, but the women only Kaffir, or rather "Makatees;" for there are many Kaffir languages. I may here remark that the Makatees' language is a very unpleasing Kaffir dialect, and that the Makatees[70] people are, by universal admission, a very nasty Kaffir people.

 I remained here several days, and then went on a short distance to a Missionary station. Here the women and girls wore European dress, and many of even the little children were clothed. I think it was here that I was amused to hear Mr. Egerton trying to convert a Kaffir to republican principles. The fellow admitted that Andreas Mayepee was, so far as he knew, of no particular use, and yet that all his subjects had to pay him tribute; but there he stuck fast. "One must have a chief—some chief—we couldn't get on without a chief," he said; and farther than that he could not be got by any arguments.

 We had a long trek without water between this place and the next water at Marullo-kop, or Marullo-hill, so-called from a picturesque hill crowned by a large marullo [marula] tree near the spring of water. Oxen do not care to drink late at night, or early in the morning, so, as one is obliged to outspan once between the Missionary station and Marullo-kop, we started late, in order to outspan after dark. The trader I mentioned before (Mr. N.) treked along with us. I left Roughy in the waggon, for he was rather footsore, and Mr. Egerton and I rode on; but to my dismay, when the waggons came up, I heard that the poor little dog had jumped out, and run after me as the boys supposed—but in fact had lost himself. It was pitch dark, but I hoped he might find his way to the campfire. Morning, however, came, and no Roughy. I could not keep the waggon waiting, for there was no water for the oxen, and it was useless to ride back to the kraal, as, even if I had found him there, he was too heavy to carry far on the horse, and too bad a runner to run after me, so I regretfully had to leave him to his fate, and go on.

We saw several spring-bucks [springboks] as we rode along, but none near enough to allow of Mr. Egerton trying his skill as a marksman; and early in the day we got to Marullo-kop. The little precipitous hill rises suddenly from the flat thickly-wooded plain, and the spring of water makes a very little lake at its foot. Tucked in among the trees were some Boer tents; saddles, skins, and dried quagga[71] flesh were hanging on the trees close to them, and various implements, strewed around, showed that one at least of their occupants carried on the trade of a blacksmith and a mender of waggons.

This individual came to greet us, as Mr. N., Mr. Egerton, and I rode up. He was a fine, sturdy-looking fellow, with an open smile and a yellow beard. After greeting him, I led my horse to where I wished the waggon to outspann, off-saddled, and sat down, while Mr. Egerton departed with his gun. Presently the pleasant-looking Boer came over from his tent with a glass of wine in his hand, and accompanied by Mr. N. He said, that, at home, he would have offered me something better, but here in the bush-veldt he had nothing else to offer. I thought more of this attention afterwards, when I learned from himself and others that he was a leader amongst the malcontents. His name was Barend Englesberg. I went with him to his tent, and was introduced to his wife, an enormously fat woman, with a very merry face, also to his daughter-in-law, Liza, and to several other women and girls—relations of his.

The waggons soon came up, the goods were spread out, and a great deal of bargaining ensued; also a great pulling about of goods, during which we had to keep our eyes about us; for it is a well-known thing amongst traders that Dutch women and girls are very light-fingered. Barend Englesberg told me there were numbers of wild quaggas about, but that they were shy and difficult to get close to. He also told me that there were several lions, and that they often came down to the water at night. He evidently wished to frighten me. In the evening he even took the trouble to send me over word that he had heard a distant roar, and that I had better be on my guard; but that was all I heard of a lion during my stay.

On leaving this place Mr. N. and I parted company—he taking one road into Waterberg, and I another. My road led through thick bush until we crossed a chain of hills and descended into a wide valley, intersected by the "Nilstrom" or Nile river, and saw, in front of us, the magnificent, solitary, and precipitous hill, called "Kranz-kop;" whilst, across the valley, the view was bounded by the range of the Waterberg hills (for they cannot be called mountains).

We outspanned for dinner near to a Kaffir house in the valley, whence a woman came with a cup of coffee for me, and told me, she had seen me while I was with the Jennings. She had relations living on their place, and had been there on a visit. She was dressed in European costume, and talked Dutch. She told me she belonged to the Mission station, which I could see tucked away in a fold of a hill just opposite, where she informed me I should find a very nice lady, the wife of a German Missionary, who had passed me on his way to Andreas Mayepee's while I was outspanned at Marullo-kop. She said also that I should do a good trade, not only at the Mission station, but at the Kaffir kraals round Kranz-kop.

It was sunset as we rode up to the pretty little Waterberg Mission station, which will ever remain impressed on my memory, with its little cluster of white huts, its mealea gardens, its rambling parsonage, shaded by blue gum trees, and its little church with a tiny spire, all nestled in amongst the hills—as the prettiest although not the most striking picture I have seen in the Transvaal—a picture that was sadly pleasant, as reminding one of home.

Chapter 24

The next morning I went to pay a visit to Mrs. B—— who received me most kindly. The whole house spoke of true homely comfort; the face of the mistress of it beamed comfort at you, although she was still crippled from the effects of the fever which had desolated Waterberg that summer, and which had made her desolate by the loss of her baby; but she had many older children, and they looked as if they had just stepped out of a German "Randzeichnung,"[72] or of Retzsch's[73] etchings to the "Lied von der Glocke."[74] There was something wonderfully refreshing and wholesome about the whole establishment, and the Kaffirs in this place were certainly the best I came across—mainly, I fancy, from the good influence of Mr. B and his wife, of whom I heard a high character from every one, and of whom I can only say that it is a sad pity there are not more missionaries like them. Their flock were certainly fond of them; but Mrs. B——, and afterwards Mr. B——, told me that the Kaffirs were very disobedient, lazy, deceitful, selfish, and grasping in their dealings, even with them; and that many whom they had helped at great personal inconvenience at the time of the fever epidemic, had afterwards refused to assist them in putting their land in order, even for pay. They never varied in their kindness, however, towards these people, although they were firm with them. This was the character I heard of them from their neighbours among the Boers, and my own observation certainly tallied with it.

On returning from my visit I found Mr. Egerton and Hendrick doing a roaring trade; and this was kept up for the whole day, and for some succeeding days, Kaffirs coming in from the neighbourhood to buy. Some of these were "Knopnase,"[75] perfect savages, with tassels of fur tied on to their woolly heads, and a girdle, with a fringe of wild cats' tails, as their only garment. We spent Sunday here. The service in the church was conducted in the Makatees' language, and some of the girls and young men came out very smart. After a few days we moved down the valley, trading at various Kaffir kraals and Boer farms (for now we were out of the bush-veldt), then crossed the Nile river, and traded amongst the wild Kranz-kop Kaffirs, until I had no more Kaffir goods left. I remember being greatly amused one evening, at the astonishment and delight caused by my appearance on horseback amongst some girls and women we met on their way to a kraal. They clapped their hands and danced about the horses (I was leading Violin), crying out, "Oh, the missus! the pretty missus on the horse!" And when I broke into a canter, their screams of delight, as they ran after me, made me laugh so much, that I had to interrupt the performance and return to a walk.

Having got rid of all my Kaffir goods, I thought I would try to get rid of a few more of my Boer goods before returning to replenish my stock at Pretoria. I therefore passed through the mission station again, and followed the course of the river towards Makapan's-poort, thus once more getting into the bush-veldt.

At one of my outspanns I came across a man who lived near Nooitgedacht [Surprise]. I was riding Eclipse and leading Violin, and Mr. Egerton was on Dandy, when we rode up to his encampment. He asked me if I would sell Eclipse; and on my saying that I would not part with him, asked me if the other horses were for sale. I said he could have the pony for thirty, the colt for eighteen pounds—that the pony was salted. He said I asked a dreadful price; but later on, after he and some other Boers had done a little trade with me, he said a friend of his, De Clerc, wanted Violin. There was a deal of bargaining, for he wanted me to exchange him for two oxen, and at last we struck a bargain. I was to have the oxen and some money to boot; but in the morning he changed his mind—he would have Dandy instead. I insisted upon having the full sum in cash for Dandy, and this was a sore point. It turned out that it was not De Clerc who was buying the horse; he was buying him for his son-in-law, Willem de Plessis. He tried every way to get me to lower the price; but I was really sorry to part with the pony, and I stuck out. They had him up, and asked me if he would stand fire, upon which I told them he always trotted away when his rider dismounted to fire; so young De Plessis tried him, and found my statement to be correct; but he still wanted the pony. At last the money bag was pulled out, and the counting out began. He got up as far as twenty-eight pounds, then his courage failed him. He asked—could I not take twenty-eight pounds? I said I could not. He said it was all he had got. I said that was all right, then; I should keep the pony. He got up from the disselboom, on which he had been sitting alongside of me, and going to another Boer who was standing a little way off, brought the two sovereigns, and gave them to me.

"Give him the pony," said I to Hendrick. "Take off the saddle and bridle."

"Oh, but you will include them in the price," said he; but I shook my head. "Then you will let me have the stable head-stall?"

"No, not unless you pay for it."

"But the knee-band you will give in?"

[It is the fashion in Africa to spancel a horse by tying its head to one of its legs, and a knee-band is often used to prevent the leg from being frayed by tying the rein round it.]

"No," I said; "not unless you buy it."

"You will, at least, let me have the rein? "

I let him have that. It was worth about sixpence. He looked at the gold lovingly as I put it into my bag.

"You will give me a written guarantee that he is salted?" he said ruefully. "It is a terrible lot of money."

"No, I won't," said I.

"Then, at least," said De Clerc cheerfully, "you will sell us a bottle of your brandy?"

"Yes, if you will pay me ten shillings;" and they did so, and departed rejoicing.

I did not go much farther along the river, for I met Mr. N——, who told me that there was no trade to be done with the Boers farther up; and, as I said before, my Kaffir goods were exhausted. My last outspann, before I turned back, was close to the encampment of an old woman of the name of Nell, related to the De Clercs and Engelsbergs in some inextricable manner, as is often the case with Boer relationships. This is natural, when it is the custom for people of both sexes to marry so often as they do in Boer-land, for each succeeding wife to call her actual husband's mother "ma," her former husband's or husbands' mother "ma," and her husband's former wives' mothers "ma." The husbands observe the same rule, one that includes the various fathers as well, who are called "pa" by a variety of people hardly related to them according to our ideas. The relationships become still more bewilderingly intricate, when one considers that the "pa" and "ma" may marry half-a-dozen times themselves, and may thus multiply their children's fathers or mothers, and grandfathers, and grandmothers to an appalling extent. I once made, or at least attempted, a calculation of the number of grandmothers a Boer might have, but I felt that to grapple with the subject was to court insanity, and so desisted.

The old Mrs. Nell had had several husbands, and it was an endeavour on her part to make me understand how a certain individual I knew was related to her, through his being related to some relation of a former wife of one of these husbands, that started me off on the abovementioned calculation. She was an old woman who wished to do business, and evidently thought me very verdant—as I was in those days—still her expectations were beyond my merits, for when she wished me to purchase an old and rather vicious bull, and explained to me that all I had to do to get him to walk along with my waggon was also to buy a cow or two—I respectfully declined. A grandson of hers was a boy with a sharp turn for business, which I suppose he had inherited from her. I had bought a young falcon and a pair of turtle doves at the mission station, and I conclude the fame of that purchase had reached this young gentleman's ears. On riding up to old Mrs. Nell's tent I remarked a sort of magpie tied to the stump of a tree close by. In the course of conversation Mrs. Nell directed my attention to it, and said her grandson had caught it. I said it was an amusing pet; and she said that it was so indeed. Some little time after she hinted that perhaps if I liked to have it her grandson might be induced to part with it, but I took little notice of the remark. Later on she came with the grandson and the magpie to my waggon, I admired the bird, to please the boy as I thought, but was rather amused when he suggested that I should give him a bottle of sweets for it. I assured him that if I had the misfortune to own the bird, I would give him a bottle of sweets to take it away. This disconcerted him, and I heard him whisper to his grandmother, "If the aunt" [Little Boers call all women "aunt"] "won't buy it, what shall I do with it?" He then returned to the charge, and at last came down to begging me to give him threepence for the bird. Finding that I would not give him anything, he walked off looking very sulky, carrying the poor bird; and I heard afterwards from Mr. N—— (who was at Mrs. Nell's tent when he returned) that he said it was a horrid shame of the aunt not to buy the bird when he had caught it expressly to sell to her—and forthwith proceeded to wring its neck. On my way back I traded two cows, which I sold afterwards at a gain, but otherwise trade was very slack. [. . . Having sold most of her trade goods,

Heckford begins the trip back.] Mr. N—— and I came into Andreas Mayepee's kraal together, and found there another trader, a very jolly young fellow, who spent the evening by my campfire, telling stories of hunting adventures and smuggling adventures in which he had been engaged. My driver, Hendrick, had served the firm to which he belonged for a long time, and Mr. S——, the young trader, gave me a very high character of him, and told me one of his great recommendations was that he could be trusted to go trading alone with a waggon amongst the Kaffirs.

I inquired here about my little dog, but all I could hear, was that he had been seen some days after I left. I felt pretty sure that he was hidden away in some Kaffir hut; for Kaffirs have a great fancy for pretty little dogs.

We three traders parted company the next day, and I took my course once more towards the Eland river. That evening I rode over to a Boer encampment to ask if I might outspann near it for the night. The owner, a fine-looking man, who was just putting his sheep in the kraal, answered courteously in the affirmative, and, after I had ridden back to the waggon and told Hendrick where to outspann, I cantered once more towards the tents, with a view to paying a visit to their occupants, when I suddenly saw a little black and white dog standing looking at me and flourishing his tail in a most surprising way. It was my Roughy! I jumped off the horse and caught the small beast up. He screamed with delight as he cuddled up to me, then suddenly leapt down and performed a frantic dance round me, letting off such a volley of little barks that I thought he would have choked, whilst the Boer family looked on in high satisfaction. It seems that, some time before, the poor little thing had come across the river to their tent, thin and so footsore that he could go no farther, and they had taken him in and cared for him, and had refused to sell him once, because they wanted to find his true owner. The name of these good Samaritans was Briet. Very nice people they were, clean and tidy in all their arrangements, and keeping their little adopted child (a rosy urchin of four, with laughing black eyes) as neat and fresh as any English child could be—very unlike the generality of Boers, whose children are filthy.

I stayed there the whole of the next day. They told me that, owing to the want of rain causing the grass to be dry, their sheep and young lambs were dying. Just across the river were the broad lands of an enormously rich Boer, a man who counts his cattle by thousands, as also his sheep, who has numbers of large farms, and plenty of money in hard cash besides. His name is Erasmus, and he is known in Boerdom as the "rich Erasmus." Now it so happened that, some time before, the grass on the other side of the river had caught fire, and he had sent to ask the Briets to help him in putting it out. They had done so, toiling all through the night with might and main. The burnt grass had now shot forth sweet green leaves, such as sheep delight in, and the Briets asked if they might hire a run for their starving flock—but were refused it by the old miser! I heard that this enormously rich man refuses himself sugar in his coffee, and wears his coats until they almost fall into rags.

There were some pretty young girls, relations of the Briets, in a tent close by. When I was starting the next day, one of them in a pretty coaxing way asked me to make her a present as a remembrance of me. She was too pretty and too young to rebuff, so I said I would give her something, I forget what.

"No," she said, holding my hand, "you must let me choose my own present"

For the same somewhat unreasonable reason as before, I said she should do so, when judge of my astonishment as she tried to draw a valuable ring off my finger, saying: "You shall give me this!"

"No," I said, "I can't give you that."

"Oh, but I don't want anything else," she answered; and she looked very much disappointed when I explained to her that the ring was a keepsake, and under no circumstances could be removed from my finger.

Chapter 25

Nothing worth relating occurred on my road to Pretoria [. . .] My own house being let, [I] pitched a tent in the Felman's erf, where I still retained possession of the eligible residence I mentioned before. This, however, I did not now occupy, but used as a storeroom.

I had determined upon parting with Mr. Egerton, as, in the life I was now leading, I no longer required his services. I think we were both sorry to say goodbye; and I was the more sorry, because I could not see any chance of an opening for him. He got an employment of a very laborious nature before I left Pretoria once more, and I left him the key of the eligible residence, which he determined to use as his domicile, so as not to incur the expense of an hotel. And this brings me to what has been my reason for recounting so much of Mr. Egerton's history; a reason which, if he ever reads this record of my adventures in South Africa, I believe he will deem a good one. His story points the moral of what I am about to remark.

For two years before I bade goodbye to Mr. Egerton, and, as an act of friendship, offered him the key of that miserable little hole, wherein to eat his meals and make his bed, subscriptions had been asked for and obtained for the erection of a new church—for embellishments of that new church—and even (if I mistake not) for an organ for it; and from its pulpit had been thundered forth denunciations of the drunkenness and consequent vices, only too common, alas! amongst the dwellers in Pretoria. These denunciations were so frequent, that they became the topic of general conversation, and reached the ears of even those who, like myself, never heard them from the pulpit; but no effort was made to provide the means to enable men (not exceptionally determined) to avoid being dragged into the cardinal vice.

It is not an easy thing for a man to avoid frequenting a canteen when he comes as a stranger to Pretoria. He cannot get furnished lodgings—there are not such things to be had—the nearest approach is board and residence in a family; and not only is there no comfortable reading room to be found in the hotels, but the bedrooms are small and uncomfortable. The natural and almost inevitable resource is the "bar," where he can find companionship.

If he does not get employment at once (which is very possible), or supposing that on arriving in Pretoria he has but a very little money in his pocket (which is often the case), then, not being able to afford to stay at an hotel, he must try to get a bed or some sort of shakedown at a canteen, where he is bound to drink or he would not get the shakedown.

If he does succeed in procuring employment, but without getting introduced to some quiet family where he can board, and lodge, the difficulty of spending his evenings anywhere but in a "bar" remains, for there is nowhere else to spend them if he does not sit in his bedroom. If he does not succeed in getting employment, or can only procure work for which he receives pay too small to meet his daily expenses, (even rough living is expensive in Pretoria), then it is not easy for him to avoid, after a time, finding it expedient to take his blanket and make his bed upon fine nights under a rose hedge in the vicinity of the town, so as to save the expense of a bed; and when in the chill, damp morning he gets up, I personally do not wonder that the temptation to have a "tot" at the canteen is too strong for him. The time may very easily come when he cannot afford to look whether the night be fine or not, before making his bed under the rose hedge, and then the morning "tot" seems still more alluring, I fancy—and so on, and so on, until he becomes one of the denounced.

Would not (under these circumstances) a subscription to start a cheap but self-supporting lodging house, with a restaurant and reading room attached, be more to the point than a subscription for an ornamental church, from whose pulpit the poor homeless victims to a strong temptation may be denounced, after a hymn has been sung to the accompaniment of an organ also bought by subscription? As I regretfully shook hands with Mr. Egerton, in the market square of Pretoria, with the moonlight streaming over it, and turned after my waggon, once more on my way to the bush-veldt, I wondered whether, were I he, I should have the strength of mind to go back to that dismal hut by the swamp, every evening, to cook my dinner with wood I should have to gather and blow into a flame after a hard day's toil, and, having eaten, to sit down on a box to read, by the light of a single candle, unless I spread my blankets on the ground and went to sleep, amidst the litter of a storeroom. This too with a dreary consciousness that I should wake up in the grey morning to discomfort, loneliness, and toil—while, all the time, there were lights and there were warmth and rest to be had in many a canteen, and something to drink—which meant to feel jolly for a little time, and to go to sleep without thinking of the morrow.

I believe it is a fact that gentlemen's sons go more quickly and certainly to the dogs in this, and I suppose in every colony, than the sons of working men. Putting aside that they cannot obtain work so easily as the latter, the reason is self-evident; they cannot battle so strongly against the privations and discomfort they are exposed to, and hence they are more liable to seek temporary solace in drink. The habit once formed, will hardly be abandoned, even if the origin of it ceases.

I do not mean to say that all the drunkenness which prevails in Pretoria is originally caused by a desire to forget discomfort, but I am confident that a great deal of it is, and that much misery and vice might be prevented by the adoption of some such plan as I have suggested.

Before leaving Pretoria, I had dismissed Hans, my leader—he was too fond of smoking "daccha," [76] an intoxicating leaf, the constant use of which drives its votaries at times almost to insanity—and in his place I had engaged the services of a Zulu Kaffir called Pete, recommended to me by my driver, Hendrick. The boy, little Hendrick, remained with me by his own desire; and I was glad to keep him, for he was a bright, intelligent, and yet wonderfully innocent-minded child. When he first came to me he used to amuse me by turning out of his blankets of a morning without a scrap of clothing on him, although the sharp wind might be blowing, and the hoar frost be lying thick on the ground, reserving his dressing arrangements until after he had lit the fire and set the kettle on to boil for early coffee; but by this time, he was beginning to think it incumbent upon him to put on his shirt before he performed these duties.

Another change had come o'er the spirit of my dream. I was now the possessor not only of a house in Pretoria, but of a small farm, about twenty-five miles from Pretoria, going the shortest way, and which carried with it the right of free grazing and water on the large farm of which it originally formed a part. The place was noted as being healthy for horses and sheep, and was an excellent stand for a Boer-store; and I got it for a price which even the Boers near considered cheap.

My load consisted principally of Kaffir goods, and I had a barrel of Cape brandy up as well. This speculation I had been recommended by many who knew about trading, and I had been asked for brandy so frequently by Boers, that I thought I would try it. So I took out a bottle licence. This reminds me of an absurd old magistrate who gave me the said licence, and who took me up very sharp for wanting a bottle and not a retail licence (I think that is the correct name for a licence to sell by the glass).

"I don't want to sell by the glass," said I.

"Oh! don't you?" quoth he; "but I am very much afraid you will." And he held up a long finger, and shook it and his head, in a manner that would have suggested to a bystander, that I already stood convicted of several similar offences.

"It is not probable," I remarked, "that I should like to have a lot of tipsy Kaffirs round my wagon." But up went the forefinger again, and with a terrible shake of the head he answered,—

"Well, mind, if I catch you at it, I shall fine you heavily—very heavily."

"I will give you permission to fine me as heavily as you like, when you catch me," said I, pocketing my licence; and I conveyed to my old friend, doubtless, the idea that I was a hardened sinner, up to all the dodges necessary to evade the law successfully.

There was another thing about this brandy which amused me. A friendly store-man at the store where I bought it, who had previously given me many little hints about trading, beckoned me aside when it was loaded up.

"When you get well out from amongst the Boers," he said—"for I understand you are going right in amongst the Kaffirs this time—just fill up the cask with water; the Kaffirs won't remark it. I wouldn't advise you to put tobacco into it; that I don't think right. But just fill up with water; it won't pay well enough if you don't."

I thanked him and departed.

This time I took my way through Buckonoo's kloof (I spell as pronounced in English), instead of through Derdepoort. It was a very pleasant change; the gorge, or kloof, with its craggy sides so thickly wooded that only here and there a bold mass of grey rock could be seen, jutting out at some curve of the river, or of the road that ran between them, looked quite delightful in the morning light; and I several times stopped to look at the pretty picture the waggon made, as, with its long team of oxen, it wound its way through the chequered sunlight and shadow. There were thousands of monkeys in this leafy retreat, and they hooted at us as we went by, not coming close, however, but affording an immense amount of excitement to the dogs and to little Hendrick, who was riding with me on Violin. On emerging from this gorge we came to several pretty farms; at one of them I was hospitably received by an old Dutchman and his family, who were in favour of English rule. They had a farm on the high-veldt, and used this farm only as a bush-veldt farm. I went along slowly, trading as I went, at the various places I had visited before, and at last got to Marullo-kop. The Engelsbergs seemed very much pleased to see me, and I met young De Plessis there. He had come over to have something done to a waggon of his, and had brought his wife and his youngest child with him. As I sat in the Engelsbergs' tent, waiting for the waggon to come up, the men—amongst whom, if I remember aright, was De Clerc—talked much of the Beeinkommste that had just been held, to discuss the advisability of starting Boer stores, the goods to be imported direct, so as to oust English traders from the Transvaal [. . .]. There was a doubt about whom they should import from. They said that the Americans and the Germans had made very liberal offers. My friends in the tent seemed to think that the American offer would be accepted. I had been listening to the men talking, while the women chatted about their babies and other domestic topics. I doubt whether they thought I understood much of what they were saying, so that there was a little hush of surprise when at this point I said "I think the plan you propose, or that has been proposed at your Beeinkommste, is a very good one, and you will, I dare say, get your things much cheaper than you now do; but I would advise any of you who may have any influence with the committee you speak of, to avoid dealing with the Americans; they are first-rate men of business, but they would be too sharp for you probably. I think it would be much safer for you to deal with the Germans." It was a great surprise to them, in more ways than one, to hear me say this; and some time after De Clerc asked me if I was born English. I said, "Yes, I am born English—at least an English subject; but I was born in Ireland, and my parents were both Irish." Upon which he said, "Ah!" as if he were making a note of it in his mind.

The next morning, as I was sitting by the waggon a number of girls of various ages came over, and sitting down, after they had made some purchases, talked to me. One of them, who seemed rather a nice girl, had bought a pair of gloves I remember, and she laid them on the grass between herself and her two little cousins. These two little girls bade me goodbye before she did, and, when she rose to go, she missed her gloves. She searched everywhere for them in vain. At last she said, "Oh, I remember; they were close to my cousins; they have taken them." And I saw the tears in her eyes.

"Well," said I, "then you can get them back; they will have found them amongst their things."

"Oh, no," she said simply; "you know of course they will keep them. That was why they went away so soon."

"Then tell their mother," I suggested rather indignantly, "and get them given back to you."

The girl almost laughed at my ignorance. "Why that would be of no use," she said. "She would never give them to me, even if she knew they were there" [. . . .]

When I reached the mission station I found that Mr. B—— had resigned his position as missionary, and was just removing to a farm at some distance, called Sandfontein. He came to see me at the waggon, but I did not go to the house, as I was very busy trading and had no time. Pete, my leader, distinguished himself by getting drunk on Kaffir beer while I was here, and sitting under the waggon the following day, loudly deploring his headache and general wretchedness, caused partly by the drink, and partly by the disgrace I kept him in.

My way now lay past some warm springs, of which there are several in Waterberg, to Makapan's-poort. On my way I once more passed the encampment of the De Clerc and young De Plessis, the size of which was increased by the addition of several tents and waggons belonging to Boers who had been encamped further along the river, but were now on their way from the bush-veldt to their farms on the ur-veldt or elsewhere. Amongst these Boers was old Mrs. Nell, who had tried to sell the bull to me.

The stories about lions being in the vicinity, and having killed horses and cattle, belonging in some cases to Boers whom I knew, were so numerous, and so well authenticated, that I thought it best to keep fires burning all night, and that we should sleep in a ring round the horses, leaving one boy to sleep by the fore-oxen. I saw Dandy again, and he knew me, and could with difficulty be got away from the waggon, but he was evidently well cared for and kindly treated. I must describe his master and his master's family. They are the best Boers I have come across. Young De Plessis himself—a man of about middle height, wiry, and full of energy, with bright laughing eyes, a merry mouth, and clustering hair, with a manner in accordance, bold and free, and with something pleasantly boy-like in his way of enjoying a joke or asking a favour—was known amongst his mates as a sure shot, a daring hunter, and a first-rate horseman; yet always ready to help his wife with the baby (she told me herself he always weaned the children for her), and withal a most diligent and energetic farmer. He was the only Boer I ever saw who groomed his horse regularly every day.

His wife was tall, and made on a large scale; but her every movement was graceful. Her face, with its regular features, large steady eyes, with long dark eyelashes and pencilled eyebrows, was a picture of serene cheerfulness, and the set of her well-shaped head on her finely-formed neck and bust was statuesque. I have seen her doing all sorts of little domestic work with the air of a Juno, except that Juno, according to Homer, never can have looked serene. She was always dressed neatly, with a fresh kerchief folded across her breast, and her hair was always tidy, her hands always clean, and she never seemed disturbed or hurried about anything. Her tent was a model of neatness, and her children never looked dirty.

The baby was a delightful baby, with big brown eyes and round cheeks; and it was always speckless. I am sure I don't know how she kept it so, but I never saw that infant otherwise than spotlessly clean from the top of its head to the tip of its little pink toe; and its garments always seemed to have been just put on. There were two older urchins—one a handsome dark-eyed fellow, as brown as a berry, and full of mischief; the other blue-eyed and shy, with a tendency to hold by his mother's apron and put his fingers in his mouth when in the presence of a stranger, but a pretty child. These youngsters were often superficially dirty, but one could always see their little white shirts peeping out at their collars and cuffs, and when, at meal times, they were told to wash before sitting down, a very little soap and water made them look refreshingly clean. I have described this family, not as a type of Boer families, but because it is the only Transvaal Boer family, amongst the many I have seen, of which all these nice things could be said, unless I except the Briets, and the Briets were rich, whereas young De Plessis was very poor. I dined one Sunday in the De Plessis' tent, and had a very nice dinner, of wild buck's meat and a sort of sweet suet pudding with cinnamon in it, served up with thick meat sauce. Several neighbours came in, and we were very merry. De Plessis and his friends were laughing over a "grand spree" they had had the night before, when, as a finish up, they had smeared each other's coats all over with fat. Some very distinguishable marks of the practical joke yet remained. Trade was good here, and I stayed for some time.

There was one man, of the name of Jan Smith, who was always coming to the waggon to beg me to sell him a "tot," and when I said I could not sell one, begging me to give him one. It was wonderful how these Boers would beg of me to infringe the law, and assure me that they would never tell of me, and that no trader minded adhering to it. I soon began to be sorry I had got brandy up, for, when they found that I would not sell them "tots," they would club together and buy a bottle, drink it in a surprisingly short time, and come back for more, until the whole encampment was several sheets in the wind. They were only gay and festive during the day, but at night I rather think they used to quarrel; and in order to get rid of the liquor, which I saw would prove a bother to me, I offered it to the whole encampment at cost price, and said I would trade it in cattle. They were much inclined to take it, but could not quite make up their minds as to how they would manage to bottle it off, and so, much to my regret, the thing fell through. [. . . The Boers try to get her to buy ostrich plumes they have illegally obtained.] De Clerc used often to come with other Boers to my waggon. He was an oldish man, but handsome in a rugged sort of way, was a bold hunter and a good horseman, and a leading man amongst the Waterberg Boers, being a fairly well-educated man for a Boer, and having held office under the Boer Government. He used often to talk politics to me, and always introduced me to his friends as an Irishwoman. Once one of the friends remarked that the Irish hated the English; upon which I told him that I did not, and that although I thought that in many ways the English Government had behaved badly to the Boers, yet that if ever it came to war I should take the English side. De Clerc said he understood my feeling; that he believed it was best for the country that the English should govern it; that England was a strong and rich country, and that the land would be more secure and more prosperous under her auspices than it would otherwise be; but that yet in his heart he felt sore about the English dominion. He went on to say that he always dissuaded his friends from any thoughts of fighting; that he meant to bring up his boy as a friend to the English; that he believed that fighting would only end in a complete overthrow of the Boers; but yet—and I could see his dark eyes flash under his shaggy brow—that, if there was fighting, his life and all he had should be thrown into the balance for his own race. "I quite understand that" I said; "it would be the same with me were I a Boer."

"But you are English, and of course if war comes you will go with your nation, as I with mine," he answered. [. . . Heckford is invited to a lion hunt that never occurs by her Boer friends; she leaves them to continue trading.] I was now approaching the last tent belonging to white men. After passing one of my old acquaintances near to the warm baths, I entered a country prettier than any I had traversed before. I rode along a wooded valley, skirting the hills that bounded it at one side. The scene was a mixture of wildness and resemblance to an English park. There were many very good trees, the bush was thick, and there was a sprinkling of tropical-looking and enormous cacti or cactus trees. One day I came on a group of Kaffirs on their way to the diamond fields, sitting under a spreading tree. I knew that I was near water—the horses were very thirsty—but I could not make out where the spring was; the course of the rivulet coming from it, was in parts dry, and in parts spread out into a half-marsh thickly overgrown with reeds. One of the men volunteered to show me the way. The spring was some distance from the spot, deep and clear, and Eclipse plunged into it eagerly.

"I have brought you to the spring," said the Kaffir, while I sat enjoying the enjoyment of my horse and little Hendrick and Dandy in the cool water. I took out a small piece of money to give him.

"I did not want any money," he said; "I merely said I had showed you the water." And he seemed quite satisfied with thanks. I afterwards gave him and his companions some brandy, and one man came forward after they had all drunk, and said they wished him to thank me very much. These were very raw Kaffirs, and could hardly speak anything but Kaffir, but they were wonderful in the matter of courtesy; for Kaffirs generally are either rude like monkeys, or like Boers—and the latter is a very bad and disagreeable form of rudeness, characterized by much staring, talking of and laughing at anything which may strike them as unusual in a stranger.

My last outspann by a white man's tent was on a beautiful evening, and the scene struck me very much. I emerged from a thick wood on a delicious greensward, almost like an ornamental lawn, interspersed with a few fine trees. The road wound through this, and it was bounded on one side by the thickly-wooded hills, on the other by the forest. A large herd of cattle were making their way to three white tents pitched on the border of this, and partially concealed by its foliage; and the last rays of the sun, as it sank behind the hills, were tinting all near objects with gold, while in the distance the hills of Makapan looked blue and misty. The family from these tents soon came to see me. Three of the men had been severely injured by fire. They had been hunting on the hills, and had set fire to the grass to hunt out the animals; but the wind suddenly rose, and, in rising, changed its direction, so that the fire hunted them out instead.

Early the next morning I passed the last white habitation; the owner was a woodcutter, and had pitched his tent under a superb tree, not with the intention of cutting it down, however. Close by I saw a very curious animal.

It was an enormous lizard, so large that it was like a little crocodile. It was close by the path when I saw it, and I frightened little Hendrick very much by riding up to it. He assured me that it had extraordinary power in its tail, and that if it struck Eclipse it would kill him. The little beast looked at me for a moment, then, slashing his long scaly tail in a most extraordinary manner, ran away with extreme agility, the tail vibrating from side to side all the time. I followed it on Eclipse, but it suddenly disappeared, I suppose down some hole. Our midday outspann was by the side of a rivulet, and in such thick bush that, no sooner were the oxen and horses loose, than they were lost to sight. It was said that there were lions close to this place, and thieving Kaffirs also, so I cautioned Pete and little Hendrick to keep the animals in sight, whilst Hendrick prepared the food. When it was prepared, and he went to call them to eat and make a fresh start, they were nowhere to be found, and neither were the animals, and it was some time before they came up. I had eaten, and was impatient to start, so I told them to up-saddle and inspann at once. I rode Dandy and led Eclipse this time, and I did not look specially at the latter until I had ridden a little way, then I saw he was sweated, which excited my suspicion. It was late when I reached Moer-drift, the place for outspanning. The valley here begins to narrow, and the hills of Makapan's-poort can be plainly seen; the valley itself is but little wooded, but the hills are covered with trees, and the effect is very pretty. I off-saddled, and it was not till almost dark that the waggon came up. Pete was running in front of it, and a glance showed me that he was quite drunk. The oxen were hardly outspanned when he fell down under the waggon and went fast asleep. I perceived also that little Hendrick was tipsy. I asked Hendrick how this was, and he told me that Pete had taken little Hendrick to a Kaffir kraal, instead of minding the animals at the last outspan, and had given him some of the beer upon which he himself had got tipsy. I said nothing about Eclipse, but I felt sure now that Pete had either ridden him, or hunted him very hard on Dandy. I called up little Hendrick and told him that I would give him something to make him remember that the after-consequences of drink were disagreeable, and ordered Hendrick to give him some good cuts with a reim [leather strap]; Pete had to be left till morning. In the early dawn I saw him arise, wrap a blanket round him, loose the oxen and take them off to graze. "He is trying to get into favour," thought I. I also heard little Hendrick laugh at him slyly for having been thrown by Eclipse—so I was quite sure about my affair now. The boys thought I was asleep, for I did not move.

I had breakfast, but no Pete appeared. At last I sent Hendrick on horseback to look for the oxen. He found them far off, but Pete was missing. However, I had no mind to wait for him, so inspanned and got on near to a settlement of Knopnase Kaffirs, where I outspanned and was trading with them when Mr. Pete slinked up. I was too busy to speak to him then, and presently inspanned to go on to Makapan's-poort.

It was a pretty ride, and when I got to the place itself I thought it a very pretty place. Right in the middle of the pass, a precipitous hill, crowned with Makapan's kraal, forms a sort of natural fortress. A small river (the Nile river, I think) winds round its base; trees of various sorts cluster round, and are scattered over it, and the ruins of a once large mission station, and the pomegranates, syringas, and other shrubs of the garden that used to be, add a charm to the scene. Numbers of women and children stared at me as I crossed the river with the two horses, and waited for the waggon to come up, for I did not know where to outspan. Hendrick could not talk the pure Makatees, spoken by these Kaffirs, sufficiently well to trust entirely to him, so I had taken a Kaffir from the mission station to act as interpreter and guide. This Kaffir's name was Nicholas, commonly called "Clas."

So soon as the waggon arrived, Clas showed me a pretty little dell at the foot of the hill, where we outspanned. I sent him to the kraal, with the present of a bottle of French brandy to Makapan, and a message that I wished to have his permission to trade with his tribe. And in return the chief sent me his thanks, and said that he was glad I had come, and would protect me.

Chapter 26

Makapan, or rather Clas Makapan, for the latter is only his surname or family name, is the son of a chief who, after a fearful massacre of the Boers, was at last reduced to submission by them. Clas was taken as hostage, and brought up in a Boer family. When his father died the Kaffirs determined to get the child back, and, fearful that the Boers would not give him willingly, they stole him one night, and having got him, made peace with the Boers by paying for him in cattle. One of the old Kaffirs told me that the little Clas had been very much frightened when he found himself a prisoner amongst the Kaffirs, and had cried and kicked to get away.

I soon found that unless I traded for corn, I should be able to do but little here, for the taxes were just being called for by the Government, and the Kaffirs were very much afraid of not having money to pay them in, as cattle were taken at a ridiculously low value for the amount, if the cash was not there when called for. I determined therefore to trade for mealeas and Kaffir corn, as I got them very cheap, and they were likely to fetch a good price in Pretoria. When I made this intention known, the Kaffirs came in swarms, the men walking in front, followed by the women and girls, bearing on their heads baskets filled with grain. There were hundreds assembled, between those who came to trade and those who came to look on; it was hard to prevent their crowding too close to the waggon, and many a time had Pete to rush at the ever-narrowing circle formed round it, with a big whip to keep the intruders off.

It takes a long time trading for grain, for the grain has all to be measured off into sacks, or sometimes by buckets-full; besides this, one has to examine its quality. The din of all these savages, talking, yelling, laughing, was deafening, and at the end of a day's work, which lasted without intermission from seven o'clock in the morning until the same hour in the evening, I was not only tired in body, but I felt nearly mad. This lasted several days. It was amusing, however, and I had a good opportunity of observing the Kaffir in his natural state. The women were dressed much like those at the Eland river, except that they had two long, thin pieces of leather hanging from their girdles behind like tails. These were ornamented with beads, brass or white buttons, &c., according to the taste or means of the wearer, and the young ladies were in the habit of holding one of these appendages in one hand and switching it about. I may here remark that Makatees young ladies are as fond of flirting as any other young ladies I have had the pleasure of studying. The girls were rather graceful, and had a way of entwining their arms round each other and falling into groups, which was absolutely artistic. I remember one group which seemed to have arranged itself with a consciousness of "The Graces." These three young ladies had rubbed their bodies and their hair or wool with a mixture of fat and red earth which, although it does not sound nice, was by no means unbecoming. Mother's darlings were also to be distinguished from urchins who were not darlings, by the former being reddish-brown and the latter of a natural black colour. The girls wore a variety of ornaments, some very prettily made—of grass and wire, also of beads. A disease much resembling scabies[77]—called, I believe, Kaffir-pock—was very prevalent at Makapan's-poort, and I observed that the persons of those who rubbed themselves, or were rubbed by their fond mammas, with the unguent I have described, had escaped it.

The men wore all sorts of costumes. Some of the aristocracy of the place wore European dress, others skins curiously sewn together and prepared, others blankets, others girdles fringed with the tails of wild cats, others again a shirt, sometimes tied by its sleeves round the neck, sometimes properly worn; while many had just a rag or a little strip of soft leather round the loins. Many had their wool ornamented with little rosettes made of the tail of the rock rabbit, or by meer-cats' tails, tied on like tassels. I often saw the men going out hunting, armed with assegai and tomahawk, and often with a rifle. They would start off early in the morning, whooping and dancing, with a troop of dogs after them.

One day I noticed a girl who was quite pretty, and also modest-looking, in the crowd that surrounded me, but at a little distance. I took aim at her with a small circular looking glass, and successfully. She was delighted when she saw herself, but after giving me one beaming smile, she turned shy, and ran away.

From that moment I had no peace. The girls were not so bad as the women, who had no excuse, for they were all ugly. One old wretch who, although she had been brought up amongst the Boers for years, and had been accustomed to dress, now wore a fringed girdle and a skin over her shoulders, pestered me every day for a glass. At last I said, "You ask me why I gave that young woman one, and won't give you one? That is easily answered. She is pretty, and has some use for a looking glass; whereas you are old, and if you had one, would have nothing pretty to see if you looked in it: when I was young I often looked in the glass, but I don't now: looking glasses are for young people."

How that woman laughed and clapped her hands, and laughed again. Then she called several of her friends, and told them; and they cried out, "True! true!" and laughed until I began to feel that I had perpetrated a wonderful witticism. They were, however, quite as anxious to get a peep into a looking glass afterwards as before, though no elderly female ever asked me for a glass again as a present.

I had almost forgotten to tell about Pete.

On the evening of our arrival at Makapan's-poort, I went over to the campfire where the boys were sitting, although it was very warm, and the moonlight was as bright as day, and said, "Pete, this is your second offence; and you made it worse by attempting to ride my horse without my permission; now remember, I never speak three times; the third offence I punish; and as I object to punishing either a servant or an animal, I never punish either, unless I give them something they are not likely to forget in a hurry." Pete stared hard at me, and said, "Yes, missus;" and I walked off. I may here remark that although I have always found the giving of a certain grace a good plan with European servants, I have found it a bad plan with African servants. I think personally that they are too much like animals to be treated in this way, and that the best way to manage them is to punish severely the first offence (I mean, of course, an offence whose culpability they understand) just as one does with an animal one has to train. At the time of which I am now writing, however, although I greatly doubted whether a Kaffir ought to be treated otherwise than as an animal, I thought it right to give him the benefit of the doubt.

The heat even at night was now very great; and the irritation caused by the biting and crawling over one of microscopical ticks was very great. I found it difficult to sleep at night, and I have often got up and walked about in the moonlight, or watched the sleeping horses lying comfortably by the waggon, and sometimes giving little ghostly neighs in their sleep that testified to their dreaming. I never slept in the tent, for I was always afraid of some robbery going on, and once my suspicions were aroused by missing Pete from where he ought to have been sleeping. He turned up shortly after, however, so I thought no more about it, as I noticed nothing else remarkable.

A serious difficulty now began to claim my attention. I had been led to believe that I should be able to get meal from some of the Boer houses in Waterberg (at the other side of the mission station), but I had not been able to procure any, and in consequence of finding very little game and no meat towards and at Makapan's-poort, the meal I had was beginning to run short. I could buy but very little milk; and the coffee was getting low. I determined to start for Pretoria, but deferred my departure a little in order to be present at a grand feast which Makapan was about to give. He was to "make rain" for his clan, and there was to be a grand dance.

Although brought up amongst the Boers, Makapan has not adopted any substitute for the superstition of his father and his tribe, and he has a pronounced objection to missionaries. He came to pay me a visit the day before this feast. He is a big man, with coarse features. He was dressed in a short coat, riding breeches, gaiters and boots, and a felt hat. Of course I gave him a "tot;" and gave one also to his head-man, called "Sturman," who was dressed like himself. He said he hoped I would visit him before I left the place; that he had heard that I said that I would not visit Makapan before Makapan visited me, and that now Makapan had come. I said I would go to his kraal the next day. I was greatly surprised to see how unceremoniously his subjects, and even my driver Hendrick, were allowed to treat him, and felt that it was difficult to know how to treat as a chief, a man who allowed my driver to shake hands with him; however, I promised to go, and then Makapan asked for another tot. I have heard that such chiefs as Cetawayo and Sekocooni[78] are approached by their subjects in an abject posture, and are never spoken to by them unless permission has been given. I can only suppose that chiefs like Makapan, who have adopted European costume, are by degrees losing the consideration of their subjects.

The morning of the great feast day broke splendidly, and, before the sun was up, groups of young warriors, dressed in their best, came past my encampment on their way to the chief's kraal. I was no sooner dressed than I ordered the horses to be saddled, and taking Clas as my companion, started for the kraal. I had been told that one could ride up, and indeed I had seen that Makapan and his suite had ridden both up and down. After turning a little round the hill we began the stony ascent, through a maze of little Kaffir huts, from which the children came forth yelling, at the sight of me, followed by their mothers, some trying to stop their clamorous vociferations, while others did their utmost to add to the din. At last, after a desperate scramble, which landed me on a shelving piece of rock with boulder after boulder rising above it, I declined to endanger the horses' feet any longer, and dismounting, told Clas he must lead the horses back, and give them in charge to some decent Kaffir until his and my return. At this moment, however, I saw Makapan descending from his eyrie to greet me, with a staff in his hand, which he offered to me to assist me in climbing. Having passed within the low wall that bounds his kraal, I found myself in a labyrinth of huts, each with an enclosed yard attached, and traversed by narrow paths. Makapan led me past a large stockade, and through various enclosures, each with a hut in it (his harem, or whatever it may be called in Kaffir), to his own house, a cottage built of bricks, and with a verandah in front. He took me into his bedroom (the house had only two rooms, I think) and asked me to be seated.

The dark and dirty room was furnished with two or three chairs, a little table, and a common bedstead, on which were thrown a mattress, some gaudy blankets, and a "caross," or large mat made of skins curiously stitched together, and with the hair left on. He asked me if I would have coffee, and brought me some in a cup; then, after talking about various things, he said he hoped that I would make him a present of a very handsome rug I had for sale. I did not like to refuse, but I said I thought he ought to make me a present too; he said he would do so gladly, and sent one of his officers to get me an ostrich feather—a very indifferent specimen. I then asked him if I might attend the feast that he was about to give that day. He seemed much pleased at this proposal, and said that I should be surprised at seeing what swarms of warriors would be there. He also told me that he should kill an ox in the course of the day, and that he would send me some of the meat; this, for aforesaid reasons, I was very glad to hear. He asked me several times whether I was not surprised to see such a large place as his kraal; whether I did not think it very strong; and told me that I should be surprised at the number of his warriors. Before I went away he asked me if I would not have something to eat, but this I declined. As he was escorting me to my horses, we met a singular-looking old Kaffir carrying herbs. Makapan said, laughing, "That is my doctor, and those are his medicines; he will help me to make medicines for my Kaffirs today." He seemed to think the whole thing rather amusing; and indeed I doubt whether he was not aware, as I was, of the absurdity of his conjuring away diseases and conjuring up rain.

Chapter 27

It was still early when I got back to the waggon. The dance was not to begin till noon—a curious time, by-the-way, for a dance, for the heat was very great. In the meantime I had ample opportunities of observing the different costumes of the savages, numbers of whom came over to talk to my boys before taking their way up the hillside to the kraal. Some of the young men presented a very picturesque appearance. Their loins were girt with leathern girdles, fringed with magnificent cats'-tails, their heads were decorated with rosettes and tassels; a warhorn—beautifully and curiously worked in brass, copper, or tin wire, sometimes all three together—was hung round their necks and thrown behind them; a bright coloured scarf thrown over one shoulder and passed under the opposite arm; their legs were covered with buskins made from the white skin from under the belly of a buck, and each carried an assegai, often ornamented with wire embroidery on the handle, a short club, also ornamented, a tomahawk or a rifle, or sometimes an assortment of these different articles. At a little before twelve I took Clas with me, and began the ascent of the hill. I went by a different way this time, one which led me in and out of rocks and boulders, overhung by trees, a scrambling, delightful way, giving one pretty glimpses of the valley and of the Kaffir huts clustering at the base of the hill. Every now and then some of Makapan's warriors would rush by me with a leap and a bound, and as they scaled the hill rapidly I could hear their yell and the discharge of their rifles as a salute to the chief's stockade as they entered it. Groups of girls also passed me, their arms intertwined, chattering and laughing until they saw me, when they would stare for a minute and then go on [. . .].

Makapan met me at the entrance of the stockade, and spoke to me, but I could not hear what he said for the din. Lining the stockade was a dense mass of women and children, talking, laughing, singing, yelling, and clapping their hands. Makapan made way for me to the front ranks and got me a chair. Just opposite to me there was a crowd of men, some dressed as I have described, some with bright coloured shirts, some with a waistcoat and a girdle of cats'-tails, some with only a woollen comforter crossed over their breasts, and a rag round their loins as their holiday costume; others again in half-European dress, and others painted, some to represent skeletons, some merely daubed with colour, but all armed. Ever and anon one or more of these would rush into the area of the stockade with a yell, and dancing the war dance, then enact some scene of warfare, casting himself on the ground, looking around cautiously, taking aim, firing, then perhaps tomahawking or assegaing his imaginary foe with such savage exultation that it made my blood curdle, while the women clapped their hands, yelled, and even—sometimes becoming over-excited—rushed into the arena and did a frantic war dance. Then after each exhibition there would be a race of a group of girls from one side to the other, before the next performer stepped forth, evidently to compare notes with friends as to the relative merits of the dancers. Four men particularly attracted my attention, not by their costumes, but by their good acting. One of these acted alone. His play was that he was defending the stockade from enemies who were creeping up through the mass of rock and tree below. He would look over the stockade, taking cover carefully, peer hither and thither, then swiftly level his rifle, and fire. He always killed his man, and then the haughty way in which he would throw up his arm as he turned on his heel and pretended to reload (for I conclude they were firing blank cartridge) was more expressive of defiance and satisfaction than any war dance. The other three acted together. They were defending themselves from enemies who were close around them, but their imagination had transformed the stockade into brushwood, the sand that strewed it into long grass. I then, for the first time, saw what we have all read of at some time, I suppose, in some novel about the North American Indians—I mean the snake-like movement of a savage as he draws near his victim. These three savages darted into the arena and looked cautiously round, then suddenly dropped on the ground, their every muscle tense, their eyes strained; suddenly one raising himself a little, appeared to catch a glimpse of something, his eyes literally seemed to start from their sockets, and as he grasped his comrade's arm with one hand, and pointed with the other towards some imaginary object, he trembled with excitement; then each grasping his arms they all moved—how, I really cannot say—they did not rise from the ground, they wriggled quickly along it like snakes; in longish grass all that one would have seen would have been a slight waving; now they were close to the stockade; to bound up, fire, and fall prostrate once more was the work of a moment. These men were actors by nature. Sometimes their fire told, sometimes it did not; sometimes an enemy would fall near them, and they would tomahawk or assegai him with savage delight, but with no waste of time; at last one of them was wounded; he crawled painfully back, and was helped by his comrades; and that ended their play. But numbers now were rushing forward; the arena was a mass of yelling, whooping savages [. . .].

Just then Makapan asked me to excuse him, he said he had a dog of a friend of his under his charge, that he had just heard it had broken loose, that no one could catch it but he, and that he must go and do so. As he was turning away, my attention was suddenly arrested by seeing a gentleman, apparently an Englishman, step from the crowd and speak to him. Makapan shook hands with him, and clapped him on the shoulder, then turned, and introduced him to me as Mr. N——. He was a trader coming down from far up country with oxen, cows, and sheep, which he had traded. He was an Austrian, not an Englishman, and an educated, gentlemanly man—a wonderful person to meet in this out-of-the-way part, of the world.

As Makapan left me he clapped his acquaintance once more on the shoulder, and I blessed my stars that I was a woman, for I suppose it was owing to this fact that Makapan did not testify his friendly feelings to me in the same manner. I do not remember what became of Mr. N——, for my attention was occupied with the savages; I imagine he went away. Not long after, one of the men, painted like a skeleton, made a set at me: first he glared at me till he caught my eye; then he took me as his imaginary foe, and ended by bringing his assegai within half an inch of my nose. I think he was disappointed that I did not scream. Another savage thought he would try whether I should be proof against a rifle brought into close proximity with my head; finding that I did not faint, he turned it towards a group of girls, who screamed loudly enough to satisfy any one [. . .].

Shortly after this, the sun being very hot, the odours from the crowd oppressive, and considerable monotony prevailing in the performances, I rose to depart, when the woman who had asked me for the looking glass, and who could speak Boer dialect, told me I ought to remain until Makapan led his guard, the flower of his warriors, into the stockade; that, she said, would be a very splendid sight. I waited accordingly. Presently there was a lull amongst the savages, and the crowd opening nearly opposite to where I sat, a band of fine-looking Kaffirs, all be-cattailed, armed to the teeth, and with their long shields slung on their arms, advanced, dancing their slow war dance, singing the accompanying war song, and rattling their assegais against their shields. There is a peculiarity about this dance and song. I had seen and heard them once before, performed by some Kaffir levies on their way to the Zulu war. The dancers move very slightly, and their song is a chant more than a song, but it gives one the creeps to see and hear it; it looks like the movement of men held in a leash, impatient for it to be slipped; and it sounds so threatening, like the muttering of a storm: one can imagine the yell that would burst forth if the leash were slipped and the bloodhounds let loose. They advanced thus into the middle of the arena, a hundred men perhaps; then opening their ranks Makapan and Sturman jumped forth from their centre. Oh! such a pair! Makapan was carefully attired in a gentleman's morning wrapper—brown, edged with red—and the girdle with its tassels bobbed up and down behind him; under this he had a riding suit and heavy boots with gaiters; on his head was a white French hat, very narrow in the brim and well turned up, with three ostrich feathers stuck in it, all pointing straight forward; a kyrie (or short club) in his hand, completed his "get up," and in this attire he did the clumsiest "breakdown" I have ever witnessed, dancing opposite to his admiring subjects, and followed by his savage guard, who I think must have despised their leader.

Sturman, in the meantime, dressed in a riding costume, booted and gaitered, with a pith helmet on his head, a red handkerchief round his throat, and a kyrie in his hand, did a very frantic breakdown indeed—so frantic, that it made him very hot; so he pulled off his neckerchief and threw it aside, then flung away his helmet; and the last that I saw of Mr. Sturman in the arena, just as I left the stockade, was that his attire had diminished to his shirt and breeches—the former article of dress having been freed from its confinement in the latter. The breakdown was as frantic as ever [. . .].

As I was going down the hill I met some women coming up, and they spoke to Clas. I asked him what they had said, and he hesitated. This of course made me inquisitive, so I pressed the point. Then he told me that these women had said that the feast was not yet ended; that as a finale an ox was to be killed; that one of its fore legs and one of its hind legs were to be hacked off at the hip and shoulder, and that then it was to be goaded until it died. This was to be the finale of the scene of which I had been a spectator. This was to be the culminating-point of the entertainment I had participated in—the *bonne-bouche*[79] reserved for the people I had spoken to in friendliness!

I could not attempt to describe my feelings. To do Clas justice he expressed utter horror of the hideous idea. He said he had learnt better things since he knew the Christian religion—that he knew it was a sin to torture an animal; and although I am certain missionaries have done a great deal of harm in some ways in Africa, if they only did this one piece of good, taught but this one lesson—they have certainly done one great work.

When I reached my encampment I found a good many Kaffirs assembled talking to my boys, many of whom understood Boer dialect. I told Hendrick what I had heard.

"Mind," said I, "if Makapan sends me any beef as he said he would, send it back, and say that we English do not eat the meat of an animal that has been tortured to death, or let it be eaten by our servants; that we would rather starve than encourage such an atrocity as he allows to be committed in his kraal."

Hendrick remonstrated in a low voice, to the effect that it was not prudent to offend Makapan; but I was too much disgusted with the savage and his savages to care; and, as from Hendrick's remarks I became aware that the Kaffirs understood what I was saying, I said something stronger for their benefit. The result of this was that Makapan sent me some goat's meat, and a message to the effect that not only was it not his custom to kill oxen as above described, but that he had killed no ox at all on this occasion—only a goat. I knew this was a lie told to calm me down, and I said so to Sturman who brought the message. As to the meat, I let the boys eat it, and contented myself with some fat pork I had bought the day before—and horrible greasy stuff it was.

Chapter 28

I had traded too much corn to take on one waggon, but I heard that I could get a waggon and oxen at the Mission Station to bring it up to Pretoria for me. I bought several large closed baskets of a curious manufacture special to the Kaffirs, to store what I had to leave behind me in, and Makapan promised to take care of it for me. He and Mapeela, a greater chief than Makapan, who came to visit him, rode down to my waggon the next day. Makapan wanted me to lend him one of my horses, but I told him I never lent my horses. The chiefs and Hendrick had a shooting-match with their rifles and my rifle for a bottle of brandy; Hendrick, not I, to stand the brandy. I think Mapeela won; I do not quite remember whether it was he or Makapan. I left them to their own devices, as they thought fit to let my driver enter into competition with them. Mapeela pretended not to be able to understand Boer dialect, but he could both understand and speak it.

Hendrick informed me that he wished to buy Eclipse; I could see in his eye that he coveted the horse as he looked at him; but whether he offered a hundred pounds for him as Hendrick said, I do not know, for I refused any offer that he might make. I fancy his offer was a high one, for he looked surprised at my refusal. At that moment I admitted distinctly to myself that trading was not my forte. Fancy a "Smouse" refusing to make eighty pounds clear profit! After this I found that it was a standing joke amongst Boers I passed, that I would not sell Eclipse for any money. I think they somehow respected me for it, probably because it gave them an idea that I was very rich—I don't think it could be for any other reason. Thinking of Eclipse, I was very near forgetting to describe Mapeela. He is a big, sensual, and violent-looking man. He was dressed in a riding suit and a white French hat; wore his waistcoat a little open, and showed a white shirt; had a necktie and a pin in it, white cuffs, and a ring on his finger. He affected more airs and graces than Makapan, and I liked him less.

And now, before leaving Makapan, I must record two things: one, that it struck me that Hendrick was a little afraid of these wild Kaffirs; and secondly, that my brandy gave me a great deal of trouble. The difficulty I had to prevent myself being forced into doing what I had said I would not do, was a constant worry. It was impossible to sell by the bottle, for the good reason that my purchasers had no bottles, or at least very few. They had old tins that had once had paraffin in them, and old oil tins, and tin mugs, and little and big gourds hollowed out, and sometimes they had small medicine bottles, or old sauce bottles. Then they would worry me perpetually to sell them sixpence worth of brandy; but this I always refused to do; and I used to hunt them away from the waggon when they wanted to drink brandy there.

"We won't tell" they used to say. Of course I knew that. "Every trader sells us 'tots'—what is the law here?" they would say. Of course I knew that too. One old gentleman, after vainly begging me to sell him a sixpenny "tot," paused, then said, "I want to make you a present," and offered me a sixpence. This is a common way of evading the law; you don't sell, you accept, and give a present! I astonished the old gentleman by dismissing him summarily. He was a curious specimen. He had been brought up amongst the Boers, had lived amongst them and dressed like them for years, and now he was accustomed to walk about in the most outrageously light costume, not from poverty but from choice.

The day I left Makapan's-poort, as I was crossing the stream after the waggon, which had gone a little ahead, I heard horses' hoofs coming rapidly after me. The riders were Makapan and an attendant bearing an empty paraffin tin. He wanted another pull at the brandy! He got it; shook hands with Hendrick and Clas, then put out his paw to me, as Mapeela had done the day before. That affair about the ox made me extremely dislike to touch the savage; but one can hardly refuse to give a man one's hand when one has voluntarily gone into his territory; so I held out mine, which he shook heartily; and turning our horses we cantered away in opposite directions.

The bush-veldt was now a desert, all the Boers had treked to their farms. It was getting late in the season, the weather was very hot—so hot that it was impossible to trek in the middle of the day. At noon one lay under a bush, or under the waggon if one could not get a leafy bush (and most of the bushes are thorn and don't give much shade), and panted. Under these circumstances to be reduced to eat rice and pig's fat, and drink tea without milk, for breakfast, luncheon and dinner, is the reverse of agreeable, but there was nothing else to eat.

One morning as I was riding in front of the waggon I saw Mr. N—— outspanned and having early coffee. I rode over, and as I did so a young zebra frisked up to Eclipse, and turned up his pretty little nose at him with a vicious grin, which affected Eclipse's nerves so much that he pretended he was going to rear. Mr. N—— asked me to dismount, and while he was giving me some coffee the zebra tried to upset the sugar bowl, and being hunted away, watched his opportunity, kicked the little table over, and having broken some crockery, and sent the sugar bowl flying, ate up the sugar, and then trotted up to his master in a perfectly artless way, and rubbed his taper white nose on that gentleman's coat. Mr. N—— had a young leopard there who excited Roughy's curiosity, and who nearly caught hold of Roughy's tail, to the great discomfiture of the latter.

A little farther on we met a Boer, going, I think, to the wood bush. Hendrick managed to get some Boer biscuits from this man, who came over afterwards to my waggon, and to whom, at his request, I gave some pig's fat. He, and a friend who was with him, had not tasted anything but biscuits for several days, so the fat was a luxury to them, and the biscuits were a luxury to me.

A little farther on Mr. N—— picked me up. He wanted to buy some Kaffir corn and came to my waggon. His zebra came with him, and thought he would like to taste the corn as it was being measured out; so he put his head in the sack and twirled round and round, with his head representing a pivot, kicking the whole time until he gratified his fancy. He kicked even at his master, whose feelings were so hurt that he asked for the whip. [. . . There is trouble with Pete; he goes off without permission; Hendrick and Pete fight. Heckford forces them to stop, but suspects Pete of mischief.] The next morning I had business at a farm lying at some little distance. Just as I was saddling, the Boer whose waggon had been outspanned near mine asked me to sell him two bottles of brandy. I drew the brandy for him, and mounted my horse. Now I always carried the key of the tap of the brandy cask and the key of the waggon-box in a leather pocket on a broad belt which I wore day and night, and it was so much my habit to put my finger in this pocket every time I mounted, to see that all was safe, that it had become purely a mechanical movement. I cannot absolutely remember whether I did this or not on that occasion, but I have little doubt that

I did. I rode to and from the farm pretty sharply, for I was in a hurry to get back to the waggon. When I got back I found the keys were not in my pocket. I looked everywhere for them fruitlessly, but at last I discovered that the stitching of the leather to the belt had given way in one part, and although it would have been difficult for the keys to slip through, still I had ridden at a very sharp canter, and it was possible. This was vexatious, but it could not be helped.

I started the next day for Pretoria, taking the direct Waterberg transport road. I found that I could not get a waggon to return for the corn left at Makapan's-poort, and I had only to make up my mind to return for it from Pretoria, after selling what I had up. I started the waggon, and rode over to Sandfontein myself to bid goodbye to Mr. and Mrs. B———. After having no one to talk to except Boers for a long time, it is refreshing to get amongst such people as the B———s. I remained to dinner, and then delayed, talking and thinking very little of the time, until the rays of the setting sun shone into my eyes through the window, and awakened me to the fact that I had a long ride across country before me, and a country that I did not know into the bargain, and that I had not an hour of daylight, or even twilight to count on. I was off as soon as possible. I knew that I had to keep in towards the Waterberg hills, until I came to a road running close to their base through thick high bush. The wind had become very high, and there were heavy clouds gathering swiftly. I rode as fast as I could, but it is not easy to ride very fast over a veldt full of holes, covered with long grass, and thickly studded in many parts with little thorn bushes; besides, it was soon pitch dark. However, I got the road, and, soon after crossing a stream, I saw a light which I knew must be in the farmhouse of Jan Steen, near which my waggon was to outspann. After a few minutes more I was greeted by Hendrick and Pete. The campfire was made in a hollow of the ground to try to keep the wind off, but it was blowing a hurricane now, and the fire had become so disorderly that cooking was not to be attempted, and Hendrick had cooked and kept my supper for me in the house of an old Kaffir "Swartboy," Clas's father, and a retainer of De Clerc's and De Plessis, whose houses were quite close to Jan Steen's. Young De Plessis came over to the waggon, and asked me to sleep in his house but I felt too anxious about the waggon; besides that, in such a storm, the horses, or at least Eclipse, were likely to get frightened, and to listen to reason from me alone. So I slept close to the waggon under an enormous tree, and sheltered by its trunk. Behind it I could not sleep, the sand was driving so furiously before the wind. During the night the dogs seemed restless, but I could neither hear nor see anything. To say the truth the wind roared so much, and the darkness was so dense, that it would have been strange if I could

The next day it was evident that rain was near—heavy rain too. The Boers were very unhappy about my having lost the key of the tap, because I could not get them any brandy. They tried to put an old tap which had a key into the barrel, but it did not work. Then they showed me a way of displacing the tap, drawing off a bucket of brandy, and replacing it without its appearing to have been removed; and this suggested certain novel ideas to me. They got their brandy, however, and were happy. There was a perpetual trotting backwards and forwards from their cottages to the waggon. A Boer or Boeress delights in buying by driblets, thus spinning out the amusement.

On one of these occasions I asked De Clerc if he could sell me a sheep. He said he would consult his wife. After a time he came back, and said that sheep were scarce, but as he regarded me as a friend, he would let me have one for a pound; and of course I had to give him the pound, which he pocketed, assuring me all the while that if his father had not taught him that he ought to help travellers he would not have let me have the sheep at all. He then asked me to give him a "tot," but as I found that the giving of "tots" was a very losing concern, I declined. He looked very angry.

"Well," said he, "it is of no consequence. I have plenty of money to buy with; but if you do not help others you cannot expect others to help you. Who can tell? a little act of kindness done to me might pay you in the long-run," &c., &c.

He evidently wished me to see the giving of "tots" in the light of a Christian duty.

"Now," he went on, "I let you have that sheep."

This was rather too much.

"I think, Mr. De Clerc," said I very politely, "you forget that I let you have that hat for nothing, for you did not even take me to the lion hunt,[80] and all because you said you had no money, but wanted it very badly."

The old fellow collapsed at once.

"You are right," he said, looking very sheepish. "Let us talk no more about it. I will buy a bottle of brandy."

He did so.

"Now," said he, "let us drink to our friendship."

"I will pledge you in water, if that will do," said I. So we pledged each other. [. . . A long discussion of the illegally obtained ostrich plumes that Heckford refused to buy follows.] On returning late from this farm I missed Pete, and on asking where he was, I heard that he had left the oxen committed to his care to stray where they would, and had disappeared. Now at this time of the year a plant grows in certain parts of the feldt which is poisonous to oxen, and I was very much displeased. He did not come back either that night or the next morning. On cross-questioning little Hendrick, he said that he had heard Pete's voice in a large Kaffir kraal which was on Jan Steen's farm. I felt sure that he wanted to hide away until I had gone, being afraid of punishment, so I went to the magistrate I have mentioned above, and requested that Pete might be caught and punished. Two Kaffirs were despatched secretly to the kraal to catch him; in the meantime I looked at some oxen, and arranged to buy them. The magistrate was at De Clere's house paying a visit, and two of the oxen were his. Presently there was a general stir noticeable among the Kaffirs hanging about the place, and I knew that Pete was coming—and the next minute I saw him running, with his hands tied behind him, in front of the two Kaffirs who had been sent for him. I felt I was in for it now. I had said that this man was to have twenty-five lashes the next time he offended, and he had offended very grossly; of course, he must have them, but it was the first time I had ever seen a man flogged. The instant that Pete reached the waggon, looking like a hunted baboon, Hendrick flew at him, tripped him up, and had him tied to the disselboom by his wrists in a twinkling of the eye. The demon in the man was loose, he looked as if he would have liked to tear Pete to pieces, and he scowled at me when I made him untie the prisoner, and told him to wait until the magistrate should come. In the meantime I explained to Pete that he was going to get his twenty-five lashes all the same. How that fellow did grovel to me, to be sure! How he called me his dear missus! his good, kind missus! How abjectly he twisted himself about before me! At last he started the happy thought that he would pay a fine to me, which was absurd on the face of it; for he had to my knowledge no money, having drawn on his wages for clothing until all I owed him was about four shillings. In the meantime the magistrate and the other Boers, besides a crowd of Kaffirs, had arrived on the scene of action. Jan Steen, a funny-looking man with a crumpled up face, bristling black hair, and bead-like eyes, looked like a weasel that has caught sight of a rat; De Clerc had a bloodthirsty look about him, and gloated hungrily on Pete; even Willem De Plessis looked excited. The magistrate alone was calm. He began to examine Pete, and asked him whether he had any complaint against me. Pete said, "No; never have I had such a good mistress; I eat the same food that she does; and even the other evening she gave up some of her own dinner to me because she thought I had not had enough."

The men sent to fetch him deposed that they had found him in the kraal, and that he had pulled out a knife and resisted fiercely until they tied his hands. Of his repeated offences there could be no doubt; it only remained to be decided what his punishment was to be.

"Twenty-five lashes," said the magistrate.

There was an eager movement amongst the Dutch; Jan Steen seized him.

"Sir! sir!" cried Pete; "I will pay—I will pay."

"Stop," said the magistrate; "what did you say, that you will pay?"

"I will pay three pounds," cried Pete.

"Don't let him! off with him! flog him!" snarled the assembled Boers.

"He can't pay," said I, "for he has no money."

"This man will lend me money," cried Pete, pointing to a Kaffir, who that very morning had assured me that he had no money and wanted me to let him have a pair of boots on credit.

"Stay," said the magistrate, "by law, Pete, if you can pay three pounds you can escape the flogging."

The Boers were furious, and between them and the Kaffirs, all of whom were talking at the top of their voices, it was very difficult to make my voice heard.

"Have I, as Pete's employer, any voice in this matter?" asked I.

"Of course you have," shouted the Boers; "flog him!"

"But have I by law?" I asked again.

The magistrate hesitated, then said,—

"Yes; you can insist on his being flogged if you choose."

"Then," said I, "I do insist."

"I daresay he will be better in future," said the poor magistrate, whilst the assembled Boers scowled at him.

"I don't think he is likely to be improved by finding that I don't carry out my threat, or by another man paying three pounds to get him off," said I; "you have said I can choose his punishment, and I choose twenty-five lashes; the quicker he gets it, the quicker this painful scene will be over."

They were round him in a minute those Boers and Hendrick, like hounds round a fox. They tripped him up, they pulled him about and yelped over him. Jan Steen was the foremost. It was a disgusting spectacle.

"Look here," cried I, in a rage, "if you don't leave that man alone I'll send every one of you away from my waggon; he is to be punished—not tortured; stand back all of you."

A very cool speech, as it struck me afterwards, considering that my waggon was outspanned on these men's ground, but they stood back. He got his five-and-twenty. I waited to see him get up before I made up my mind as to whether I would keep him in my service or not; as he stood up, he turned savagely to me,—

"Thank you, missis," he said, "give me something to drink; I am almost dead."

He had not had a severe beating by any means, but his rage was almost killing him I could see.

"Give him some water quickly," I said, but he dashed it from him.

"I want brandy, brandy," he said hoarsely, and then in Zulu he said, what I understood (and rightly) to be, that he would complain of me in Pretoria, which under the circumstances was of course absurd.

I took the money I owed him out of my purse and gave it to him.

"I may stop [stay], may I not, missus?" he said.

He was cooling rapidly.

"No," I said, "you have had your punishment and been insolent—now go," and he went.

I was sitting by the waggon in the evening, at the campfire, little Hendrick and a few Kaffirs from the kraal were squatted chatting. They were talking Boer dialect, and as I sat apart from them they probably, if they remembered that I was there at all, thought I could not understand them. A little time before I should not have understood their gabble. One man was telling how Pete had bought a goat, and some fowls, and how he had seen him pull a handful of sovereigns out of his pocket. I let the fellow go on until he changed his subject; then I called to him and asked him to repeat what he had said about

Pete. He instantly shuffled, but as I told him that I had understood what he had said at the fire, he repeated it all correctly to me. I then sent him back to the others, got out my account book, and examined my money. It was all quite correct—the inference therefore was, that Pete had been robbing the waggon, and selling. I knew that he had no money honestly come by, and this discovery only corroborated a suspicion I had conceived when his friend offered to pay three pounds for him. I said nothing, but the next morning, instead of starting, I told what I had heard to the magistrate, and he agreed that Pete should be caught again and examined. The Kaffirs said they were afraid to go to catch him, and the gentle magistrate was obliged to ask me to bribe to the extent of half-a-crown each if they brought him; to this I agreed.

This time there was a grand conclave in Jan Steen's cottage. [. . .] After a sitting of several hours, it was made evident that Pete had stolen articles from my waggon, and had disposed of them to the Kaffirs, and had afterwards treated them and been treated in return with brandy bought from me, and not only this, but at the very time that we were searching for Pete gold had been brought to Jan Steen by a Kaffir of his own, to be changed into silver, the money being brought from and returned to Pete. [. . .] In the meantime, Pete was committed for trial before the Landrost[81] of Nilstrom. I may here mention that I found out on taking stock that I had lost about 50*l*. worth of different sorts of goods.

As the trial of Pete could not come on for a few days I was obliged to postpone my departure. This was inconvenient. Rain had not fallen, but it was evidently imminent. There was a long stretch of turf-country to be crossed—country which is frightful to pull through, except after a long continuance of dry weather. The waggon was very heavy, and so full that it would be impossible for me to get any shelter by creeping inside in case of rain. Added to this the weather was intensely hot, and I felt the fever beginning to creep over me. Under these circumstances I determined to buy from De Plessis a very good new waggon with a tent on it, to make two spans of the old span and of those oxen I had recently bought, and to divide the load.

On the day of the trial I rode over to Nilstrom early in the morning. Nilstrom, the capital of Waterberg, consisted then of four rather tumble-down buildings. One was the prison, another the Landrost's office, a third his dwelling house, and the fourth the church. The imaginary town is situated in the ugliest part of Waterberg that I have seen, and in a particularly unhealthy locality.

The Landrost, an educated German gentleman, must, in my estimation, be a person of very decided character, not to have (at some unguarded moment) committed suicide. Pete would not confess, and, on account of his contumacy, was sentenced to twenty-five lashes as well as six months' imprisonment with hard labour. As he got out of the crazy old prison before many days, and disappeared, his punishment was not a particularly severe one [. . .]. The next day I started. Some of the oxen I had bought had strayed, and were missing. But the people said they would send them after me to my first outspann, and I could get on well without them till I got into the turf. The next morning, however, they had not arrived; so, before the sun was up, I started back to fetch them. I had breakfast with the De Plessis, and the oxen having been found, Willem De Plessis, De Clerc's young son, and I started for the waggon, driving them in front of us. It was now very hot, with a hot wind blowing; and in the evening, as I was sitting by the waggon, I remarked a fever sore coming on my hand, and I knew I was in for it.

We treked that night, and I felt very ill. Little Hendrick had to act forelooper, and so I rode Dandy and led Eclipse. I did some trade along the road, but pushed on as quickly as I could, fearing that the rain would catch me before I got through the turf. It was very hot, and there was very little water to be got, some of the springs were quite dried up. The fever came on strong, and I was soon all covered with fever-sores, which made it very painful to ride, particularly as I had a led horse. But at last we were through the turf and through the Pinaar's river. As I crossed it the river was barely up to the horses' knees in the deepest part, and was a mere little rivulet running between very high banks; but the sky was heavy with clouds, the sun sometimes scorching, sometimes hidden, and there was a gusty wind. I off-saddled near to a Boer's house, and threw myself down on the grass quite exhausted. I had been wondering whether I should be able to keep up until I had passed this river, for an hour or more; it was done now. Presently the waggons came over, the oxen looking very much knocked up. They had had nothing to drink for nearly twenty-four hours. By the time that they and the horses had to be tied up for the night, the first drops of the storm were beginning to fall. I saw the horses well blanketed and with their hoods on, then got into the tent-waggon myself. That night the rain came down in floods, and the next morning when I emerged from the waggon I saw an enormous lake stretching far and wide, with the tops of trees showing like little islands here and there with the current swirling round them. The waters were out over miles and miles of country along the little rivulet of the day before.

For the next few days it rained off and on, and I was laid up with fever. I used to crawl out of the waggon occasionally, but it would have been impossible for me to ride. The Boers, whose home was close by, were not very nice specimens, but were civil enough. At last the weather and I were sufficiently improved for a move to be made, and two days after, late in the evening, I rode into Pretoria, though still burning and shivering with fever. The weather was still uncertain, and that very day I had had to ride through the rain, owing to there being no one but myself to mind the horses. I passed my Irish acquaintance's house as I rode in, and he gave me some wine, for which I am still grateful to him, and told me that the Basuto war[82] had broken out, and that grain of all sorts was commanding a high price so my speculation of trading grain turned out a success so far.

Chapter 29

Before I left Pretoria on this expedition Mrs. Felman had told me that I might have the use of the stable, and of a very tiny room partitioned off from it by a half-high wall, for my own occupation. This had two advantages—it saved me expense, and allowed of my being near the horses and the oxen and waggons. During my tenure of this room I repeatedly pressed her to receive payment for it, and for the stable, as well as for my food (for I was always invited to join the family at meal times), but she persistently refused.

To the Felmans, therefore, I betook myself on this evening, and was greeted heartily. Going out to see to the oxen in the dark, I tumbled against Mr. Egerton. He still lived in my mansion by the swamp, but soon after this he left it, and went off with the volunteers to Basutoland. I had meant, after selling my loads, to return with the waggons for the grain I had left behind, but the fever had me in its grip now. I would never lie by completely, but the weakness and the intense pain from the dreadful sores quite prostrated me. I hired a groom (a half-caste Hottentot) called "Soldat," and sent the waggons back, with a few goods to trade with the Boers and Kaffirs, under the charge of Hendrick, and a son of Swartboy's, called "Boy," whom I had engaged as driver to the new waggon at Jan Steen's farm. He had been brought up amongst the Boers there, and they gave him an excellent character. I was very averse to trusting these men alone, but under the circumstances I did not know anything better to do, considering the high character I had received of Hendrick, a character confirmed to me by various Boers.

Jimmy was in Pretoria now. He had left the Higginses' store, and had got employment as clerk to a surveyor. So soon as I felt a little better, although still far from well, I determined to go and put my new farm a little in order. So I bought an old half-tent waggon cheap, and a span of salted oxen. I had a long time to wait before I could get the oxen, and then there was a difficulty about getting a driver—for most of the drivers were off with the volunteers to Basutoland.

There was beginning to be a feeling of insecurity in Pretoria. There was nothing to be seen, but people felt that the air was electric. I was pretty sure that the Boers would fight, after a certain conversation I had with De Clerc at his farm. On this occasion he had been talking with me about political affairs, asking me if I thought the Boers would be supported by any of the European powers or by America; and he suddenly said, "But in any case we shall fight;" then after a moment's pause continued, "I will tell you our plans. I don't count you as an enemy. This is what you will hear. Some man will refuse to pay his taxes; then your government will seize property to the amount of what is due; and then we shall rise; and we shall take that property out of the hands of the authorities, and if they interfere with us we shall fight; but until then we have done with talking."

"I should be sorry if you did what you say," I replied. "We have not many troops in the country now; but for you to go to war with the English nation is like a little child going to fight a man."

He assented to this, but in the conversation that ensued he told me that the Boers were not afraid of our cannon.

"We don't fight as you do," he said. "What is the use of cannon against men who scurry round singly on horseback, and who shoot at you from behind stones and trees without your seeing them? We shall not meet your troops in the open Urfeldt, [field] don't you believe it; we shall go into Natal to meet you."

On my return to Pretoria I was still so impressed by De Clerc's words and manner, that I considered whether it might not be the right thing to do, to tell what I had heard and who I had heard it from to Sir Owen Lanyon.[83] But I determined not to do so, as I had not stopped De Clerc when he said he did not count me as an enemy, and had not cautioned him that I would not undertake to observe secrecy in respect to what he was about to tell me. Just before I started for Jackallsfontein the news came from Potchefstrom [Potchefstroom] that a Boer had refused to pay his taxes, that his waggon had been seized in consequence, and that the Boers had taken violent possession of it in defiance of the law. Then I felt quite sure of my affair. The De Clerc programme was going to be attempted.

My waggon was ready packed; I had got my new driver and leader, and had kept them under my eye all the morning to take care that they did not get drunk. I saw the oxen brought up to span in, and then, having to transact a little business before starting, I told the driver that he was to meet me in a quarter of an hour at a particular store, and cantered off. My business was with the tenant of my house, a matter which I should have transacted in five minutes, but by the time I was at his door a tremendous and sudden storm had burst over the town, and it was half an hour before I could get away. As I rode into the market square I saw the waggon rounding a corner into it, the oxen all mixed up together, the driver drunk and swearing at them, the leader drunk and running about in front of them, entangling them more hopelessly every minute. They were turning another corner by the time I was alongside of them; the waggon was on the point of being upset. "Pull out the fore oxen—straight out!" I am afraid I shouted in a very unladylike manner, to the horror of some Pretorians who were spectators. The leader answered with a drunken laugh. There was no time to be lost. I gave him a sharp cut with my riding whip, and he sprang forward pulling the oxen out. But it was no good, the two fellows were too hopelessly drunk to be fit for anything. I got the waggon on to an open space and outspanned, left Soldat and his Kaffir wife, "Clara," whose services I had engaged, in charge, took the oxen to the Felmans' kraal, then looked up Jimmy, and asked him to oblige me by sleeping at the waggon for that night, which he did. The next day the driver and forelooper were sober, but the man, although he was said to be able to drive, could not, and broke the disselboom before we were out of the village. I then dismissed him; and had to get the disselboom mended, and also to get a new driver. After considerable trouble I got one fairly recommended, but when I took him to the waggon I found the forelooper had run away. However, I managed to get another forelooper, and early the next morning we started. Hardly had we got on the camp-common when the leader threw up the tow, and leaving the waggon, sat down on the grass. I rode up and asked him why he did so.

"I am going no farther," he said.

"Indeed," said I, "you forget that you engaged to go to the farm with me."

The end of it was that I put Eclipse at him, and having made him stand up, hunted him, although he tried doubling, up to the head of the team, and then rode alongside with my whip raised. So we got out of the village. I never saw anything so bad as that man's driving. It was a wonder that the waggon was not upset and the oxen hurt. We did seven miles in five hours, and then stuck hopelessly in what is called the "seven-mile spruit," close to what is called the Red House[84]—a place which has a tragic interest attached to it now.

The spruit was an absurd place to stick in, but the oxen were bullied by the bad driving, and had been too long in the yoke. I outspanned them, and off-loaded. Shortly after the guns and military train that were being sent to Potchefstrom came over the hill and down to the spruit, and crossed, the men looking at my waggon in disgust, for it was a good deal in their way. To the credit of the men be it said that only one swore at it, and he was reproved by a comrade, who remarked that probably I was more annoyed by its sticking than they were. They pitched their camp close by, and as soon as the oxen were rested I inspanned and tried to drag the waggon out. But my wretched driver only got the oxen more hopelessly entangled than ever, and at last I had to ask the Boer on whose farm we were to pull it out, which he very kindly did. I saw the things loaded up, and then told the driver to saddle the horses and take his blanket, as I was going to ride back to Pretoria. The sun had set, but there was a beautiful moon, and I got into Pretoria in good time. The next morning I discharged the driver and engaged a new one; and in the meantime Jimmy turned up, and told me that his employer had discharged him, having no farther need of his services, and that he was unable to obtain any other employment, as everything was very slack in Pretoria. Under these circumstances I proposed to him to come with me, to which he gladly assented. So in the evening we started; Jimmy and I riding, and the new driver, a half-caste named Andreas, walking, and carrying his own and Jimmy's bundles. We were only on the outskirts of the village when we saw that a great storm was imminent, and turned back to the Felmans' house just in time to escape it, fortunately, for it was very severe. The next morning we started again, and when we arrived at the waggon, found Soldat, Clara, and the dogs anxiously expecting us; and here I must beg to introduce a third dog to my readers. He was a sort of sheep-dog, black and white, called "Nero," a most unappropriate name, for a milder dog never existed, although he was a very good hunting dog. I had bought him, and a splendid half-bred mastiff, Prince, for waggon dogs. Prince had gone with the waggons, but Nero gave the boys the slip, and ran back to me.

There had been heavy rain at the Red House as well as at Pretoria, and the spruit was very much swollen. The worst was that the weather looked very threatening. I inspanned after lunch, and started. This time the oxen pulled much better, and it was evident that, although not a good driver, Andreas was much superior to his two predecessors.

We had only got a few miles, however, and were on a bleak hillside, when the storm I had seen approaching for some time, burst upon us. It was something terrific. There was no making head against it. I had the oxen outspanned, blanketed the horses, and sheltered them as well as I could in the lee of the waggon. The flashes of lightning and the roar of thunder were almost continuous, the rain poured down in torrents, and the wind howled and raved until I thought the waggon would have been blown over. I was afraid that the horses would get alarmed, and stood by them until the fury of the storm abated, which was not for some hours. The rain was still falling heavily, and it was quite dark, when, at last, drenched through in spite of my mackintosh, I crept into the waggon along with Clara, whilst Jimmy made his bed (such as it was) under it, in the wet. When I woke next morning the rain was still falling, nor did it cease till midday, when it cleared up. The waggon had sunk very deep in the soft ground, which was slippery for the oxen's feet, and after various efforts to pull it out, I was obliged to make up my mind to off-load partially again. The evening was very fine, and I trusted to being able to load up in the morning after pulling the waggon out. The whole ground was so wet and swampy that I determined to let the horses and oxen remain loose during the night; the moon was bright, and from time to time I inspected them. The morning dawned beautifully, but hardly had the first rays of the sun become visible, when I saw a heavy bank of clouds, which threatened hail, sweeping rapidly up from the horizon. I ordered all haste to be made to get whatever had been off-loaded up on the waggon, but before everything was ready the storm burst—such a storm, almost worse than the previous one, although the thunder and lightning was less severe.

Fortunately there was but little hail, for about this time there were hailstorms in other districts, which would have cut the tent of the waggon into shreds, and killed or maimed the animals and us. The rain poured down the whole day. Clara at last managed to make a sort of little tent with a tarpaulin and some sheets of iron roofing I had with me, and got some coffee made, which Jimmy and I, crouching in the waggon-tent together, were very thankful for; and she also managed to make some very bad griddlecakes, but the only wonder was that she was able to make them at all. Night came on, and it was still raining and blowing—it was useless to attempt to tie up the animals, the waggon was standing in a swamp, so they had to take their chance. Jimmy and I slept in the waggon, the tent of which had begun to leak, and little Roughy and Moustache begged so to come in also, that I let the poor little brutes have their desire. When the morning dawned it was still raining, the horses were in sight, but the oxen were gone, and so was the leader. I sent Andreas on foot and Soldat on Dandy to look for them, and while they were away, seeing two government waggons going to Potchefstrom with strong spans of oxen, I asked the conductor to pull my waggon out, which he obligingly did.

It rained on and off the whole day, and in the evening the two boys returned, having seen nothing of the oxen. Soldat reported that the spruit was at flood. I determined to go to look for the oxen the next day myself, as I very much suspected that they had treked off to the farm they had been feeding on shortly before I bought them. This is a favourite pastime of oxen. Unfortunately I did not know where this farm was, and hence I knew it would be necessary first to go to Pretoria to see the man I had bought the animals from, and inquire the way to it. The next morning was Sunday, and the weather was beautiful. Jimmy and I saddled up early, and taking Nero with us, started for Pretoria. We got in there about nine o'clock, and having found the gentleman I wanted, and got the direction to the farm, and a note to its proprietor, we rode to the Felmans' to give the horses a rest and try to get a little breakfast for ourselves. On our way I met a Kaffir who had just come in from Waterberg, and he gave me a letter written by "Boy," who had learned to write at the Mission station. It was a very funny production, but Mrs. Felman and I managed to decipher it, and it corroborated what I had previously heard from a Boer, viz., that Hendrick was doing a good trade, and that the oxen were well.

We were, as usual, hospitably entertained at the Felmans', who had pressed me to come to them whenever I should be in Pretoria, and had told me that I might always consider the little room next the stable as my own, although I had given up the mansion by the swamp after Mr. Egerton left Pretoria, Mrs. Felman having taken charge of all things which I had not loaded up on the waggon to go to the farm. These articles which she took charge of, were goods for trading, which I did not care to take there until I had got the place into some order. It was very hot when Jimmy and I started once more. The road was rather pretty, and for a time was sufficiently good for us to be able to push along pretty quickly. At last we came to a very steep decline, and after following the road in its windings between the hills, we saw a thick line of brushwood marking the course of the river we had to cross, and at the same time heard the rush of the water, telling of its being in flood. The spruit we had crossed in the morning was part of this river that was before us; where we had forded it, we had not found it very deep, but it was evident that it was considerably deeper here. When we rode down to the ford, it looked very ugly. There was a farmhouse on the opposite side, and presently a small boy made his appearance, and looked across at us. I hailed this boy, and inquired if the ford was passable; his answer was, "Come across." It was not altogether a satisfactory answer, because he might be a truculent young Boer, anxious to drown the enemies of the liberties of his nation; but as no other answer was to be got from him, I put Eclipse at the stream. Eclipse did not like the look of it at all, sniffed and snorted, and even, when he got into the full current, wanted to turn back; however, we got through with a good wetting, Jimmy followed, and poor Nero swam through after a struggle, for the current was very strong. Arrived on the bank, I said to the boy that I had a letter for Mr. P———, and felt much gratified by hearing that Mr. P———'s farm was some way down the stream on the side I had just left, so we had to ford back again!

A short canter took us to Mr. P———'s house, where we were very kindly received. Mr. P——— is an English Africander, I believe. Mrs. P——— gave us some coffee, which was very acceptable after our wetting, but Mr. P——— could tell us nothing about the oxen, except that that morning, looking with his field-glass for some oxen he had lost, he had seen, on a hillside far away, a number of oxen which he had not recognized as his or as any belonging to his neighbours. The hill was in the direction of my waggon, so I thought this sounded hopeful. Mr. P——— told us that a number of his sheep had been killed by the late storms, and that several of his oxen were missing. We mounted once more, and fording the river again at the same spot, took our way towards the hill Mr. P——— had pointed out to us, when suddenly Jimmy exclaimed that he was sure that he could see the oxen grazing in a valley at some distance. I could not make them out; but he was so confident that we altered our course, and presently coming to a farm, we asked the Boer who owned it, if he had seen any strange oxen, and he told us that he had seen fourteen strange oxen that morning with their heads towards the spot Jimmy had indicated. Thus encouraged we pushed on, and soon came in sight of our friends peaceably grazing.

It is an odd thing that oxen who play truant know quite well when they are found out. They are wonderfully sly about sneaking away; if they mean to run away in the daytime, they do not do so ostentatiously. They will graze quietly until they think they have lulled suspicion, and then walk off more quickly than any one not accustomed to their ways would think it possible for them to do. If they mean to run away at night, they set about it very softly, so as not to wake any one, but whenever they go, their expression upon being found out is the same. They do not, like the Elfin page, "fall to the ground," oxen being of a less emotional and demonstrative nature than elfins, but if there be any expression in an eye, they most unmistakably mutter to themselves, "found, found, found," and having so muttered, they visibly, to the least imaginative observer, turn round, "form," to use a military expression, and move off in front of their captor. In the case of my oxen, there was one daring spirit of the name of "Blauberg," who had always been mutinous. He now maintained his character by perpetually trying to run away, tossing his head, and flicking his tuftless tail—for, like many of his brethren, he had lost a portion of that appendage during the illness consequent upon inoculation with "lungsickness." We had to take the oxen over the veldt to the waggon, which was not an easy operation, for we did not know the country, there was no road, and our only guides were the slopes of the hills. Added to this the night was coming on quickly, and the moon did not rise until late. Blauberg's antics were, therefore, very inconvenient, and caused feelings the reverse of charitable towards that erring ox to arise in Jimmy's breast and my own. At last, some time after it was dark, Jimmy caught sight of our campfire, much to my delight, and after we got the oxen tied up, and the horses blanketed and fed, we sat down to the dinner Clara had been keeping warm for us. She had, by my orders, bought a sheep from a neighbouring farmer during my absence.

We started the nest morning; but to make a long story short, we had a miserable trek. The weather was very bad; the road was very bad in places; the drift or ford of the Yokeskey river, which we had to pass, was in such a state, that I had to hire a span of oxen from a neighbouring Boer to put on to my span, and then, with three drivers, the oxen had a difficult job to pull the waggon out. I do not think that this Boer would have hired me his oxen had it not been for the persuasions of his good-natured wife. His name was "Durks." He had a good reason for not wanting to hire them, for they, and all the young cattle, were being used for tramping out the corn: rain was threatening, and it is no joke for rain to come on while the corn is on the tramping-floor. Of course, the fact of rain being imminent made it very desirable for me to get across the river, and kind, fat Mrs. Durks saw this.

The rain did come on heavily shortly after I outspanned, but the weather cleared after an hour or so, and we treked again; to add trouble to trouble Jimmy was taken ill, and had to go in the waggon; so that I had to ride Dandy and to lead Eclipse, as well as drive the two loose oxen (for I had yokes for twelve oxen only with the waggon I was using). That evening we outspanned by the farm of an English Africander, of the name of Williams. He was from home, but his wife was very kind, giving us nice bread, milk, and eggs, which were all very acceptable, the more so as one required a little inner consolation to withstand the rain and wind which, coming on shortly after we outspanned, continued nearly all night. I here met a man who had just come from Waterberg, and who told me that the storms there had been something terrific. I afterwards saw in a paper the intelligence that "the public buildings at Nilstrom had been blown down by the hurricane!"

We at last reached Jackallsfontein in a storm, and found, alas! that the cottage had shared the fate of the "public buildings at Nilstrom." It had been blown down!

Chapter 30

There is not much to describe in Jackallsfontein in the way of scenery; no comparison between it and Grünfontein could be instituted. Jackallsfontein is undeniably ugly; it lies on a gentle slope of what, in England, we should call the "Downs" of the Wittwaters Randt. The few trees around it have all been planted, and not only around Jackallsfontein itself, but in all the country for miles round. But to counterbalance this, the material advantages of Jackallsfontein over Grünfontein are manifold.

At Jackallsfontein horses can be safely bred; they can be let run summer and winter without fear; sheep, too, thrive well, not being plagued with the ailments or by the ticks which render their lives a burden to themselves and to their proprietors, on the slopes of the Magaliesberg, and in a great part of the Transvaal. No herbs poisonous to cattle or sheep grow near Jackallsfontein, and that is a point greatly in favour of any farm in the Transvaal, where poisonous herbs are very common. Although I took great care of my sheep at Grünfontein, I had lost several through their being allowed to stray into pasture which was poisonous; and not far from my property there (although at too great a distance to endanger my oxen) a farmer had in one day lost sixty head of cattle through the carelessness of his herd, who had let the animals in his charge stray on to unhealthy grazing. Added to the above-mentioned advantages, the quality of the soil at Jackallsfontein is excellent, the water good, and the site very favourable for opening a general Boer store. Kaffir labour there is none, but Boer labour can be easily obtained from adjoining small farms, whose owners are glad for younger members of their family to earn something to assist in the general housekeeping.

My house being uninhabitable, I was obliged to engage a room in the house of some Boers whose farm adjoins mine. The name of these people is De Plessis, but they are no relations of Willem De Plessis.

Their house consisted of three rooms and kitchen, and one of these rooms, separated from the family sleeping room by a half-wall, they made over to me. It was not a very eligible apartment, having no window, and the door being composed of dilapidated reeds—however, it was better than nothing. I pitched my tent as a room for Jimmy, the servants had the waggon, and the horses were accommodated at night in a deserted house at a little distance, which once had been a dwelling of some pretensions, having several rooms, and bearing traces on the walls of the sitting room of having been tastefully painted. There was yet another cottage quite close to the one in which I lodged, tenanted by members of the same family as mine hosts, and numberless small farms were dotted about the environs. The owner of the deserted house I have mentioned was an English Africander, who, I was told, was bankrupt, and the property was held by his creditors.

I cannot give a very lucid account of my hosts and their neighbours, they were all so mixed up, owing to the curiosity my appearance excited having a stimulating effect on the custom amongst Boers of running backwards and forwards between one another's houses. There was a very large number of dirty little children of all ages, and a sprinkling of dirty but helpful boys—boys who could drive a plough, or hold it, as well as their fathers; there was an entanglement of slatternly women with loud voices, who have left shadowy pictures on my mind, as bearing the more or less depressed expression common to the Boeress. With a life of dull toil stretching from childhood to the grave, it is no wonder that it should be so; and yet, those who have known the peasantry of other lands, must feel the question arise in their minds, "Why should the Boer peasant woman look depressed, when the South Italian peasant woman (for instance) does not?" I think the answer to the question is, "Look at the men." It is not want of education, or rather of book-learning, that makes a life of toil dull, and the men and women who live such lives generation after generation incarnations of dulness. It is but in the latest generation that a gleam from the sun of knowledge has fallen on the peasantry of South Italy, yet who would have ever called them "dull?" Who would have discovered that their women wore a general air of depression? The women of a race will not look depressed if the men be not "dull;" and vice versa, if the women look depressed the men must be "dull."

Although the Boers are in many ways cunning, anyone who has any knowledge of them will corroborate the statement that the vast majority of them are dull, and that the vast majority of Boeresses bear a stamp of depression, although in the elder women this stamp is somewhat effaced by a tendency to fat, which on first sight gives an appearance of jollity. I do not mean to say that I have not seen cheerful women amongst the Boers, but they are rare exceptions.

Besides the children, lads, and women, there was a group of big, rough-handed, grimy-looking, rough-voiced men, the only individual member of which I can distinctly remember was "Lo," a fine stalwart fellow, with kindly blue eyes, and whom I distinguished sufficiently from the general relationship to know that he was the son of mine host, and that he was unmarried.

These people were very kind in their way, but very annoying at the same time. They were willing to help at settling my room, so as to make it inhabitable, and willing also to help with the ploughing and sowing that had to be done; but they invaded me incessantly. To be certain of privacy, I had, from early dawn until the family retired to rest, to tie the reed door to with a piece of string, and then an enterprising youngster or an inquisitive female was as likely as not to push the reeds aside and peep in. Of course as there was no window the door had usually to be left open to afford light, and then the whole troop disported themselves from morning till night. If I did not talk to them, or even if I was engaged in writing, it did not matter; they would talk amongst themselves, and the children would scramble about at their mothers' feet, and the men would smoke, whilst all would spit on the ground in a manner trying to weak nerves. They, as indeed all the Boers I have met, treated me to a certain extent differently from the way in which they treat most people. They never called me by any familiar name, although they were all very friendly. Perhaps they had some vague perception that if they had attempted to do so I should have stopped them; whatever the reason may be, although playful conversation amongst the Boers is frequently what we should consider both coarse and impertinent, I had only twice any occasion to check any acquaintance of mine. This point being attained, I felt that it would be unwise to try to put limits, marked out by my sense of the proprieties, upon conduct which these people considered as a proof of their friendly feeling, and which besides afforded to them a source of innocent amusement. I felt this to be the more imperative owing to the dislike existing between the Boers and the English; a feeling which, in so thinly populated a country as the Transvaal, each individual settler could either augment or diminish; for it is wonderful how trifling information respecting individuals spreads in the Transvaal. I may mention an instance of this in illustration.

In the month of April I had telegraphed from Pretoria to my banker's in London to ask how my balance with them stood. In the following September old Mrs. Nell in Waterberg asked me why I was trading when I had so much money in the bank! Neither is this a solitary instance of private matters, connected with an unknown individual, being subjects of common conversation amongst people who perhaps never saw him or could be supposed to take any interest in him. Certainly, so far as my experience goes, a Boer loves gossip as well as any man or woman in existence. [. . .]

In the meantime the tenant I had had in my house left Pretoria; and as, owing to the unsettled state of affairs, it was a bad time to let a house, I determined to prepare it for my own occupation, at least temporarily, although, with a view to the possibility of an outbreak, I determined only to put the most necessary things into it. The garden had been much neglected, and I employed two Kaffirs to set it in order.

Day after day passed, and my waggons did not come in, and in the meanwhile alarming rumours were on the increase. The very morning that I left Jackallsfontein, a Boer had ridden over from a neighbouring farm with news that Paul Kruger and Pretorius had sent a message to the effect that every man who could ought, in the name of God, to attend the now famous meeting at Perdekraal,[85] which was to be held forthwith. [. . . Rumors of impending war intensify; many English settlers leave for Pretoria.] It was on Monday, the 13th of December, that at seven o'clock in the morning I started for Jackallsfontein.

The morning was fresh after the rain, and I pushed on pretty quickly, taking a shorter road to the farm than I had taken with the waggon, and hopeful of escaping rain, although very heavy masses of cloud were lowering round the horizon. I was already near the Yokeskey river, and the rain appeared not far off, when I met a Boer on horseback. We both drew rein, and he asked me where I was going; I told him to my farm.

"Then" said he, "you will have to swim the river, there is no passing it otherwise."

He then asked me if I meant to stay at the farm or return to Pretoria. I told him that I was going to bring up my waggon to sell, with, I hoped, a light load of farm produce.

"Look at the clouds!" said the Boer; "the river is impassable now, and if it rains, as I think there is no doubt it will, it will be still deeper by the time you get your waggon back to it."

It struck me that what he said was true; so, much disgusted, I turned my horse and we rode alongside of each other for a short time. My companion asked me if I had heard any news of the deliberation of the Beeinkommste at Perdekraal (Perdekraal was within a ride of my farm). I told him that no one in Pretoria had any news about it. He then asked me whether it was true that no Boers were allowed to enter Pretoria, saying that such was the current report; and this I was able to contradict. Shortly after he bade me goodbye, and cantered off across the veldt in one direction, whilst I held on, likewise across the veldt, towards Pretoria.

My way lay past a large farmhouse, belonging to a well-known man amongst the Boers called Guillaume Pretorius. As I was passing he came out, and I stopped and saluted him. He asked where I was going, and I told him how I had turned back from going to my farm.

"If you mean to get into Pretoria, then," said he, "you had better push on: the Beeinkommste is broken up, and the commando rides today to Pretoria."

"Does it?" said I; "then I am in luck; I should like to see it."

The old fellow looked at me with an odd expression—I think he did not quite know what to make of my speech. He had never seen me before, although I knew about him, but with that habit of hospitality which has become a second nature to a Boer, he said, "Will you not off-saddle? Although perhaps you had better push on if your horses are not tired."

At this moment we both caught sight of the Potchefstrom post-cart approaching the house, which was a post-station, and a minute after I recognized Mr. Cooper, the attorney, as one of the passengers in it. Our rencontre was a mutual surprise, and as he shook hands I noticed that his feet were bare, the result of the cart having been upset, one of the mules having been nearly drowned, and the passengers having to scramble and shift to set things straight in fording the river. Mr. Cooper introduced me to his fellow passenger, the Attorney-General De Wett; and, hopeful now of hearing some authentic news from Potchefstrom, I dismounted, off-saddled, and went into the house with the others, while the fresh horses or mules for the post-cart were being brought up and harnessed. Seated in a large and rather comfortable sitting room at the back of the house, the three men talked of the present and coming events, and I listened.

Mr. De Wett told us that the commando was not to ride into Pretoria until Thursday, and then only in case no compromise had been arrived at. He said that the Beeinkommste had appointed all necessary officers, both civil and military, and had despatched a messenger to Pretoria that very day to tell the administrator that if the Government offices were not delivered over to the republic on Thursday, they would be taken by force, and that on Thursday the heads of the new government would ride into Pretoria with the commando to take possession. Mr. De Wett assured Pretorius that he had seen the Boer leaders, and that he was certain that by a little tact things might still be arranged. It struck me that it was very little use to think of compromises when things had come to such a pass, but I held my peace, and listened, whilst Pretorius expressed himself to the effect that the Boers would accept of no compromise so far as the complete restoration of their independence was concerned. This Pretorius struck me as being a good old fellow, rough enough, but yet a superior man to the ordinary Boer. All this time we had been sipping coffee brought to us by Mrs. Pretorius, who must have been good-looking in her time, and been looked at by two or three pretty little girls, in much neater trim than the generality of Boer maidens.

The post-cart being now inspanned, Mr. Cooper and Mr. De Wett started; I waited, for I was anxious to hear what Pretorius would say when they were gone, as I observed that he spoke with reticence before them, and I thought he might perhaps speak more freely when I was his only English listener; I talked first about my farm, which he knew, and was interested in, then a neighbour came in, and the conversation drifted back again to politics, while we removed into another more homely sitting room, and, upon hearing that I had had no breakfast before leaving Pretoria, Mrs. Pretorius brought me some Boer biscuits and more coffee.

It has always been my opinion that although the English Government were perfectly justified in annexing the Transvaal, the manner in which it was annexed was not only an unjustifiable blunder but an unjust act. My reasons for thinking that the annexation in itself was justifiable are based on general principles, which it would be a hopeless task to attempt to explain to any Boer I ever met; but my reasons for thinking that the manner of annexation was altogether wrong are completely within the grasp of every one of them. In any expression of opinion to them, they inevitably missed my allusion to the general principles, which were unintelligible to them, and only remarked that I coincided with them in thinking that they had been very badly treated. All the Boers I knew spoke before me with great frankness, and when (in order to prevent the idea that I sided with them from obtaining) I said that in case of war I should, in spite of what I had expressed, side with the English, they accepted that as simply an inevitable consequence of my not being able to change my nationality, and it would have been a useless task to attempt to explain to them that under given circumstances I should feel myself bound to side against my own nation; but that in the Transvaal case I did not feel myself so bound. I confess I often felt seriously annoyed and depressed by this state of things in my intercourse with the Boers, so much so, that in the case of De Clerc, Willem De Plessis, Pretorius, as also of Barend Englesberg, all men superior to the common run of Boers, I should have attempted what I yet knew was impossible, namely, to explain my opinion thoroughly to them, but for my still imperfect knowledge of Boer language. That language is unfit in itself for the expression of abstract thought, because formed by people who never think abstractly; and this deterred me from the effort whenever I felt impelled towards it, and in after-reflection I always admitted that it was well that I had been restrained from so doing.

The party assembled in Pretorius's house talked, as usual, freely before me; and I heard it confidently asserted that if the public offices were not given up on the appointed day an attack would be made on Pretoria, and that even the presence of women and children would not deter the Boers from fighting from street to street until they had occupied the whole town. The innocent blood shed would be on the head of the English Government. As to all English on outstanding farms, Pretorius, his friend, and his wife (who took an animated part in the conversation), seemed to think that those who remained strictly neutral would be left unharmed, or even protected in case of necessity. Having heard all I needed, I changed my mind as to returning to Pretoria. Rain or no rain, it was evident that I must give Jimmy a choice whether he would remain on the farm or run into Pretoria before it was too late, for I felt sure that an outbreak was imminent; so, saddling-up once more, I turned towards the Yokeskey river. [. . . Despite a storm Heckford arrives safely at Jackallsfontein.] Just as I got on the highest part of the randt, the wind and rain came whirling up, but it was only the tail of a storm which went roaring away over the hills to one side, while another storm was pouring its fury on the distant hills at the other; and by the time Eclipse was picking his way down the stony slope above the De Plessis' cottage, all that remained of the rain was a watery sort of haze, gradually dissipating under the rays of the moon, which did not allow the party assembled outside the house, to see me until I was close to it. Then I was welcomed with a cordiality which would have made a stranger suppose that I had known, not only Jimmy, but the Boers, for years, while little Roughy, after executing some antics highly creditable to such a soft little mass of hair as he was, discharged a volley of little barks, and rushed at Moustache, who had offended him by espying and welcoming me first, and bit his long ears until they were forcibly separated, Nero, the while, wagging his short tail and giving little bounds indicative of satisfaction.

What a chattering; what an anxious asking and answering of questions; what a retailing of my news to each member of the small community—who, hearing of my arrival, hastened to the cottage—took place that night by the light of the moon! My last evening in the yet unmade home, before all the plans that I had carefully thought over, and toiled hard to realize, were to be swept away into a past as remote as if years lay between it and today!

At last, after I had retired to the interior of the cottage, and had eaten my supper, surrounded at first by the whole family, but with a gradually diminishing company, as sleepiness caused first one and then another to drop off to their beds, until Lo De Plessis bade me goodnight, I was alone with Jimmy. Then for the first time I confessed to him that I was anxious, and told him all that I had heard with regard to the treatment the Boers had it in their minds to bestow upon the English; told him not only what Pretorius had said, but what a farmer, whose cottage I had passed between Pretorius's farm and Durks' Drift, had said. This farmer's name was Joubert. He had called to me as I was riding past his cottage, and I had ridden up to the stoop, where he and some members of his family were congregated. A big, bony, black-haired man was Joubert; with a stubbly beard, high jawbones, and eager eyes.

"Where are you from?" he cried, as I drew rein.

"From Pretoria."

"What is the news?"

I told him.

"Yes, yes," he exclaimed, "that is well. Will your Government give up the public offices, think you?"

"I am in no position to know what are the intentions of the Government," I answered; "but I do not think it likely they will."

He drew his breath, and said, in a savagely suppressed manner,—

"Then the streets of Pretoria shall run with blood like water on Thursday."

He asked me eagerly what I thought of the action of the Government; asked if I were going back to Pretoria; called Heaven to witness that the blood spilt would cry vengeance on us; his eyes glittering, his whole frame absolutely quivering with passion. He had laid his hand on my horse's neck as he spoke; there was a look in his eyes unlike anything I had ever seen before—a bloodthirsty look that made me involuntarily shiver.

"Then you don't think they will give us the country back?" he cried again. "Then we will fight; we will drive you from the country; not one of your nation shall remain alive; your blood shall run as water on Thursday; we will kill all—all of you! Where are your troops? sent away to fight against the enemies that are attacking you—the Russians—the Irish—the Americans."

"No, no," said I, "now there you are mistaken."

The blood rushed to his head, suffusing his very eyes until they looked red.

"Now I know you lie," he cried, his voice shaking with passion. "There is your path—begone!"

"Not like this," said I, not moving. "I am not the Government. I wish the Boers no harm and although I am English and you a Boer, there is no reason for our quarrelling personally. Give me your hand before I go;" and I held out mine. Joubert looked—hesitated—then out came the rough paw; and he bade me a civil goodbye.

All this I told Jimmy; and told him he must choose for himself whether he would remain on the farm or return to Pretoria with me. He chose the former alternative; and after a sleepless night, I called up Soldat and the Kaffir at four in the morning to span in. I had packed up some things I required to take with me, but the waggon could not have got across the Yokeskey river with even a light load on it. The Boers before leaving me in the evening had promised that, in the event of hostilities breaking out, and of my being detained in Pretoria, they would protect Jimmy, and had also promised to give him his food until I returned, for Clara was going with me as well as Soldat.

The early dawn was just breaking when the waggon started, and I, mounted on Dandy, and with Eclipse by my side, bade Jimmy, who was holding Roughy in his arms, goodbye. They both looked so forlorn as he stood there in the cold, faint light. "It is not too late to change your mind yet," said I; "you have only to say the word." But be preferred remaining, and indeed I thought myself it was safer for him where he was than in Pretoria. The words I had heard that morning, when some movement I made had wakened the sleepers in the next room, were still in my ears.

"She is getting ready to inspann," said a sleepy female voice. "Well, she will never come back."

"Ah," remarked another equally sleepy female voice; "and if she don't, then who will pay us for the little Englishman's food?"

We forded the Yokeskey in a torrent of rain, the current running strong and deep, and outspanned at Durks' farm. Nero and Moustache had broken loose, and followed me. Nero was nearly washed away, and little Moustache was only saved by being caught by his neck as he was sinking—the leader himself could hardly keep his legs. Mrs. Durks was friendly, her husband civil. He advised me, if my waggons had come in, to come out of Pretoria with them on Thursday as early as I could. He said even if I met the commando that I, as a woman working for herself, should be let pass, with the waggons and oxen, if I explained that I was going to my farm; but that if I remained in Pretoria I should hold my life in my hand. They gave me some milk and bread; and shortly after I inspanned, and that night I outspanned about three miles from the Red House, by a spring of water.

The moon was at its full, and I inspanned before dawn, and came into Pretoria as the clock was pointing to seven in the morning—to find, alas! that the whole village was in a panic, and that not only were most places of business shut, but that the auction I had counted upon for selling my waggon was postponed, owing to the unsettled state of things. My Waterberg waggons were not in!

I left the waggon at the auctioneer's for private sale; but I saw that, as I had failed in selling it on Wednesday, it would, in all probability, be too late to sell it at all; for, after Thursday, people were afraid to leave the village. In the meantime I took possession of my house, and sent for a carpenter to make shutters for the windows, in order to bring thither with safety the goods I had left in Mrs Felman's care. I had only a rough shake-down for a bed, a chair or two, and a rough table; for, in the unsettled state of things and in the absence of my waggons, I did not care to go to any expense; indeed, could not have done so without incurring debt.

The dreaded Thursday came and passed quietly. I had gone to bed, when, at about eleven o'clock, I heard a tap at my window, and the voice of my next neighbour calling me. I got up and opened the door.

"I hope I did not frighten you," he began, in the usual formula, "but I have just had news that the Boers are coming in tonight;" and he told his story.

His great point was that the band-master's wife, whom he knew, and whom he had been to visit, was sitting up, expecting the signal to be given to go into camp for protection, and that she had told him that the colonel's wife was doing the same. He said that the Boers were coming over the hill singly or in small parties, to avoid detection, and were to form at a given spot and attack the town; that all sorts of preparations were being secretly made, and that the signal for going into camp was to be a bugle call.

I thought the whole story sounded odd, particularly the bugle call as a signal.

"It is odd that no notice has been given publicly of the likelihood of an attack, and of the signal to seek protection in camp," said I.

"That is because there are so many traitors about" was the answer.

My neighbour was deeply impressed evidently, and I thought it best to take some precautions; so I waked Soldat and Clara, told Clara to put a few things together for herself and for me, in case of our having to run for it, and then dressing myself, I started to walk down the village to old Mrs. Parker's cottage, for I knew that she was likely to be alone, her sons being in the country, and I thought I might be able to be of use to her in case of a sudden alarm. I told Soldat that, as soon as the bugle sounded, he was to saddle the horses and bring them down sharp to her cottage, after leaving Clara with my neighbour's family to be taken into camp with them. My oxen were all kraaled in Mr. Felman's kraal, so nothing could be done about them.

It was a beautiful moonlight night, by no means a favourable night for a surprise, and I knew it to be against the usual tactics of Boers to attack at night at all; and as I stepped out I felt pretty sure that there was some mistake. As I passed my neighbour's cottage I saw lights inside, and through the open door I was aware of some commotion.

I had not gone far when I saw two orderlies with a saddled horse at the door of a cottage. I thought I might as well inquire of them if they knew of any report as to the Boer attack. They said that they had heard of nothing, but that in another minute Captain C—— would be coming out, and that he would be able to tell me. I waited accordingly. There was no special report as to an attack, only the possibility of such an event caused a certain anxiety. The officer was just on his way to visit the outposts, and seemed much amused at the idea that a bugle call had been suggested as an improvement on the three cannon shots always fired as a signal of danger, whereupon I went back and to bed.

The next day I heard that Mrs. Parker's sons had come in. The village was in a state of suppressed panic; but as I had a good deal to do in the matter of setting my garden in order, I went out but little the next day or Saturday, when at last my waggons came in late in the evening. They brought bad news. A good deal of the corn I had left at Makapan's-poort had been damaged by the floods of rain that had fallen there. Hendrick had traded grain and cattle, but on coming to the Pinaars river had found it impossible to cross it with heavily loaded waggons, or with loose cattle. He had therefore waited for it to run down, until he had been told by the Boers that if he did not get the waggons that night into Pretoria by Saturday, they would seize them and the oxen. He had then left the cattle and part of the loads behind with some Kaffirs, and had swum the oxen through, the loads getting partly wet. It was a comfort that the oxen were in splendid condition, but a terrible disappointment otherwise.

The next day, Sunday, I spent writing, when, towards evening, Hendrick, who had been "on the spree," as is the custom with drivers in general when they come off a long trek, rushed up to me in a state of wild excitement. The Boers were coming in—the market square was being fortified—rifles were being given out—we should all be massacred that night—the danger for the half-castes and Kaffirs serving in Pretoria was even greater than for the English—they must all have rifles, &c, &c. He quite took my breath away, but then I saw he had been drinking, although he was not absolutely drunk.

I ordered Eclipse to be saddled, and rode into the village, taking Hendrick with me on foot. My house lies at the outskirts, near to the camp; but I was soon close to the market square. Then I saw that Hendrick had not exaggerated. Crowds of Kaffirs, superintended by an engineer officer, were hastily throwing up earthworks round the church in the centre, whilst a mass of frantically excited white men and lads of all ranks, was rushing after and crushing round a cart laden with rifles, that was being driven through it to the place appointed for distributing them.

It was with difficulty that I made my way through, and learned from an acquaintance that no rifles were to be given to the coloured population, till all the white population had been provided. The rifles in the cart were not nearly sufficient for those who crowded round it, so it was not worthwhile staying. I turned into the square, and approaching the little group of officers, waited till the one in command was at liberty. I then asked him whether it was true that an attack was expected that night. He said that there was reason to believe that such would be the case; and I then inquired what provision had been made for the protection of the horses and oxen belonging to people in the town.

"Where are you going for refuge?" he asked, disregarding my question.

"I was not asking about protection for myself, but for my oxen and horses," I answered.

"But what ward are you in?" he asked.

I said I did not know, but that my house was near the camp common.

"Well, then, you had better go to the convent," he said.

"I shall remain at my own house," I answered. "What I want to know is, whether any place of comparative safety has been appointed for the oxen in the town. I have three valuable spans; I don't want to lose them."

"Oh!" he exclaimed, "have you any waggons?"

"Yes—three."

"I am greatly in want of waggons for barricading," he went on eagerly. "The best thing you can do is to bring them up here to me."

"But the oxen?" I remarked.

"I think," he answered, "the best plan for them would just be to let them loose in the square."

"Between the barricades and the earthworks?" I said, "just let them go loose?"

"Yes," was the reply.

I thanked him very politely, and rode off, thinking to myself how singularly beneficial to all parties it would be to have thirty-eight oxen, maddened with fear, rushing about a small square that was being desperately defended; unless, indeed, one looked upon the arrangement from a Boer point of view.

When the waggons were mentioned I had glanced in the direction of my old waggon, which I had left at the auctioneer's. It was gone; and the next day I discovered it in the barricade of one of the streets approaching the market square, from whence, of course, I was not allowed to remove it

Having been unable to get any information from the engineer officer, I cantered quickly towards the camp to try to find Colonel Gildea, for it seemed almost impossible to me that some plan for protecting the large numbers of oxen and horses belonging to people in the village had not been devised, considering that in case of a siege of even a few days' length, such a provision was of the greatest public importance.

On my way across the common I met Mr. Hudson, the Colonial Secretary, hurrying down to the village on foot, behind a hand-cart drawn by Kaffirs, and full of rifles. He told me that Colonel Gildea was not in camp; he did not know where he was, but as to the oxen, he said there was no place set apart for them; that he thought the best thing I could do was to let them run about the town loose that night. As this idea seemed inadmissible to me, I asked him whether, in case of an attack, the fire from the guns at the camp was likely to be directed so as to injure my house, which I pointed out to him. He said he thought it was in a safe position; so I determined to keep my oxen with me.

I had, since the arrival of my waggons, brought my other oxen from the Felmans' kraal, and let all the spans feed together; so now I had them all tied to the yokes inside the erf, barricaded the entrance to it with the two waggons, made my boys sleep close to the stable and the oxen, and determined to sit up myself.

The streets, by the time I was returning from the common to my house, were full of people wending their way to the various places of refuge; men with rifles on their shoulders, going off on patrol; women and girls carrying hastily-made-up bundles, mattresses, and infants, and dragging little children after them. There was no attack, but the morning brought the news of massacre of the 94th [86] and the panic and excitement increased.

I managed that day to get old muzzle-loading rifles for my boys from the Ordnance Department; and, as I was riding back from camp, I saw a commissariat officer superintending the moving of stores into camp, in preparation for the siege which was now undoubtedly imminent.

There was evidently a great deficiency of waggons to convey all the stores, and yet haste was imperative, for the news that the Boers were close by was expected at any moment. All coloured men seen in the streets were being seized; horses, waggons, and oxen also. Now I had been revolving in my mind whether or not I would save my property by a trick. My waggons I did not think of moving, but my oxen were all grazing far out of the village. I had only to mount little Hendrick on Dandy, and with him as my companion ride out to them, drive them through a poort at some little distance, and not much under observation, and get them away to my farm. I knew pretty surely that what Durks and other Boers had told me was true—there was but little danger of the Boers robbing me, unless in some case of necessity; and should I meet the commando, I had little doubt that by speaking fair I could induce the commander to let me pass, even if I could not wheedle him out of a safe-conduct, which I deemed it very probable I should be able to manage. It was a temptation to do this, not only on account of my own pecuniary advantage, but because I am very fond of my animals; and I thought it likely that they would get hard usage in government employ; but on the other hand it seemed, and seems to me, that when matters have been brought to the war-test in any country in which one happens to be residing, one is bound in honour to side distinctly with either one or the other of the combatants. On general principles I believed, and believe, that a vindication of British authority in the Transvaal would benefit, or rather would have benefited the majority of its inhabitants; and hence I determined not to ask favours from the Boers, but to do all that lay in my small sphere of action to help the side that I felt was the one I ought to wish to win. I therefore, of my own accord, offered my waggons and oxen to the officer in question. He gladly accepted the offer, telling me that he should like to have the waggons and spans in an hour's time; and I sent out for my poor oxen, and by the given time had delivered them and their drivers and foreloopers over to the government. I did not know that such would be the case at the time, but by doing so I gained several advantages which, had I not come forward in this manner, I should have missed. And as I am on the subject of my animals, I may as well say that I succeeded in saving my horses from being seized for mounting the so-called volunteers, by offering them to the government for a special service—which service, as matters turned out, was never required of them.

Everything was now confusion. The streets were full of waggons, Kaffirs, half-castes, and white people, intermingled here and there with officers, orderlies, or volunteers on horseback. In every house the women were busy packing up, unless they were stupefied with fear, as they were in some cases. Arrests were being made every now and then on charges of conspiracy with the enemy, which were in some cases I know of made very lightly, although the suspicion may have been strong. Numbers of farmers from the immediate vicinity of Pretoria had come in with their families for protection, and swelled the already thick ranks of the emigrant population. I rode to the Felmans, and found them in a state of distraction. I had meant to speak about my goods, but it was impossible to obtain a hearing.

On Tuesday the order circulated that all the inhabitants were to go into camp, and we were also told that all those who adhered to the loyal cause should receive full compensation for any loss they might receive from so doing. I hastened to the Commissariat Yard, to see if I could get Major W——, who was in command, to let me have back my large tent-waggon. He was not there, but as I was riding away I heard a horse's gallop behind me, and turning saw him. He said he had seen me, and guessed what I wanted, so had followed me, and we cantered to where the waggons were working, and he gave me the order I required. The oxen were to be sent to him again the next day.

Once more I loaded up, not leaving anything in the house, and just as the oxen were inspanned, we heard the report of a cannon. Oh! the terror of those boys of mine! The Boers were upon us! We should not be in time to get into camp! All the roads to the camp were crammed with ox-waggons being hurried along, with mule-waggons dashing along, with people on foot, women, little children, some carrying a bundle, some a mattress, or a chair, some pulling a hand-cart piled up with articles hastily snatched from their dwellings; and all this in mud, and with the thunder growling overhead. Suddenly a rattling peal came through the poort near the camp, and a cloud of thick rain driven by the wind came sweeping towards us from it.

"The Boers! look at the smoke of the firing!" cried the boys.

But soon a torrent of rain showed them their mistake. Through this pelting shower I, and the rest of the Pretorian wanderers, made our way to headquarters, and were there told what?—That there had been a mistake as to our going into camp that day, that the camp was not ready to receive us, that we must go back and return the next day. So all the poor women and little children, who had toiled up through the mud and wet, had to toil back again to the homes they had dismantled. It was a sad procession to look at. That evening, I, as having but little to move, a horse to ride, and last, not least, no little children, wet, cold, and tired, to console and feel anxious about, was probably the happiest person in Pretoria.

The next day we all fairly went into camp and prepared for the siege.

Chapter 31

Any one who has paid me the compliment of reading this story of my adventures will, perhaps, remember that in the earlier chapters I mentioned that I was writing in the besieged camp of Pretoria; and, indeed, the principal part of my book was written there, partly with a view of recording facts which might prove interesting, and possibly instructive, to a few, and partly to while away the time. I am finishing the story when the war, of which the siege formed a small episode, is a thing of the past—a past which, if I do not mistake, will have an important influence on numbers to whom the Transvaal is, and will remain, utterly unknown, except as a small part of Africa, which gave rise to a peculiar exhibition of political incapacity on the part of those who sway the British nation at the present time, and have swayed it for some time past. Our colonial policy is not a thing of today, nor are the ideas which have had their outcome in a convention—which, if it has not pleased, has certainly astonished everybody—ideas of sudden growth. Before attempting to describe the life we led in camp, I must try and describe the camp itself. Although I talk of the camp, there were in reality three camps on the hill above Pretoria, exclusive of the camps formed in the convent, and in the prison within the village, of which I knew little. On the hill there was the military camp, which, although composed in great part of civilians, was called military, partly, I fancy, because most of the able-bodied men attached to families quartered in it were either members of the mounted volunteers, or in what was called the Reserve Force, and principally because it was circumscribed by the military lines. At a short distance from this, there was what was called the civil camp, the able-bodied men in which belonged to no corps, but had to do picket-duty; and at some distance from it, higher up on the hill, was a camp inhabited by coloured people. Just below the military camp was the great kraal where the cows and slaughter cattle were kept at night, and a little above it was the so-called Government kraal, made of waggons impressed by the Government, or belonging to them, in which the Government oxen, and all the impressed trek oxen but mine, and one span belonging to my old acquaintance, Mr. Brown, of Rustemberg, were kept [. . .]. The native camp was composed of tents pitched round an old hut or two, and from its position it certainly struck me very forcibly that it was very possible for continual communication to be kept up between it and the insurgents. It is an absolute fact that their leaders knew most of our movements, and as it certainly was impossible for any doubt to exist that, if so inclined, a Kaffir could any night have slipped in and out of the camp without being observed by the outposts, I have very little doubt that such communication took place. The civil camp was composed of waggons with awnings, or side-tents made to them with buck-sails or other canvas; of tents, and of a few little canvas houses, although these last were only erected a week or so after the siege commenced. Some of these had boards put down for the floors, and were in some cases divided into rooms. The military camp consisted of all these elements, and besides of the ordinary soldier's bungalows (long, low, stone buildings), and of other so-called bungalows, made of wooden framework with canvas drawn over it. All of these bungalows were given up to accommodating the women and children who could not be accommodated with tents, or who had no waggons of their own in the military camp; and the beds in them were almost touching each other. Every night the women and children of the civil camp had to come up to one or other of these bungalows to sleep, so as for them to be within the military lines in case of attack; and wretched work, indeed, it was for the poor things on wet evenings and mornings. The first evening that the order came out, it happened to rain, and to continue raining all night. At the last moment it was found that there was not sufficient accommodation for all of them. Some, after standing in the wet, were obliged to paddle back through the running water to the civil camp, others got into tents not yet properly protected by trenches from the rain, and I saw them in the damp morning shivering with cold, their bedding, which they had had to bring with them, soaked through, and the floor of the tent one big puddle. On the whole, however, I think, considering all things, the camp was well managed as far as the comfort and health of its inmates were concerned. With a number of people all crammed together in a confined space, discomfort is, of course, unavoidable; and the discomfort naturally tends to cause irritation between the members of the community. I had my own waggon in the military camp, and made a comfortable side-tent to it, and had besides the advantage of having my waggon at the end of a line of waggons facing a main road through the camp, so that I was not subject to the same annoyances as most of my neighbours.

A most miserable sight was that camp, early on a rainy morning, when I would be coming back from the lines where the horses were picketed, with my waterproof over me, and the water running, very likely, over my boots. Women of various ranks emerging from their tents, or from their waggons, slipping in the mud, or plashing into the water so soon as they stepped on the ground; making their coffee, or preparing the breakfast over the little fire some shivering Kaffir was trying to blow into a blaze, while a little child, perhaps, held on to them and cried, or bewailed itself from within the tent. In many cases numbers of people were stowed away in one waggon, and both in these waggons and in the bungalows ablutions had to be very much restricted, and many people both looked and were very dirty.

Against this picture I may set that of a fine evening, after the band had ceased playing. Then all the various habitations were alight, and one caught glimpses of illuminated interiors, with, dashes of bright colour in them, arranged in long vistas. The campfires burnt cheerily, and one heard nothing but merry voices and laughter from the groups of coloured people assembled round them and from the promenaders, whilst here and there a gay party would be assembled, and one would hear snatches of song—and even, in one bungalow, the sound of a piano.

Of course there was an unlimited amount of scandal and gossip of all sorts, and of course there was also an unlimited amount of squabbling, more or less serious, varying from the quarrel between Mrs. A——and Mrs. B——, which raged femininely and furiously, but nevertheless privately, to the noisy vociferation between another pair of ladies, which woke the neighbours from their slumbers for some fifty yards around the scene of warfare. Besides these quarrels there were, of course, occasional rows between the inhabitants of the bungalow where the less aristocratic members of society were accommodated, which took the form of unparliamentary language, and which, when human patience (in the shape of the sentry on guard) could endure it no longer, had to be suppressed by the master of the ward.

These ward-masters had a hard time of it, I fear. They were civilians, appointed over different blocks of the camp, to see that the orders issued from headquarters were observed, and to be general referees on disputed matters. The smoke grievance, which was perpetually recurring, must have caused many of these persecuted mortals to become prematurely grey. It was a general conviction of the camp-mind that the owner of a fire could prevent the smoke from the said fire drifting into his neighbours' nostrils. This peculiar mental epidemic was not peculiar to females. Many a time an indignant head of the family would exclaim, appealing to his particular ward-master, "It is outrageous. I cannot allow the ladies of my family to be inconvenienced in this manner." And then, if the bewildered official shrugged his shoulders in despair, an appeal would be made to the camp-quartermaster. This office was held by a youthful officer, who, I think, had a quiet enjoyment of a joke—a young officer who, although he never in my presence did wear them, always impressed me with the idea that he wore pale kid gloves—a young officer who never appeared to be in a hurry, although he worked hard, and who (as I learnt from many a conversation) had a singularly exasperating effect upon minds excited by the influences of camp life. I remember seeing this young gentleman seized upon in his tent by an infuriated neighbour of mine, and carried off to decide a smoke dispute between her and an equally impassioned neighbour of hers.

"The smoke of that lady's fire absolutely suffocates us," cried the one.

"I declare I can't endure her smoke any longer," retorted the accused. "You really must do something to alter this state of things, Mr. H——."

But it was not only on the subject of smoke that the camp-quartermaster was assailed. Once, when he was speaking to some one just in front of my tent, a well-dressed woman rushed at him, exclaiming,—

"Mr. H——, I want some soap. Where can I get it?"

I must give credit to the ward-masters for keeping their wards very fairly clean. There was one ward in particular which was particularly nicely kept, but of which the ward-master was of course particularly obnoxious.

Then there was the light grievance. At first all lights had to be out at nine, but the hour was advanced to ten. Of course there were refractory spirits who would not put out their lights, if only to show their free and independent spirit.

"Put it out now, ma'am," I have heard the soldier who went the rounds say. "You can light it again after I'm gone."

But then sometimes the ward-master or the quartermaster was inconveniently active, and one was caught, as I was once, and had my candle ordered out, interrupting me in a species of hunt attended with much anxiety in camp, viz., the flea-hunt! If the camp was not a paradise for man and beasts, it certainly was for fleas and flies. Not but that there were many human beings who enjoyed the camp thoroughly. I have heard more than one girl and child aver it would be "nice" to have it over again. There were lots of flirting and lots of playing to be had. Every day was a holiday to the children, who swarmed to the gates of the camp to see the volunteers, the soldiers, and the cannon go out, as if they were going on parade—who swarmed there too, I am sorry to say, in a state of half-amused, half-frightened excitement, to see the wounded men and horses come in. They became wonderfully knowing did those children.

"Hark to the boom of the gun," I said to a little girl, as we were watching the engagement at Henning Pretorius's camp; "do you see the smoke?"

"That is not firing," replied the little wretch, quite confidently. "That is dynamite. They must have got to the lager, and be blowing it up."

One great event every day was the getting the rations at the booth appointed for the purpose in each ward. It was a frightfully tedious affair, and a most grotesque picture did it offer. Old and young—men and women—Kaffirs with the name of their employer written on a piece of paper, either in their hands or fastened on to them, some carrying baskets, some dishes, cups, all sorts of things; all crowding round the unfortunate men who had to serve out the rations. There was plenty of grumbling, and also plenty of joking. One old farmer of the name of Cockcroft, who had been in the camp at Durban when the Boers besieged it, had a standing joke with me when any one grumbled about the meat being bad or the rations being small.

"They'll be glad to come to dine with us presently" he would say, chuckling. "I'm glad you've got that leather fore-tow.[87] It'll make good soup yet."

He remembered eating soup made of the same ingredient, just before relief came to that gallant little band in Natal.

Mr. Cockcroft was a very fine old fellow, and very touching it was to see him leading his blind wife. They had lately bought a fine farm not far from Pretoria. They had worked hard and had got on well, and had invested their earnings in it. Their son was in the volunteers—a hard-working young farmer. When we were listening to the firing from Swartkopjee, two officers rode up to where he was standing near to me.

"Heavy firing, Mr. Cockcroft," said one of them, "I'm afraid there won't be much of your house left; they must be just close to it."

"Let it go," cried the old man, with kindling eyes; "if only it gives some shelter first to our poor fellows."

"Ah!" exclaimed one of the officers, "that's the right sort of spirit, Mr. Cockcroft."

Yet this gallant old farmer is now a ruined man.

As time went on, little concerts, bazaars, and theatrical entertainments were got up in camp—open air performances of course—and there was a little camp newspaper. The band of the 21st played every evening, except, indeed, for some while after the disastrous fight at the Red House,[88] for then there were many dangerously wounded, and it was thought that the noise would disturb them. There were invitations to dinner also occasionally, and on one occasion there was a grand birthday festival given by a certain old gentleman, who, on rising to make his speech returning thanks, remarked, "Little did I think this night sixty-two years ago, when I was born, that I should live to see," &c, &c, thereby, of course, bringing down the house.

My time was taken up in a routine, of which the following is the outline. I got up at dawn, and went to see the horses fed, and then walked to the Government kraal, to see how the oxen were. Early coffee. Went to fetch the rations (for by going myself, instead of sending a boy, I got better rations); then breakfast; afterwards rode down to the village and let the horses graze, while I generally lay on the grass and either worked or did nothing, except when I would take pen and paper with me, and write some of this history. Home to dinner at about five; looked to the horses being settled for the night, inspected the oxen; then paid visits. [. . .]

The weather was very stormy, and children and delicate people suffered severely. Many a coffin was taken down in a cart to the little graveyard with a few mourners walking after it; a few flowers plucked from some deserted garden strewn on it. Poor, inglorious martyrs, sacrificed for nothing! The number of deaths was at last so great that there was difficulty in obtaining planks for the coffins, and those earthworks in which wood had been used as a support, had to be demolished to supply what was necessary, the earthworks, being replaced by brick walls. I never thought the village of Pretoria so pretty as I did when riding through its deserted streets, in which the grass grew knee-high, until cut for hay for the horses in camp, whilst the neglected gardens bloomed in glorious luxuriance. The Felmans' erf was now beautiful to behold, the thick luscious green herbage covering up all signs of former disorder and dirt. The stores were all closed, the streets almost deserted. Sometimes I came across the Government horses and mules, sent out to graze under guard; and sometimes a few dropping shots would be heard, and they would be hastily collected and brought near to camp for fear of some sudden raid. On the hills around, the cattle were pastured under the surveillance of a guard, and they too were often to be seen hurrying home for fear of capture. Sometimes a storekeeper would obtain permission to leave the camp (all men had to obtain passes), and would half open his store for a few hours; then the place would be thronged by people, mostly women.

By order of the Government, mule-waggons plied between the camp and the village three times a day. I never tried them, having my horses; but I heard that those who drove in them suffered excruciating torture, owing to their being springless. Sometimes Mrs. Parker used to visit her pretty cottage (it looked so sad to see it deserted), and then she used to ask me to a picnic there. Once when I was at my own erf, and the horses grazing quietly near me, I was a spectator of a small engagement quite close to the village. A party had been sent out as an escort to a mowing-machine. The Boers made a raid, reinforcements were sent out to our men, but the Boers had the best of it. They captured the mowing-machine!

There was great demoralization among all the coloured people in camp. Very stringent orders had been issued against any violence being used to them, and the upshot of this was that they became very insolent, and that their masters and mistresses were afraid of punishing them. I openly punished a leader of mine more than once for neglecting my oxen, and was not interfered with, and I must say that my servants were better than most in camp; but I everywhere heard complaints, and saw myself that some very bad influence was at work among the coloured people. The drunkenness among them was very great, and this while civilians, not volunteers, could not obtain wine or spirits unless they got a special order from the Provost Marshal on a particular store, or an order from the doctor. Of course it was supposed to be the rule that no liquor at all was sold to coloured people, unless they presented a written order from their employers, and the requisite order from the Provost Marshal as well; but the rule was openly and constantly disregarded, while the storekeepers were obliged to be very strict with white people. For instance, I once wanted some Pontac wine, so I went to the Provost Marshal and asked for an order. He asked me what wine I wanted, what number of bottles I wanted, and at what store I was going to buy the wine. I told him, and he wrote out the order, and I went to the store; then it turned out that at this particular store there was no Pontac, so my order was of no use. In the meantime my groom often got enough liquor to get drunk upon. The fact about the coloured population was, I believe, this. The authorities were afraid of them, and winked at their sins. The immense number of them in camp helped the general demoralization, and there were doubtless many messages sent backwards and forwards between the Boers and their secret friends in camp, by means of these people.

One day my driver "boy" told me that a friend of his had come in from Waterberg, and had brought word that Mapeela had broken out and had driven off numbers of the Boers' cattle, had also put all the women and children of the Boers in that part of the country into a sort of lager, and had provided for them, saying, that he would show his respect for the English by treating them well; but had dragged a man, whom he had found hiding among them, outside the lager, and killed him then and there. It seemed odd to me to think of this self-same Mapeela sitting by my waggon in his smart dress a short time previously. I heard afterwards that the Boers in part of Waterberg had cruelly ill-used unoffending Kaffirs during the war, and this I learnt from the Landrost of Nilstrom, who came into Pretoria after the war was over. He told me he had seen them seize a Kaffir, tie him up, and give him fifty lashes on his bare back for no fault.

On Thursday, the 6th of January [1881], the first sortie from the camp took place. This was the occasion when the fighting occurred near Mr. Cockcroft's farm. The troops and volunteers went out long before dawn: we heard the firing early in the morning. This was our one successful engagement. In the afternoon the wounded and the prisoners were brought in. We had four killed. The prisoners were all Waterberg men, but I was glad to learn that none of my old acquaintances were among them. Their leader, who was severely wounded, and a prisoner, caused a good deal of not very creditable nonsense, as it seemed to me, to be talked in camp. I believe it is true that he had allowed his men to fire under a flag of truce, still I think it would have been better, had there been no talk as to the desirability of curing him of his wounds in order to hang him afterwards. This was, of course, purely unofficial talk, but it was argued that as, according to the proclamation of the Government these men were rebels, and as he, as chief, had allowed the white flag to be violated, it was evident that he must be hung, and I regret to say many who spoke thus seemed to hope he might be so treated. Now began the piteous sight of women, watching with pale, anxious faces, to catch the last glimpse of their dear ones, as they rode out in either the Pretoria Carabineers, or Nourse's Horse;[89] hastening from point to point to see the last of their retreating figures, gazing with aching eyes and hearts at the little column until it was lost to sight, and then going back with pinched faces to their waggons and tents, to wait to hear the first gun, and so to wear away the day until the first few rode in to tell the fortune of the warfare. I used to admire those women! There was no ostentatious anxiety or grief, but you would see their poor trembling lips, and nervously clasped hands, and eyes strained bravely to try to keep back their tears, as they hastened to where they could get tidings of those who might perhaps be destined never to return, or to return only to die. On Friday the funerals of those who had lost their lives cast a gloom over all, still we had been successful, and that was something. Two of Mrs. Parker's sons were in the Pretoria Carabineers as officers, and one was slightly injured in this engagement. Mrs. Farquason's husband was also an officer in this corps.

This was the only success we had. There were other small sorties without any engagement taking place, between the 6th and the 16th of January, when an attack was made on Henning Pretorius's camp, situated on the randt within view of our camp. An attempt was made to distract the attention of the Boers by exploding dynamite in an opposite direction, and the ruse partially succeeded; but after some heavy firing, which was watched with intense interest from our camp, we were obliged to retreat. While almost all our available men were absent, there was a sudden alarm that a body of Boers were advancing to attack the camp from the side opposite to Henning Pretorius's position. A shot or two from our guns caused them, however, to retire. On the return of our men we heard that two wounded men had been left in the hands of the Boers, and great dissatisfaction was expressed by the volunteers as to the management of the whole affair. The next day a Kaffir brought a flag of truce from the Boer camp, to say that we ought to send an ambulance for these two wounded men. This Kaffir said that Henning Pretorius was severely wounded, and that about thirty Boers had been killed.

With regard to the dissatisfaction of the volunteers, I may say that it increased as time went on, and that, so far as I know, the regular troops were dissatisfied also; and I think, from what I heard and observed, they had reason on their side. The volunteers said that they were sent on far in front of the guns and troops, riding in file, and were never properly supported, besides being often employed in work unsuited to their capacities; for that it was useless to try to take a lager with irregular or regular cavalry. The troops complained that they were shown off to disadvantage, being kept back from being engaged, and not receiving orders as to what they were to do. This particularly applies to the disastrous sortie on Saturday, the 12th of February.

Early in the morning of that day I heard sounds among the horses, indicating that there was going to be a move, and presently I heard the tramp and clank of the horses being harnessed to the guns; then that of the volunteers riding past my tent to headquarters. I got up and looked out. There they went—tramp, tramp, through the dark; and, as I looked at them, I felt one of those presentiments of evil, which may or may not be true, but which nevertheless affect one painfully at times. This was a large sortie, and was supposed to be a very secret one; but all the time the Boers knew all that we were planning. Colonel Gildea was in command. Captain Sanctuary, mounted on Wellington, rode at the head of the Pretoria Carabineers for the last time. I give my account of the action from what I was told by a volunteer officer who was present, and I have had corroboration of what I say from others. The Boers were quite prepared for us. Colonel Gildea was wounded early in the action; the second in command lost his head. The volunteers, pushed on in front as usual, were exposed to a galling fire from the Boers, whilst the troops and guns remained aloof, and took no part in. the engagement.

Captain Sanctuary was shot through the leg; and Mr. Mackenzie Walker took command. His men were wavering; the only orders he could get from the officer who had taken Colonel Gildea's place was an exclamation,—

"Oh! what a—mess we are in!" and then "Retire."

But Mr. Walker rallied his men to keep the Boers in check, and to try to save the ambulance, behind which the doctors were dressing Captain Sanctuary's wound. He pointed out to the commanding officer that if they retired the ambulance would be taken; it was of no use, so, on his own responsibility, Mr. Walker formed his men, and tried to rescue the ambulance.

As he passed some infantry, he exclaimed, "Good God! why don't you fire?"

"We have no orders, sir," answered one of the men. Captain Sanctuary's wound was not yet dressed; the troops were retiring; the Boers cutting the volunteers off from the main body.

"Better put him in," cried Walker, "and let us try to save him and the rest;" for there were other wounded.

No, the doctor thought he would finish the dressing first; and in despair Mr. Walker had to retire and leave the ambulance, the wounded, and the doctors. One of the Boers levelled his rifle at a man in attendance on it.

"For shame," cried the latter; "do you fire on the hospital?"

But fire he did, and killed the man; another shot at the ambulance, wounded a man already wounded, who lay in it. In the meantime the volunteers, having protected the retreat of the troops, retreated themselves. They found a mule-waggon deserted on the road by the troops who had been in it. One of the mules was killed; the men had jumped off and fled, so the volunteers cut the dead mule loose, and one of them drove the waggon into camp, or it, too, would have fallen a prey.

When the news of this defeat came into camp, great was the grief and dismay. The greatest sufferer was an old Boer lady; her only son was the man wounded a second time while in the ambulance, and left a prisoner among his enemies; his father, a Boer from the old colony and a faithful English subject, was very obnoxious to the Transvaal Boers. The name of the wounded, man was—Desiderius (commonly called Deesy) Erasmus. He was one of a large family—the youngest, and the only boy, and was the darling of his sisters, and the very apple of his father and mother's eye. A fine, young fellow, broad shouldered and strong, but a mere boy in years and in innocence. His father had gone to Colonel Gildea when Deesy had joined the corps, and had so besought him in the name of the boy's mother and his own, to place him in the reserve, that the colonel had at last consented; but the young fellow held firm.

"No, father," he said; "I have never disobeyed you or caused my mother grief before, but now I must do so; this is a matter of honour; not even for your sakes can I let myself be called a coward."

Nothing would move him, and so he rode out after Captain Sanctuary on that dark morning; now he was a prisoner, and doubly wounded, in the hands of his enemies. His mother and one of his sisters (the wife of Major Ferreira, who had gone to the Basuto war) went to Sir Owen Lanyon, and prayed to be sent to the Boer camp under a flag of truce to see him, and the Administrator granted their petition, and placed a mule-waggon at their disposal. It was the act of a kind-hearted gentleman, but surely hardly an advisable act, particularly when the enemy had been openly styled rebels. When the ladies arrived at the Boer outposts and told what they had come for, the message was sent up to headquarters, and presently some of the chief men came to them, and laughed at the idea of allowing them to see the boy; but the mother and sister would take no refusal; they wept and prayed, and besought these men, by all they held dear, to let them see their darling, and at last they prevailed. They were taken to where he lay, and all night long they nursed him in a tent, the Boer commander coming in occasionally, and asking if he could assist them in any way. Outside in camp, all was joy and festivity over their victory, and the captured ambulance.

In the morning the ladies returned to Pretoria, bringing a message, that if we wished for the prisoners to be given up, we must release the prisoners we had taken at our first engagement, and must agree to send back the ambulance to the Boers, after it had conveyed the wounded to our camp. And so it was.

The next day the prisoners were brought in, the Boers sending a slaughtered sheep along with them, which (I was told by one bred amongst them) was a covert insult; and all the Boer prisoners were released. One of them, going to Lydenburg, was fallen upon by Kaffirs, and torn in pieces. There were many wounded, most of them were severely wounded. Captain Sanctuary's leg was despaired of, and Deesy Erasmus' life, besides that of others. He had received a wound (which grazed the stomach) through the body, besides one in his leg. At first he seemed to rally, but it was a false hope, and in a few days he passed away, conscious and calm to the last—nay, almost cheerful, although he knew he was dying. One of his comrades, a Mr. Simpson, died the day before, an artilleryman had died before him, and Captain Sanctuary, after his leg being amputated, lingered to the 7th of March, and then followed his companions in arms. There was a profound feeling of sorrow through all the inhabitants of the camp on the day when the body of this kindly and gallant officer was borne, with military honours, to the little graveyard in the valley.

In the meantime we had had news of the reinforcements that were coming to relieve us, and we were counting the days until we should see Sir George Colley[90] ride through Bobian-poort at the head of a victorious column. Some said one day, some said another would be the likely one for the welcome sight to greet our eyes, but none doubted that we should see him.

On the fifteenth (Tuesday) we saw about twenty waggons, under escort, defile through a poort to the east of the camp, and crossing the valley, outspann on the opposite ridge, while a Boer, bearing a flag of truce, rode towards us. Colonel Gildea, who had only just risen from his bed, rode out to meet him in company with other officers. They brought back letters for the Administrator, and a Dutch newspaper, printed in the Free State; and the rumour that our troops had been defeated, and that Sir George Colley was killed, flew from mouth to mouth. But many would not, could not, believe it, and I was one of these. It seemed too dreadful, too incredible, to believe, until official confirmation came. Alas! it came too soon. We were now put on half-rations, but still there was enough to eat.

There was an armistice now, and it was very dreary. I used to wonder how the Administrator and some others could have the heart to play polo of an evening. The true state of affairs was not known generally, and all sorts of rumours were continually flying about; still, there was enough known to cause a great feeling of depression, though no one expected what followed.

On the evening of Monday, the 28th of March, I was sitting in Mrs. Parker's waggon talking to her, when a girl rushed up, and told us hurriedly that three officers had just ridden in from Newcastle: that there had been a great battle, in which Sir Evelyn Wood[91] had completely defeated the Boers, and that he and some of the Boer leaders would be in Pretoria the next day to discuss the terms of peace. Oh! I shall never forget that moment! To leap from the waggon and hasten to headquarters was but the work of an instant. Crowds were pouring towards the same goal. It was quite dark. Arrived in the square, we all waited breathlessly for the news to be proclaimed. The officers who had ridden in were with Colonel Gildea, the Administrator, and Colonel Bellairs. We waited and waited, but no sign was given, and then I heard whispers that there had been no victory, that peace had been concluded on the terms dictated by the Boers, that the country was to be given back! It seemed incredible; but a chill struck through all those assembled, and they dispersed gradually and silently, to wait until the morning should bring them some distinct official information. How well; I remember that morning! I woke early, as usual, but with a dull, listless feeling of impending misfortune. I had then no reason to believe that personally I should be a very heavy sufferer. It was not for myself that I felt the bitter ache at my heart, it was for the honour of England, a thousand times worse than any pain caused by personal loss: the one I could retrieve by courage and steadiness, but it made me feel almost mad to think that I was powerless to move so much as a feather's weight to retrieve the other. I went as usual to see to the horses, and as I stroked their sleek necks I thought with a keen pain, almost amounting to agony, how glad, how really thankful I was that I had been able to win a reprieve for my pets from having been uselessly, and therefore cruelly sacrificed, while many a mother was being ground to the very dust by the crushing torment of knowing that her boy, whose life she had told herself in the midst of her woe was lost in upholding a cause she cherished, had in reality been sent forth, recklessly, wantonly, to swell the ranks of death. For what? For the *dishonour* of that cause. A volunteer, an Englishman, one who had no stake whatever in the Transvaal, but who, happening to be in Pretoria, had joined Sanctuary's corps, spoke to me as I stood there. "So it has come to this," he said; "we have been fighting for nothing! The country is given back."

"It can't be true," I cried, although, after the dead silence at headquarters the previous night, I knew in my heart it was, "I won't believe it till I see it in general orders."

"It is there now," he answered; "young S—— has just seen it; he is almost mad. He was a rich man in his own belief yesterday; today he is little better than a beggar."

Yes, it was quite true. I went to see the oxen. I was luckier than most. By hard work and incessant watching them, so that I got for them every nibble of grass that was to be got while they were not working, by buying the stalks of mealeas out of private gardens for them at an enormous price, by covering them with rugs if they seemed ill, I had brought most of them through, when other oxen working for government were dying in numbers! I was the luckiest person in camp, and I felt almost as if I were selfish as I walked through the lines of tents and waggons on my way back, thinking of the ruin that had fallen on almost all in them. I went to the Higginses' little shanty. They knew they were ruined. They tried to take it bravely, did take it bravely, but you saw that the knowledge struck home. They had staked all on their faith in English trustworthiness. They had believed implicitly in the repeated asseverations of the Government that the Transvaal should remain British territory; they had broken utterly with the Boers, they had lost all their oxen and cows, all their sheep, all their crops, all but two of their horses, and they were destined henceforth to be subject to the men whom we, by our promises, had tempted them to turn from friendly neighbours into enemies. The Sturtons were close to them in their waggon and tent. It was the same with them, only worse. Their very house had been despoiled, and they were old—very old. But it is useless to particularize. Wherever you turned in that little camp you saw faces, heard voices that told you of ruin; sometimes the thought of it was patiently borne, but the thought of the disgrace, which seemed to have been thrust on them, roused the anger of these men and women.

"Look at those fellows," cried one old tradesman as two officers rode past; "look at them with their well-groomed horses and their dandy airs! It's all they're good for to look pretty. We wouldn't have disgraced ourselves." "You'd better take off your coats," cried another, as he passed some other officers; "you're only carrying about the badge of your disgrace."

Even the Kaffirs jeered at us. In the midst of all this, a large body of Boers were seen riding close past the camp. I was walking through the volunteers' lines as they did so. The excitement was great. Some cried out to muster and charge them, not to submit to the insult that was being thrust on them; some swore; others cried out that they cared for nothing now, but would go and get dead drunk. This excitement had hardly subsided when Henning Pretorius, Joubert (I think), and Hendrick Schumann rode up to headquarters on their shaggy nags, then rode through the camp to greet old acquaintances. How proud those men must have felt that day, when the handsomely dressed gentlemen in military attire had to acknowledge them (whom they had termed, and unjustly termed, "rebels") their virtual conquerors. It was of no use trying to hide the fact under the cloak of generosity; the Boers knew in their hearts that we should not have attempted to fight if there had been any generosity in the matter, and so did we all, and we both knew also, that we had found them a harder nut to crack than we expected, and that the Government at home had considered the game not worth playing out. I knew Hendrick Schumann, but I could not, and would not greet him then; but I saw him meet his only sister and kiss her, and that was a pleasant sight even to my eyes. But it was not pleasant to see men who had truckled to the English, now truckling to them—and that I also saw.

The next morning, I determined to take my waggon out, and return to my house. The whole camp was breaking up. I rode through the streets of the village early in the morning. Groups of Boers were riding about, looking proud and contented, a little insolent, perhaps, but that was not to be wondered at. Numbers of Boer waggons laden with produce had come in to the market. I saw Hendrick Schumann standing by his waggon in the midst of a knot of Boers, so I went up and spoke to him.

"I am sorry for the peace," I said, "it is a disgrace to my country; but so far as my feelings towards you are concerned, I heartily congratulate you; You have fought well and have got your reward."

He took my hand. "What you say is true," he said, "and I thank you;" and his friends gave a united grunt.

The village now became a scene of disorder. The canteens opened, the whole population, black and white crowded into them, and things got worse instead of better the next day. For some reason, the coloured men who had been impressed by Government were not immediately paid off. They wanted to get away to their families, but they had to wait, and in the meantime, having nothing else to do, they drank. The streets were full of howling, reeling wretches. All order seemed gone. Horses were stolen in the most daring manner [. . .]. Heavily as the destruction entailed by the peace has fallen on us English in the Transvaal, the real sufferer is the loyal Africander, and the loyal Boer. Our policy has robbed them not only of their property, but of their home, of even their country; and they, unlike us English, cannot face the thought of leaving the land they have been bred in, to cross the sea and carve out a home for themselves elsewhere, but, if they mean to gain a livelihood for themselves and their children, must bend their necks to the taunts which will be lavished by the Boers on those, who, having fought for and been discarded by the English, are now dependent on them. But the one person I dreaded seeing in Pretoria was Mrs. Erasmus. She had been a fine-looking old lady before Deesy died. Now she was bent, shrivelled with grief. I often saw her, but it was ever the same sad wail that I heard, and what could I, or any one, say in answer to it? "Oh! if only he had died for any purpose! Oh! I clung to the thought that I had given him for his country's sake! But he was sacrificed—murdered! Why should they have sent my boy to be killed for nothing?" His father wandered about silent, the decrepitude of grief stealing over him visibly. Only once he spoke to me of his son's loss, when asking me to let my waggon and oxen take a simple tombstone to his grave.

"I could bear it," he said; "but his mother; oh! his mother!" and he turned away.

Chapter 32

In this my concluding chapter I trust my readers will excuse me if I enter into some details as to the manner in which the war and its results affected me personally. The narrative will hardly be entertaining, but, as hundreds have been ruined in a very similar manner, it will afford an illustration of how the process has been carried out in the Transvaal generally

Not long ago an officer who sat opposite to me at breakfast in an hotel, speaking of the ruin that had befallen numbers in that part of the world, asked me whether I had suffered severely, and on my reply in the affirmative, asked whether the Boers had looted largely? I told him that they had in some few cases, but that in my case, and in the case of the majority of the sufferers, ruin was not the result of being robbed; and he then stated that he could not conceive how this could be the case.

If any one who reads my story is of the same way of thinking, perhaps the end of it may throw a little light on the question.

The animals impressed by Government were all valued some time after they were impressed, and had been working hard, while their food was stinted; they had in consequence become thin. Even in the state they were in, the valuation fell very much under the real value of the animals in a number of cases; for this reason, no allowance was made in favour of salted animals [. . .]. The consequence of this was that most people, including myself, refused the valuation. It is true that I should under no circumstances have sold my oxen to Government, for the government animals are very cruelly treated, and I am afraid there is no remedy in the matter; but in this I am an exception.

When the peace was declared, I, and others, applied to have our animals returned to us, and there was considerable delay in the matter of the oxen. We also applied for hire of them and the waggons. We were told that the Government did not intend to adhere to English law in the matter, but to Roman Dutch law—the old law of the Transvaal; and that the question whether by it we were entitled to payment had been referred to the Attorney-General for his decision. That decision was not given for almost three weeks after the declaration of peace. In my case, and no doubt in others, this was productive of evil; for my already thin oxen had to be kept in Pretoria until, the decision being given, I could leave the village. I wanted to take loads to Natal, and the winter was coming on apace, while owing to there being hardly any grass to be had near Pretoria the poor beasts were getting thinner daily.

If the Government had given over the country to the Boers at once without reserve, the results of the peace would have fallen less heavily on us; but as it was, all of us knew that the Boers would never consent to any partition of the Transvaal. The Boers themselves said so openly, but, in the face of the terms of the Convention,[92] every one believed that England meant to retain a portion of it, and this we all knew meant a renewal of war, and an alliance between the Free-State and the Transvaal. This knowledge determined numbers, at great personal loss, to leave the Transvaal, if only for a time. My belief in this eventuality made me determine to risk taking my poor oxen to Natal with loads, rather than take them to Mr. Higgins's farm for the winter; my own farm would have been too cold for them in their impoverished state.

The belief that war was imminent was prevalent amongst the military as well as civilians, and was increased by its being known that the forts round Pretoria were being strengthened. The Boers, too, spoke of the great probability of war; and indeed what official intelligence we received breathed the same thought. All work was at a standstill in Pretoria. All those who could were leaving the town. Owing to the uncertainty with regard to the settlement of the country all credit was at an end, and people were obliged to realize at a great loss in order to meet current expenses. Numbers of waggon-loads of goods had been stopped on the road. The loads that were coming up to me had been stopped and warehoused at Newcastle. I had to pay for their warehousing, and now they were coming up, at heavy rates, to be thrown on my hands, when there would be no market for them, and I should only have the choice of selling them for a quarter of their value, or warehousing them. The only things which were saleable in Pretoria, at a fair price, were horses and fat oxen, and of the latter the Boers brought in numbers; the value of everything else was wonderfully depreciated. The auctions were crowded with articles for sale, but there were no buyers, for there was no money. I saw a cart which would have been cheap at thirty-five pounds sold for five; a handsome silver-mounted biscuit box (it was real silver) sold for less than ten shillings; a very nice house with a large well-stocked garden, put up without reserve, and not a single bid made for it. There was absolutely no money in Pretoria. The shops were offering goods for cost price, to get rid of them without loss, for loads which had been stopped on the road during the war were now coming up to them, and the market was diminishing daily. The whole village was in a fearful state of demoralization, and it was hard to keep one's boys in hand at all. I have had to go personally to force a boy away from a canteen, and as a rule they were all either half or quite drunk. Thieving too was going on to a great extent in the village, for, once outside it, the thief could defy the law, so that the temptation to rob and bolt was very great.

The Felmans' house had been, I heard, broken into during the siege; I wanted Mrs. Felman to go there with me then, and see whether any of my things had been taken, but she always made some excuse, and refused to let me have the key of the house to look. I had told her husband that if I was not allowed to investigate the matter in my own interest then, so as to be able to make an affidavit as to my loss and ask for compensation, I should be obliged to hold him responsible. At the end of the siege it turned out that all my property was gone, but it was of no use holding him responsible, for he was bankrupt.

Mr. Higgins had gone to Surprise, to see how things were there. He brought me back word that all my lambs were gone—dead or stolen; that seventy of my sheep, including all my wethers and my best ewes, were stolen, some of them having been taken after peace was proclaimed, and that my ram was also gone [. . .] and he said that the remaining ewes were in a pitiable condition from neglect. All his sheep were gone, so I asked him if he would care to buy mine cheap. He answered that he had no money. Mr. Sturton had lost his sheep, but he too had no money to buy any, and, indeed, was living in Pretoria in his waggon, unable to leave, for it would have been useless for him to go, without oxen, to his desolated farm.

It appeared that the Nell family had been rejoicing greatly over the discomfiture of the Higginses and had been purloining freely. So much for gratitude!

Added to this, a notice had been sent to Mr. Higgins from the neighbouring Boers, telling him that all his standing crops, and indeed everything he had, was confiscated to the Boer Government, and that he was held responsible for nothing being wanting until the sittings of the Conference should come to an end, when he would be communicated with. I saw the letter stating this myself. Mr. Higgins returned to Pretoria, and reported the matter to the Administrator for the time, Colonel Bellairs. Hendrick Schumann heard of it, and declared, on the part of the Boer Government, that such a letter was utterly unauthorized; also that the seizure of my sheep was an act of violence not authorized by the Boer leaders; but in the meantime Mr. Higgins and I were the sufferers.

I sent a waggon to Jackallsfontein, to bring Jimmy up, and was delighted to find that he had been kindly treated, and that two oxen which I had left on the farm had been kept safe. Little Roughy, too, came up flourishing, but nothing remained of all the crops I had sown. Of course his host made a good penny out of his board, &c., but I was in no humour to haggle—only too glad to see him safe and sound. [. . .]

I was getting anxious about the answer from the Attorney-General. It was very bad for the oxen to remain in Pretoria, the grass being all eaten off; and every day the boys were going from bad to worse; besides, there were no means of making any money, for all work was at a standstill. Rumours of a fresh outbreak of war were rife, and as the Boers all vowed that they would not yield up any of their country, while it was stated distinctly by Government that this was one of the conditions of peace, it seemed likely that the rumours were true. Every day also brought accounts of the dissatisfaction of the Kaffirs, and threats of a general rising against the Boers, if the Transvaal were given back to them. People did not know what to do, and numbers were leaving every day for Natal. I determined to do the same, and agreed to take loads down there. It was the only way of making money; but the danger was that the oxen, already overworked, would not stand the journey in the winter. Every day now was of importance, so as to get over the Drachensberg before the great cold set in—and still the Attorney-General sent no answer.

My oxen were already drooping from bad feeding, and I even lost one of them, a favourite of mine; Hendrick, too, was taking to very bad courses, and I had more than once discovered him in theft, but I contented myself with speaking to him, for it was almost impossible to get drivers, and I did not want to lose him. One evening, after a very hard day's work, I felt ill; I had been on my feet, packing up, so as to be ready to start at a moment's notice, when the decision about the hire of the oxen should be given, and had been in the saddle, too, looking after the oxen that were feeding at some distance, and after the boys, who were all drunk except little Hendrick. The next morning I had hardly got up when I was obliged to lie down again, and from that day I was unable to leave my bed for three weeks! The news of the decision came two days after. It was what I expected. No one was to receive a penny for the use of their oxen and waggons. The Government decided to act on the old Boer law, and by it no hire is allowed in time of war! I believe that it was in consideration of my having given up my oxen and waggons voluntarily, that I was allowed seventy-five pounds as compensation for deterioration in the value of the oxen and waggons. I was told by other sufferers that no such compensation was allowed to them. It was a terrible blow to those who had counted on being paid, and to me the delay in giving me the answer was fatal.

During my illness of course everything went to the bad, and at last I heard that Hendrick was stealing my oxen. I was getting better; had just been moved on to the sofa-chair, and was fortunately more capable of acting than I had been. I had him and the oxen caught, and so escaped this loss; but Hendrick bolted. Weak as I was, I saddled up, and pursued him as far as Derde-poort, taking my revolver with me, but he had the start of me on horseback, and I had to turn back. As it was, I was shaking in the saddle as I rode into the village. I managed after some delay to obtain two drivers ("Boy" and my other driver had left me to go home), neither of them good; and, although still ill, I started, taking Jimmy with me, and discharging Soldat and Clara. My goods had not yet arrived, but I could wait no longer, for the season was too far advanced as it was.

It was a terrible trek. I rode by the side of the oxen myself to see that they were tenderly treated, and not over-driven. I saw them blanketed every night before lying down, and often I have got up of a cold night from where I slept close to them, to see that they were covered. I watched them as if they were children rather than oxen, but all was vain, one by one they drooped, and lay down and died. The weather was very cold. Some I left behind in charge of farmers, but I knew they were doomed. They came to know me so well that I could not only work with them myself, but they would come up to me as I sat by the campfire, would rub their noses on my shoulder, or take mealeas out of my hand, and it was real grief to me to see them wasting away. If it had not been for this, I should often have enjoyed the picture round the campfire of a moonlight night before they were tied up, for the horses too would come and stand with their noses close to my shoulder, and often would try to take a piece of bread out of my hand as I was eating.

It was an unlucky trek throughout. Poor little Roughy was bitten by a snake, and handsome Prince shot through the heart by a Boer. At last my spans were so decimated that at Harrismith they fairly gave in. I had to arrange for the loads to be brought on for me, and at first determined to try to take the oxen loose over the Drachensberg and try to get them on to a warm farm, while I, for a time, once more tried my fortune as a governess, in, if possible, the employment of the owner of the farm, so as to be able to watch over them; but the one day that I had to remain at Harrismith before starting with them showed me my error. It would have been cruelty to have exposed them to the long, toilsome ascent of the Berg, where numbers of them would have lain down in the cold never to rise again, whilst I had an offer of selling them to a man who had sheds to shelter them in, and plenty of good forage to give them. So I sold all but two of them at a third of what I paid for them, and left all of them together with a gentleman who buys half-dying oxen as a speculation, having the means of caring for them, and having a fancy for looking after them. The last thing I saw of them was comforting to a certain extent. They were all busy eating loose forage which was thrown to them with a lavish hand, and seemed to be enjoying themselves, although one of them (one of the two I left as boarders) left his forage to come over to me when he caught sight of me, and put his great wet nose against me in sign of friendship.

The depression of trade in the Transvaal was making itself felt even at Natal. Firms there were offering goods as cheap as you could buy them in some cases in England, and this applies to Harrismith as well. Large stocks of articles had been sent over to firms for transmission to the Transvaal, and were now left on their hands. Crowds of emigrants were coming down from the Transvaal, and the market was overstocked with people wanting employment. There were no good prices being offered for anything except fat oxen, and garden or dairy produce, which latter, strange to say, always commands a high price in South Africa; and instead of being able to sell my waggons well, as I had hoped, I could get no more than about half value for them. The depression was so great that the auctioneers often refused to sell rather than let articles go so much below their real value, as they would have done by accepting the highest bid.

I think what I have told will show those who read it, how ruin has come to numbers owing to the war and the subsequent Convention, without being due to any looting on the part of the Boers. The compensation offered by the Government, even if it be paid, which is doubtful, will come tardily, and only *direct* losses are to be admitted. As a fact, most of the people who have been ruined, have been ruined by *indirect* losses, and this without counting the loss entailed by the depreciation in value of landed property, which is such that properties which would have fetched a high price before the war are now unsaleable. It would be impossible so far as I see, for any government to contemplate compensation for indirect losses, but it is hard that a government can sign away that which numbers have toiled hard to earn; and yet this is what has been done in the matter of the Transvaal. All that I have to add is, that I took Jimmy with me to Natal, where he got a fairly good situation; and that Eclipse and Dandy, and little Moustache, are well, and still belong to me. Herewith I make my bow, and end my story.

THE END.

Notes

* Heckford's spelling of place names is idiosyncratic (she writes them as she hears them pronounced) and I have placed the correct or current spelling in square brackets next to the first appearance of the name. Her punctuation is equally idiosyncratic; she often uses commas to indicate pauses in speech. I have made changes only when the punctuation renders the meaning unclear. Deletions from the text are marked by elipses.

[1] The Anglo-Zulu war (1879). The conflict resulting from the British invasion of Zululand after Cetshwayo's refusal to disband his army at the command of the British High Commissioner, Sir Bartle Frere. The British and colonial forces were defeated at Isandlwana, averted the Zulu invasion of Natal through the bloody battle at Rorke's Drift, and destroyed the Zulu capital of Ulundi, ending the war. The British abolished the Zulu monarchy, exiled Cetshwayo, and divided Zululand into thirteen separate chiefdoms. This led to internal division, the intrusion of land claims from the Transvaal in the north, and, finally, formal annexation of Zululand by Britain in 1887.

[2] A lamp fed by methylated or other spirits, using for heating, boiling, or cooking.

[3] A reference to the proverbial expression (attributed to Horace) that "the mountain labored and brought forth a mouse."

[4] Probably George Warner whose actual identity remains unknown. He may have been the son or ward of Ashton Warner, a Hospital trustee and close friend of the Heckfords. If so, one wonders why he was sent away from home at such a young age. He may also have been one of the Hospital orphans given the name of the trustee.

[5] In this case the term refers to the place in which a fixed-price meal of several courses would be served.

[6] To inspan is to harness draught animals to a vehicle; to outspan is to unyoke them and allow them to rest. Both terms are frequently used in South African English to refer to the harnessing and unyoking of teams of oxen.

[7] A term usually applied to a Dutch or Afrikaans speaking white inhabitant of South Africa. However, Heckford uses the term to apply to English speaking, white South Africans, often calling them "English Afrikanders."

⁸ See note one.

⁹ One of the labors of Heracles, the Greek hero, was cleaning the huge and filthy stables of King Augeas which housed 3,000 horses. Heracles ran two rivers through the structure.

¹⁰ Spears with a pointed, sharpened iron tip and a wooden shaft which may be either short (for stabbing) or long (for throwing); both varieties are used by Africans.

¹¹ The name is probably derived from the term *huttentut* ("stutterer") applied to the Khoihoi people of Southern Africa by the early Dutch settlers on account of the "clicks" which gave Khoihoi speech its distinctive character. The term, originally descriptive of a short people with yellow-brown skin and tightly curled hair, was not considered pejorative in the nineteenth century. However, it was used in later years as an insulting form of address or reference to a person of mixed Caucasian and African race.

¹² To *jib* is to refuse to go.

¹³ A king of Israel who drove his chariot recklessly.

¹⁴ The word means "farmer" and refers to a Dutch or Afrikaans-speaking person from or in the rural areas of South Africa. The term widened to include all Caucasian Afrikaans speakers.

¹⁵ An article of women's clothing originally suggested by the wearing apparel of Polish women. It is a dress or over-dress, consisting of a bodice and overskirt open from the waist down to reveal an underskirt.

¹⁶ It is uncertain whether the questioner means the Dutch Reform Church or the Anglican Church.

¹⁷ Sir Walter Scott's famous novel of 1819 which deals with the conflict between the Norman conquerors and the Saxons they conquered. It is famous for its sympathetic portrait of the medieval Jews caught in the struggle.

¹⁸ A contagious disease of cattle marked by blood-stained urine.

¹⁹ A springbok is a small gazelle, cinnamon-brown and white in color, characterized by its high graceful leaps into the air when it is excited or disturbed.

²⁰ A small mammal similar to a mongoose, found in Southern Africa.

²¹ A nek is a narrow ridge of land, lower than but joining two hills or mountains.

²² A name given to any one of a number of chattering African birds.

²³ Metaphorically, the end of the world.

²⁴ The pseudonym Heckford gives to William Jennings, the owner of Nooitgedacht.

²⁵ This was probably a draft of *Excelsior,* the novel, now lost, that Heckford published in 1884.

²⁶ Heckford's translation of the Afrikaans name of the Higgins' Transvaal farm, Nooitgedacht.

²⁷ A sort of "crown" of rocks or trees.

[28] "Chaste Goddess," an aria from Bellini's opera *Norma* (1831) which Heckford had probably seen in London since it was performed in England from 1833 on. The famous aria is Norma's prayer to the goddess of the moon.

[29] Andries Hendrik Potgieter (1792–1852) was the leader of a group of Boer emigrants from the Cape Colony to Natal in 1836, as part of the Afrikaner migration known as the "great trek." After defeating the Ndebele (see note 21 in the Introduction), he joined forces with Andries Pretorius (see note 53) to defeat the Zulus at the battle of Blood River. He later migrated to the Western Transvaal before finally settling near the Zoutspanberg in the Northern Transvaal.

[30] The term refers to animals, especially horses, who have become immune to a disease after having either survived an attack of it or through being inoculated with weakened disease germs. Salted animals are more valuable than ordinary ones. Bots are parasitic flies that infest animals.

[31] For Cetshwayo, see note 1 above and the notes to the Introduction. Heckford's spelling is erratic; she often guesses at the spelling of African and Afrikaans words.

[32] Also *laager*. Setting up a camp within a ring of wagons or wagons placed in a circle as a defensive fortification.

[33] A military title for a country magistrate or petty official whose duty is to look into crimes committed within his ward.

[34] Usually spelled *Byeenkomste,* an assembly, gathering or meeting.

[35] The British High Commissioner of the Cape Colony sent to implement the British policy of federating Britain's South African colonies and the Boer republics. Believing that an independent Zulu kingdom stood in the way of this plan, he launched an invasion of the Zulu kingdom in Natal in 1879.

[36] A long, rocky hillock.

[37] A variety of beet used as cattle-feed; the English word for it is *mangold.*

[38] *A Day's Ride* (1863) is a novel by Charles Lever (1806–72), a once popular but now forgotten Dublin-born author. It was serialized in its original form in Charles Dickens' magazine, *All the Year Round,* but proved unpopular, prompting Dickens to insert *Great Expectations* instead. Heckford clearly enjoyed Lever's novel, especially a character with an excessively large imagination named "Potts."

[39] Usually spelled mealies or mielies. Maize or Indian corn, usually crushed or ground into meal is an important ingredient in the diets of both white and black South Africans.

[40] Märchen is the German term for fairy or nursery tales. Heckford mentions the favorite stories of nineteenth-century British children, including the tales of the Brothers Grimm, De La Motte Fouque's *Undine,* the story of a water nymph or undine who loves and is betrayed by a Christian knight, and *The Arabian Nights* or *Thousand and One Nights.* Heckford refers to herself as Scheherazade, the name of the queen (in the last mentioned book) who preserves her life by telling stories.

[41] Heckford refers to one of three species of dassy; this one is known as the rock rabbit or great mountain rat. It resembles an ordinary rabbit but is without the tail and the long ears of the European animal. A meerkat is similar to a mongoose.

[42] "Magic Music" was a popular Victorian parlor game. A player is seated at a piano and another leaves the room while the group decides what the absent person must do or find upon reentering the room. When the person is called back in, he or she is given a hint of what must be done or found by the pianist playing either loudly and/or quickly or softly and/or slowly depending on whether the person is "hot" or "cold." "Friar's Ground" is another such parlor game. I have been unable to find a description of its exact nature.

[43] To sham or pretend.

[44] *Die Volkstem* is an Afrikaner newspaper published in Pretoria beginning in 1873. *The [Cape] Argus* is a Cape Town newspaper published from 1857 on and is still in existence.

[45] A coarse woven fabric used as a table or floor covering.

[46] The popular London newspaper, famous for its prints and illustrations.

[47] A euphemism for "drunk."

[48] A Scottish ballad about John Graham, Viscount Dundee, who fought for the Jacobite cause, winning a victory at the battle of Killiecrankie but dying in the conflict.

[49] He was the brother of Stephanus Johannes Paulus Kruger (1825–1904), President of the South African Boer Republic from 1883 until 1900 and regarded by Afrikaners as one of their greatest leaders.

[50] Usually spelled *stellasie*, it is a frame set up for drying fruit.

[51] The term, usually spelled *bastaard*, is descriptive rather than pejorative in Heckford's era. It is used for persons of mixed racial ancestry, usually Khoihoi and Caucasian or sometimes Khoihoi and other African peoples.

[52] Marthinus Wiessel Pretorius (1819–1901), son of Andries Pretorius (1789–1853), the man who had been one of the leaders of the "great trek," became a member of the triumvirate who organized and led the Anglo-Boer war of 1880 in the Transvaal. Along with Piet Joubert and Paul Kruger he also negotiated the retrocession of the Transvaal from Britain. Potchefstroom was the capital of the Transvaal until 1860 when it was superceded by Pretoria. Nevertheless, it remained important as a stronghold of Afrikaner nationalism.

[53] A name for a baby carriage, shortened in British English to the word *pram*.

[54] The name, also spelled *Mosilikatze* and *Mzilikazi*, is that of the founder of the Ndebele people. See note 21 in the Introduction.

[55] Heckford's reference is unclear although it may be to the aristocrats who fled to England during the French Revolution.

[56] Heckford here alludes to Dante Alighieri whose role in the conflict over the governance of Florence led to his fine and exile. He never returned to the city.

[57] In South African parlance, this term is applied to someone of Indian rather than Chinese ancestry. It is derogatory but was commonly used in the nineteenth century.

[58] French, "hurry."

[59] A clumsy, awkward adolescent or youth.

[60] This is an allusion to Nathaniel Winkel of Charles Dickens' *Pickwick Papers*. Winkel, ostensibly the group's sportsman is a bit of a humbug and a failure at sporting activities.

[61] Secocoonees, more correctly *Sekocooni* or *Sekhukhune*, was a tribal chief of the Pedi in the Northern Transvaal against whom the Boers repeatedly fought.

[62] A disease of the skin characterized by deep red inflammations.

[63] A man or boy who assists the driver of a team of oxen by walking alongside of and guiding the animals.

[64] A small plot of land usually measuring about 100 by 200 feet.

[65] Nocturnal animals, also called "bush-babies" that resemble lemurs or small monkeys.

[66] The pole of a wagon between the cart and the oxen that connects the two.

[67] Literally "a quick glance" but here, a "quick overview."

[68] The names of two London department stores of the period.

[69] A wild or riotous dance.

[70] Heckford misspells the name of the tribe; she appears to mean the *Mantatees*. See the Introduction, note 21.

[71] Heckford probably means one of several varieties of zebra; today the term refers to the extinct *equus quagga*, once found in Southern Africa.

[72] An illustrated periodical.

[73] Friedrich August Mortiz Retzsch (1779–1857) was a well-known engraver whose work was popular in England. He illustrated scenes from Goethe, Schiller and Shakespeare and influenced British Victorian artists.

[74] *The Song of the Bell*, a work by Friedrich Schiller (1759–1803).

[75] A pejorative name for an African tribe, possibly the *Magwamba*. The name means *knob-nosed or bulbous-nosed*.

[76] Cannabis or marijuana.

[77] A general name for skin diseases characterized by scabby or scaly eruptions.

[78] See note 61.

[79] Literally, a "good mouth," meaning a delicious morsel or tidbit.

[80] Heckford here reminds De Clerc of his promise to take her on a lion hunt which never materialized, but for which she had paid.

[81] A magistrate, usually *landros* in modern Afrikaans.

[82] Basutoland was taken over by the Cape Colony in 1871, but a magisterial system imposed on the Sotho people provoked resistance and led to a widespread conflict in 1880. When the conflict ended in stalemate, Britain assumed direct responsibility for the territory.

[83] Originally an army colonel, Lanyon took over as administrator of the Transvaal from Sir Theophilus Shepstone in 1879. His inflexibility and "tough line" supposedly led to the confrontation with the Boers in the First South African War (as the war of 1879–80 is now called).

[84] The "tragic interest" attached to the Red House was the unexpected defeat of the British volunteers at a sortie at this farm, also known as the "Red House Kraal." Led by the Pretoria Carabineers, commanded by their popular leader, Captain Sanctuary, the troops attempted a night maneuver to seize the farm and the hill on which it was located. As much a fiasco as a tragedy (the Scottish Fusiliers of the regular British Army did not support the volunteers, since they had not received orders to do so), the incident resulted in a number of deaths including that of Captain Sanctuary.

[85] A mass meeting of Boers to protest British taxation; one of the causes of the Transvaal crisis.

[86] The British 94th regiment, garrisoning Lydenburg but ordered to return to Pretoria was intercepted by the Boer commando at Bronkhorstspruit (about 30 miles from Pretoria) on December 20, 1880. More than half of the regiment was killed or wounded.

[87] A rope used to attach the front horses of a team.

[88] See note 84.

[89] The Pretoria Mounted Carabineers was a cavalry unit composed of British colonial settlers and volunteers as was Nourse's Horse, named after its commander, Captain Henry Nourse. Both units were active during the siege of Pretoria. See the Introduction.

[90] Commander-in-chief of the British forces in Natal, killed at the battle of Majuba while on his way to attempt to lift the siege of Pretoria. The only footnote in Heckford's book is about his attempt to relieve Pretoria. It was thought, Heckford reports, that "he believed the people of Pretoria to be starving," and therefore made a desperate but fatal march.

[91] The High Commissioner of the Transvaal, popular among the colonists of British background since, as a member of the Commission sitting to decide on peace terms, he was considered a "hard liner." He argued for Britain's retention of part of the eastern territories of the Transvaal after the retrocession.

[92] The Convention of Pretoria of 1881 revoked Britain's annexation of the Transvaal and provided for Afrikaner self-rule subject to the suzerainty of Queen Victoria.

About the Editor

CAROLE G. SILVER is Professor of English at Yeshiva University's Stern College for Women and former chairperson of the university's humanities division. A recipient of a PhD from Columbia University and of Woodrow Wilson and National Endowment for the Humanities Fellowships, she has written widely on Victorian literature, art, and culture, notably on William Morris and Pre-Raphaelitism. Her recent works include *Strange and Secret Peoples: Fairies and Victorian Consciousness* (Oxford, 1999), a forthcoming introduction to an exhibition of the paintings of William Holman Hunt, and a collection of African folk tales, *Ubuntu: Fairytales From Southern Africa*.

Photograph of Carole G. Silver. © by Yeshiva University, 2008. Used by permission.

www.ingramcontent.com/pod-product-compliance
Lightning Source LLC
Chambersburg PA
CBHW030129240426
43672CB00005B/73